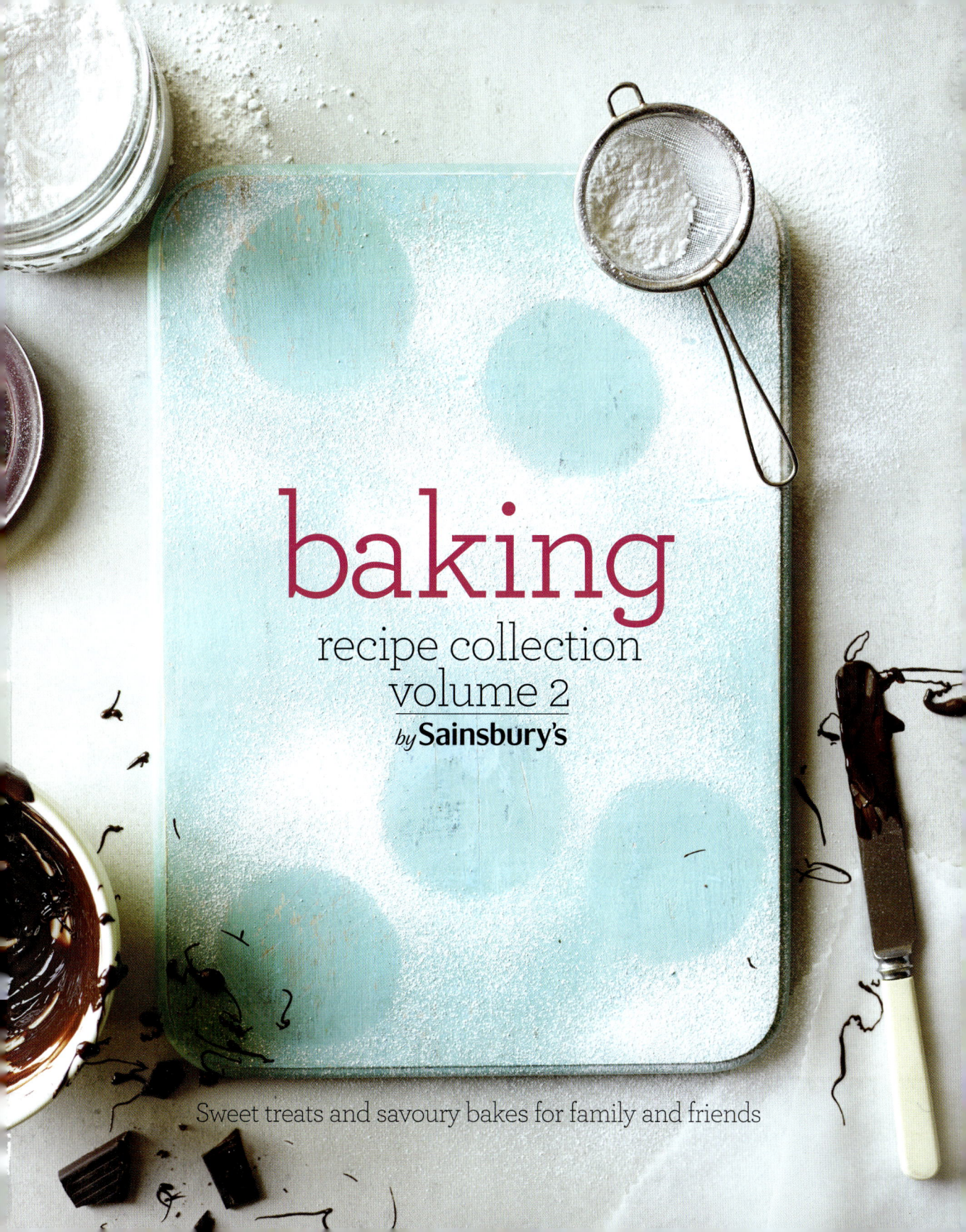

baking
recipe collection
volume 2
by Sainsbury's

Sweet treats and savoury bakes for family and friends

welcome...

Britain loves baking, and it's easy to see why. As well as being a creative, fun and relaxing way to spend some spare time, you also get the pleasure of sharing your delicious creations – and enjoying all those compliments! In this collection of baking recipes, you'll find ideas for all occasions, big and small – from family weekends at home to bake sales, picnics and parties. There are bakes to make with the kids, grown-up recipes to enjoy with friends and tempting desserts for entertaining. With unusual flavour combinations, updates on classic favourites and some brilliant bakes from around the world, these are recipes everyone will love. And there's also a generous sprinkling of simple decorating ideas throughout, so you'll have no trouble making your bakes look as good as they taste. All the recipes are tried and tested, and include nutritional information so you can see which ones are great for regular occasions, and which ones to save for that once-in-a-while treat.

Happy baking!

contents

Family weekends	8
On the move	40
Baking with kids	70
Sharing with friends	102
Entertaining	136
Celebrations	166

let's bake

Baking is great fun and everyone can do it. Even if you're new to baking, you'll find recipes in this book that you can make straight away. It's easy to get started – with a minimum of equipment and a few simple techniques, you can soon master the basics, then start getting creative and adding your own flavourings, fillings and flourishes.

Tins and trays

Sainsbury's has an extensive range of baking tins and trays in all shapes and sizes. For a starter collection of equipment, a couple of 20cm round cake tins, a baking sheet, a muffin tray, a loaf tin and a Swiss roll or traybake tin are all very useful.

Loose-bottomed or springform cake tins make it easier to remove cakes from the tin. Most bakeware has a non-stick coating, but it's also a good idea to also grease and/or line your tins and trays with baking paper. The baking paper will ensure nothing sticks and with many recipes, such as traybakes, it can be used to lift the bake from the tin. Greasing the tin before lining will help the paper stay in place. Alternatively, you may like to use silicon bakeware, which also makes turning out cakes very easy.

traybakes are a simple option for baking beginners

don't forget the lining to make cakes easy to turn out

useful techniques

Baking involves a range of techniques, but there are some you'll use over and over again. Here are four commonly used ones you'll find useful.

Beating egg whites
Beat egg whites just before you need to use them in a clean, dry glass, ceramic or metal bowl. Any traces of oil or fat in the bowl will hinder the egg whites from reaching their full volume. Use fresh eggs at room temperature. When separating the eggs, take care not to get any yolk in the whites. A pinch of cream of tartar will stabilise the egg whites and help increase their volume. Start beating on a low speed until the whites are frothy, then increase the speed to high and continue beating until they reach the desired stage. The 'soft peak' stage is when the whites will hold their shape in the bowl and on removing the beaters, the peaks that form will fall over to one side. The 'firm peak' stage is when the peaks stand up on their own and don't fall. Don't beat egg whites past the firm peak stage, as the liquids and solids will start to separate. When adding sugar for a meringue, do it gradually and beat until the sugar is dissolved and the mixture is glossy.

The rubbing method
Many baking recipes begin with the rubbing method, which involves rubbing butter into flour until it is evenly combined. Use cold, firm butter and cut it into cubes. Dust your hands in the flour, then add the butter and use your fingertips to rub the butter and flour together until you have small, even crumbs, with no large lumps of butter. Work as quickly as you can so the butter doesn't soften or melt.

Kneading
To knead dough, put it onto a lightly floured surface and hold it with one hand while pushing it firmly away from you with the heel of the other hand. Fold it up again and turn it 90 degrees on the surface, then push it away from you again. Keep repeating the pushing, folding and turning, until the dough feels smooth and elastic.

Melting chocolate
To melt chocolate, break it into small pieces and put it in a heatproof bowl set over a pan of simmering water, making sure the base of the bowl doesn't touch the water. Stir the chocolate occasionally until it's fully melted. Alternatively, put the broken up chocolate in a microwave-safe bowl and microwave at half-power for 1 minute, then remove and stir. If it's not completely melted, continue to microwave in 20-second bursts, stirring in between each one.

A 2lb loaf tin is a great all-rounder for sweet and savoury bakes

when it comes to melting chocolate, gently does it

Rising stars

These yeasty treats are light, fluffy, and unlike regular doughnuts, baked, rather than fried. They're filled with a classic combination of rhubarb and custard – find the recipe on p30.

bakes for family weekends

old favourites with new flavours, perfect for lazy Sundays

Passionfruit & lime drizzle cake	10
Plum & ginger upside-down cake	12
Cinnamon & cardamom rolls	14
Chocolate & beetroot fudge cake	16
Apricot & stem ginger scones	18
Coconut & lime Victoria sponge	20
Blackcurrant Bakewell tart	22
Salted caramel, banana & pecan muffins	24
Fig & nut roll	26
Carrot & ginger cake	28
Rhubarb & custard baked doughnuts	30
Lemon fridge cake	32
Red pepper cornbread	34
Bacon, broccoli & cheese bread pudding	36
Courgette & oregano bread	38

SERVES 10
PREP TIME 30 mins
COOK TIME 1 hour

Passionfruit & lime drizzle cake

Give a traditional drizzle loaf a modern, tropical twist by using tangy passionfruit, zesty lime and sweet coconut instead of lemon

---

8 ripe passionfruit (about 150ml of pulp and seeds)
175g sunflower spread by Sainsbury's, plus extra for greasing
275g caster sugar
3 large eggs
225g self-raising flour
75g desiccated coconut
Finely grated zest of 2 limes
4 tbsp freshly squeezed lime juice

---

1. Preheat the oven to 180°C, fan 160°C, gas 4. Grease a 900g (2lb) loaf tin and line the base and sides with baking paper. Halve the passionfruit and scoop out the pulp - this should give you about 150ml. Set aside half of the passionfruit pulp and seeds to use for the cake. Heat the rest gently in a small pan until just warm, then strain it to remove the seeds. Discard the seeds and set the juice aside - this will be used in the drizzle later.

2. In a large bowl, beat the sunflower spread and 175g of the caster sugar until light and creamy, then beat in the eggs one at a time, adding 1 tbsp of the flour with the last egg.

3. Fold in the rest of the flour and the coconut, along with the lime zest and the reserved passionfruit pulp and seeds. Spoon the mixture into the prepared tin, level the top and bake for about 55 mins or until the top of the cake springs back when lightly pressed.

4. Meanwhile, add the lime juice and the remaining sugar to the strained passionfruit juice and leave in a warm place while the cake cooks, stirring it occasionally.

5. When the cake is cooked, prick the surface all over with a skewer, leaving it in the tin. Give the drizzle mixture a stir and then spoon it over the cake. Leave to cool completely in the tin.

6. When cool, remove the cake from the tin, peel off the paper and serve cut into slices.

Each serving (101g) provides:

ENERGY	FAT	SATURATES	SUGARS	SALT
1381kJ 329kcal	14.6g	6.3g	28g	0.4g
16%	21%	32%	31%	7%

% of the Reference Intakes
Typical values per 100g: Energy 1367kJ/326kcal
Each serving provides:
43.6g carbohydrate | 1.8g fibre | 5.1g protein

family weekends

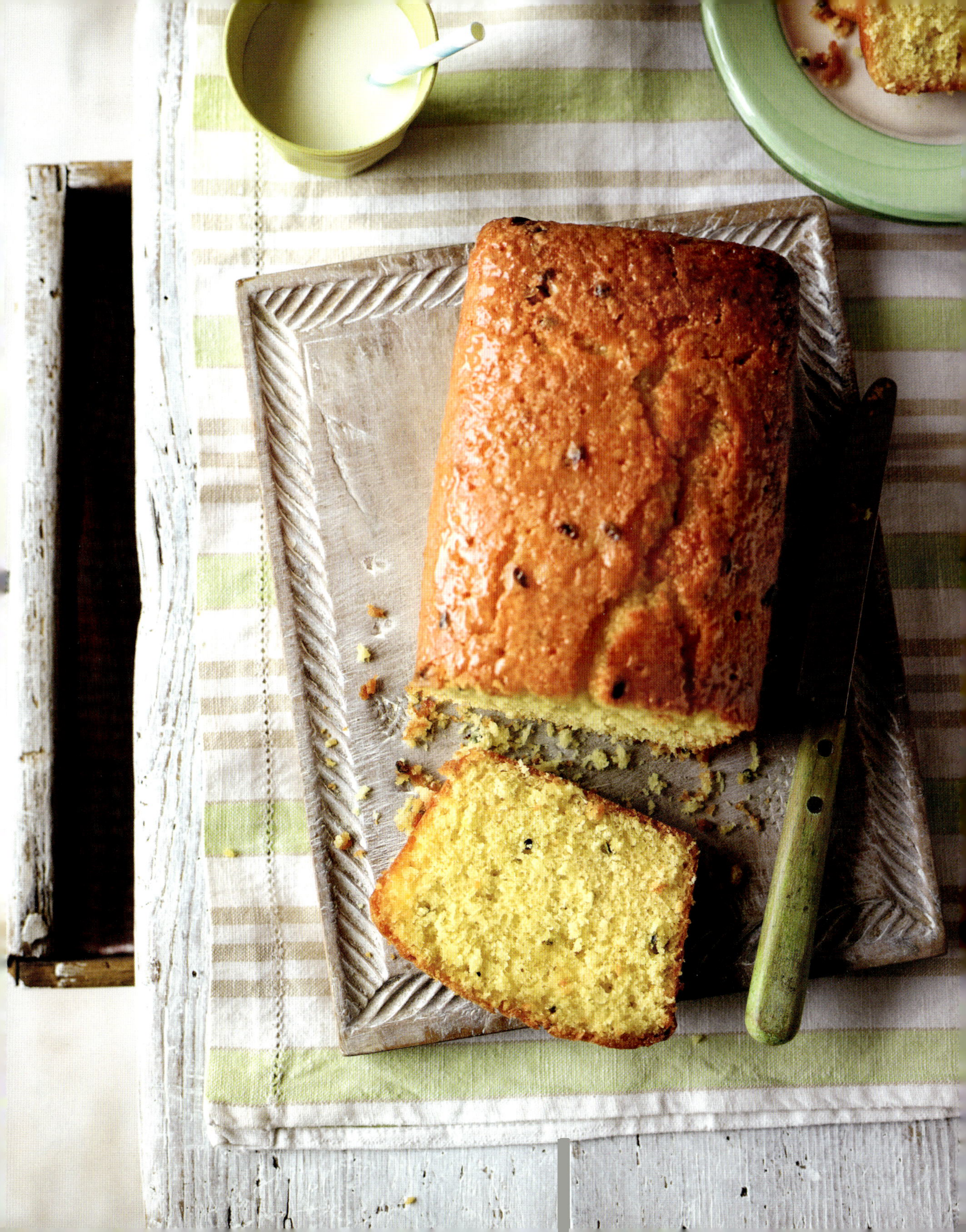

family weekends

SERVES 8
PREP TIME 25 mins
COOK TIME 40-50 mins

Plum & ginger upside-down cake

Made with plump plums and spicy stem ginger, this cake is wonderful served warm as a dessert, then as a cake for the next day or two

150g unsalted butter, softened, plus extra for greasing
160g light brown soft sugar
350g just-ripe plums, halved and de-stoned
2 pieces stem ginger in sugar syrup by Sainsbury's, drained and diced

125g self-raising flour
2 tsp ground ginger
1 tsp ground cinnamon
1 tsp baking powder
2 large eggs

1. Preheat the oven to 180°C, fan 160°C, gas 4. Grease a 20cm springform tin and line the base with baking paper. Heat 35g of the sugar and 25g butter in a small saucepan, over a medium heat, until melted and combined. Spread over the base of the prepared tin.

2. Scatter half the stem ginger pieces over the sugar and butter mixture, then arrange the plums, cut-side down, in the tin.

3. Sift the flour, ground ginger, cinnamon and baking powder into a large bowl. Add the remaining softened butter and sugar and the eggs, and beat together with a hand-held electric whisk until you have a smooth mixture. Fold in the remaining stem ginger.

4. Carefully put spoonfuls of the cake mixture on top of the plums then spread it level – it will only just cover the fruit.

5. Bake for 35-45 mins or until the cake is risen and the top springs back when lightly pressed.

6. Remove from the oven and leave to cool in the tin for 5 mins, then turn out onto a cooling rack to cool completely. Store in an air-tight container in a cool place for up to 2 days.

Each serving (100g) provides:

ENERGY	FAT	SATURATES	SUGARS	SALT
1311kJ 314kcal	17.4g	9.8g	24g	0.4g
16%	25%	49%	27%	6%

% of the Reference Intakes
Typical values per 100g: Energy 1311kJ/314kcal
Each serving provides:
35g carbohydrate | 0.9g fibre | 3.8g protein

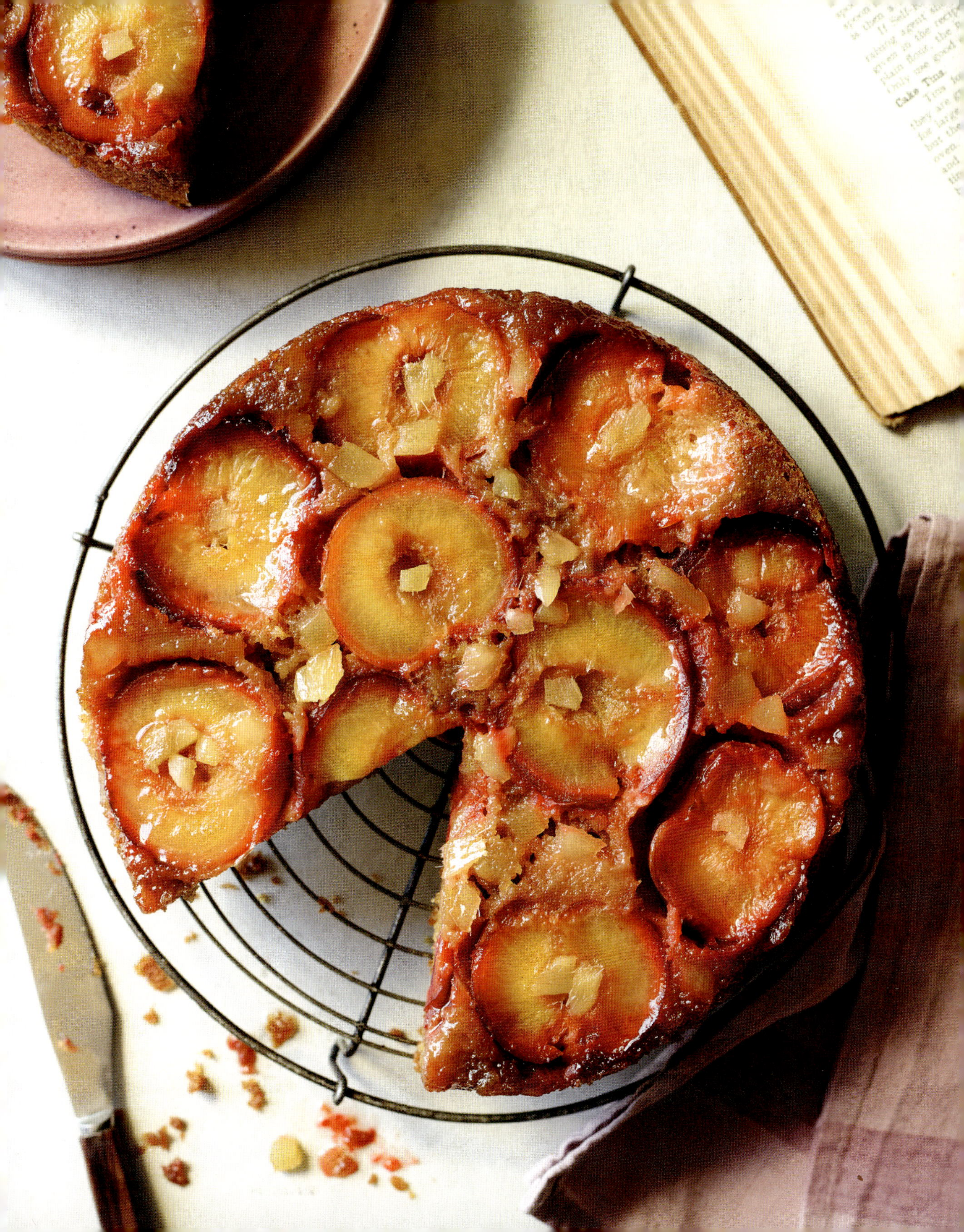
Cake Tins

family weekends

> **MAKES** 12
> **PREP TIME**
> 40 mins, plus rising and cooling
> **COOK TIME**
> 25-30 mins

Cinnamon & cardamom rolls

These sticky buns have been given a makeover with fragrant cardamom

10 cardamom pods, outer shell removed and seeds ground
175ml semi-skimmed milk
40g unsalted butter, plus 50g, softened, for the filling
350g strong white bread flour by Sainsbury's, plus extra for kneading
7g sachet fast-action dried yeast
¼ tsp salt
50g caster sugar
1 large egg, lightly beaten
Vegetable oil, for greasing
50g light brown soft sugar
½ tsp Taste the Difference Madagascan vanilla extract
2 tsp ground cinnamon
150g apricot glaze by Sainsbury's

1. Put the ground cardamom in a pan, add the milk and heat until almost boiling. Remove from the heat and set aside until the milk is just warm.

2. Cut the 40g butter into cubes. Put in a large bowl, add the flour and rub it into the butter using your fingertips. Mix in the yeast, salt and caster sugar. Strain in the cardamom-infused milk and add the egg. Stir to make a soft dough, then tip onto a lightly floured surface and knead for 10 mins (see p7), until the dough is smooth and elastic. Put the dough in a lightly greased bowl, cover with cling film and leave in a warm place until doubled in size – this will take about 1 hour.

3. Turn out onto a floured surface and knead again for just 1 min. Roll out to a square measuring about 30cm x 30cm. In a bowl, mix the 50g butter with the brown sugar, vanilla extract and cinnamon, then spread evenly over the dough. Grease a 25cm x 30cm shallow baking tray and line with baking paper.

4. Roll the dough up tightly to make a log. Using a serrated knife, cut into 12 even slices. Put on the baking tray, cut side down, in three rows of four. Cover loosely with oiled cling film and leave in a warm place for about 30 mins or until the rolls are doubled in size and just touching.

5. Preheat the oven to 190°C, fan 170°C, gas 5. Remove the cling film and bake the rolls for 20-25 mins or until golden. Warm the apricot glaze in a small pan and brush all over the rolls while they are still hot. Cool on a cooling rack.

Each roll (76g) provides:

ENERGY	FAT	SATURATES	SUGARS	SALT
971kJ 231kcal	7.8g	4.1g	14.1g	0.2g
12%	11%	21%	16%	3%

% of the Reference Intakes
Typical values per 100g: Energy 1277kJ/304kcal
Each roll provides:
33.8g carbohydrate | 1.5g fibre | 5.6g protein

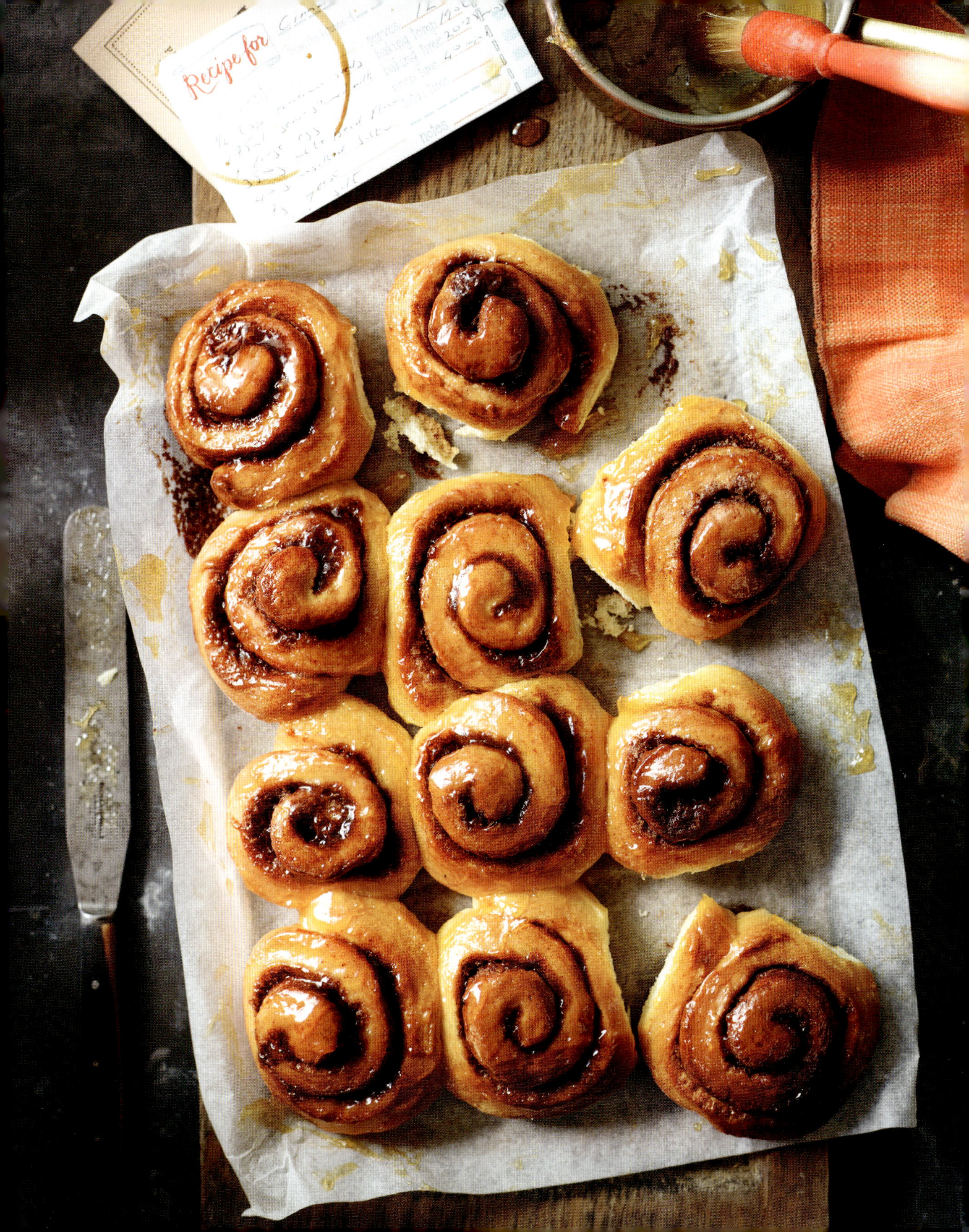
Recipe for

SERVES 10
PREP TIME 30 mins plus cooking
COOK TIME 1 hour

family weekends

Chocolate & beetroot fudge cake

Beetroot gives this chocolate cake a moist texture and natural sweetness

75g Taste The Difference Swiss dark chocolate, broken into squares
75g unsalted butter, plus extra for greasing
250g pack cooked beetroot in natural juices by Sainsbury's, drained
75g natural yogurt
175g self-raising flour
1 tbsp cocoa powder
½ tsp bicarbonate of soda
125g caster sugar
1 large egg, lightly beaten

FOR THE GANACHE
200g smooth dark chocolate by Sainsbury's, broken into squares
150ml fresh double cream

1. Preheat the oven to 180°C, fan 160°C, gas 4. Grease and line the base and sides of a 21cm round cake tin with baking paper.

2. Melt the dark chocolate and butter in a heatproof bowl set over a pan of simmering water (see p7). Remove the bowl from the pan and set aside to cool slightly.

3. Purée the beetroot and yogurt using a hand-held blender or food processor. Sift the flour, cocoa powder and bicarbonate of soda into a large bowl, then add the chocolate mixture, puréed beetroot mixture, sugar and egg. Beat with a wooden spoon or balloon whisk until just evenly mixed.

4. Pour the mixture into the prepared tin and bake for 50 mins or until a skewer inserted in the middle of the cake comes out clean. Cool on a cooling rack.

5. Make the ganache. Heat the cream over a medium heat until it just begins to simmer, then remove it from the heat and add the chocolate. Stir until the chocolate is melted. Set aside to cool slightly.

6. Put a baking sheet under the cooling rack to catch any drips. Spread the ganache over the top and sides of the cake with a palette knife. Set aside until the ganache is set, then serve.

Each serving (103g) provides:

ENERGY	FAT	SATURATES	SUGARS	SALT
1667kJ 400kcal	24.7g	15g	24.7g	0.4g
20%	35%	75%	27%	7%

% of the Reference Intakes

Typical values per 100g: Energy 1618kJ/388kcal
Each serving provides:
37.3g carbohydrate | 3.8g fibre | 5.2g protein

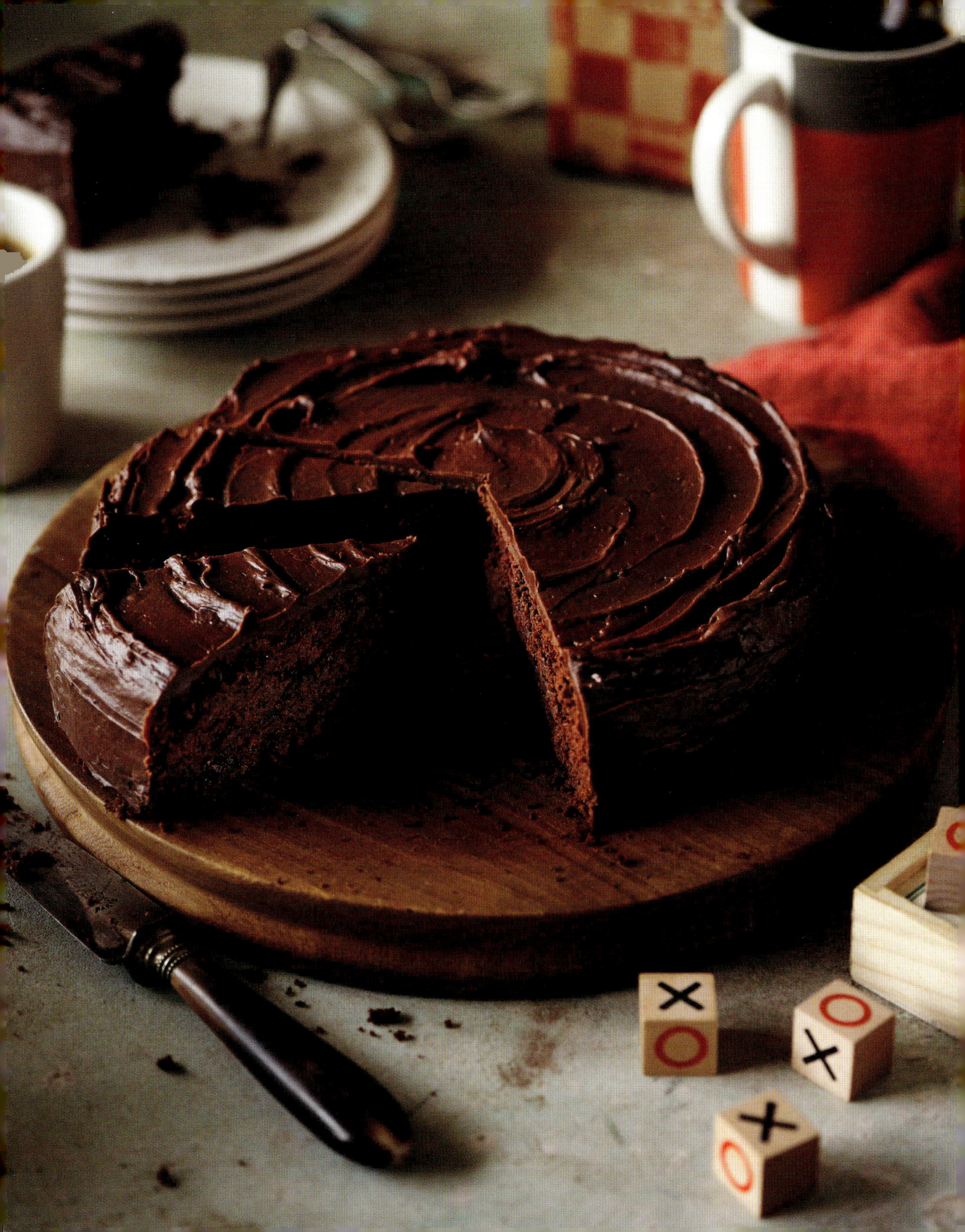

family weekends

MAKES 10
PREP TIME 15 mins
COOK TIME 10 mins

Apricot & stem ginger scones

Ready in just 25 minutes, these scones are easy to make when unexpected guests drop by. Serve them still warm from the oven!

225g self-raising flour, plus extra for dusting
1 tsp baking powder
Pinch of salt
50g unsalted butter, chilled and cut into small cubes
40g caster sugar
100g dried apricots, finely diced
2 pieces stem ginger in sugar syrup by Sainsbury's, drained and finely diced
75ml buttermilk by Sainsbury's
75ml semi-skimmed milk

1. Preheat the oven to 220°C, fan 200°C, gas 7. Line a baking tray with baking paper.

2. Sift the flour, baking powder and salt into a large bowl. Add the butter, then rub it into the flour mixture with your fingertips until it resembles breadcrumbs (see p7). Stir in the sugar, apricots and ginger.

3. Mix the buttermilk and milk together in a small jug. Set aside 1 tbsp, then add the rest, in one go, to the flour mixture and mix with a round-bladed knife until you have a soft dough.

4. Turn the dough out onto a lightly floured surface and pat it out with your hands until it's about 2cm thick. The secret of good scones is to handle the dough as little as possible. Use a 5cm cutter to cut out as many scones as possible, then gather the trimmings and pat to a 2cm thick again and cut out more scones – you should get at least 10 scones in total.

5. Put the scones on a baking tray and brush the tops with the reserved buttermilk mixture. Bake for 10 mins until well risen and golden. Cool on a wire rack and serve warm or cold.

Cook's tip
When cutting scones, press straight down and don't twist the cutter. This helps them to rise evenly. Dip the cutter in a small bowl of flour before you cut each one.

Each scone (69g) provides:

ENERGY	FAT	SATURATES	SUGARS	SALT
837kJ 199kcal	5.8g	3.3g	12.4g	0.6g
10%	8%	17%	14%	9%

% of the Reference Intakes
Typical values per 100g: Energy 1213kJ/288kcal
Each scone provides:
32.2g carbohydrate | 1g fibre | 4g protein

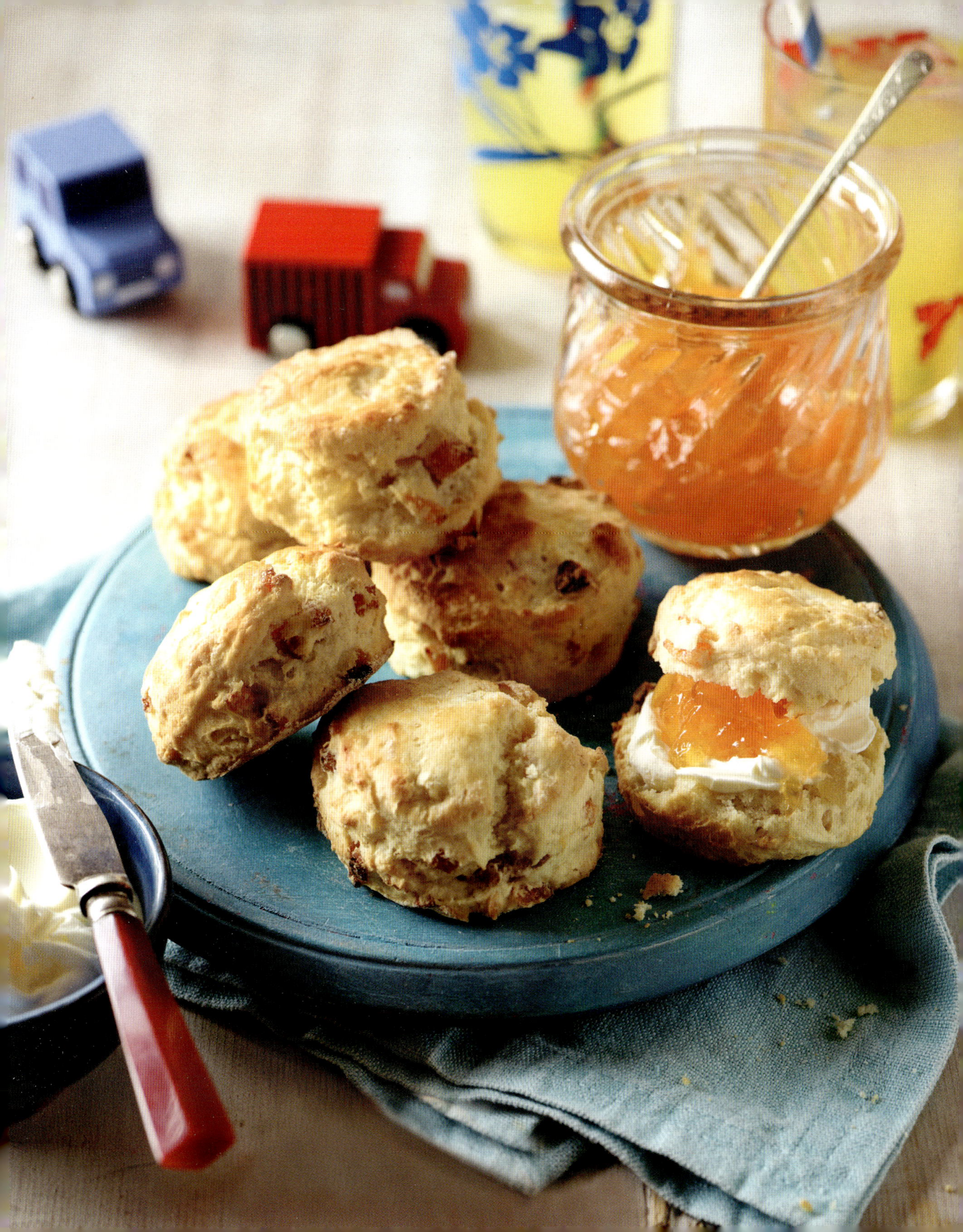

family weekends

Coconut & lime Victoria sponge

A quintessentially British teatime cake with a zesty, tropical twist

SERVES 12
PREP TIME 20 mins
COOK TIME 25 mins

220g unsalted butter, softened, plus extra for greasing
220g caster sugar
4 eggs
220g self-raising flour, sifted
1 tsp baking powder
50g desiccated coconut
2 tbsp coconut cream by Sainsbury's
Icing sugar, for dusting

FOR THE FILLING
100ml fresh double cream
150g lime curd by Sainsbury's

1. Preheat the oven to 180°C, fan 160°C, gas 4. Grease 2 x 18cm loose-bottomed cake tins and line the bases with baking paper, or use Sainsbury's cake tin liners.

2. Put the butter and sugar in a large mixing bowl. Beat well using a hand-held electric whisk for 2-3 mins until the mixture is light and creamy. Add the eggs, one at a time, and 1 tbsp of the flour, beating well between each addition. Fold in the remaining flour, the baking powder and desiccated coconut until everything is combined, then gently mix in the coconut cream. Divide the mixture between the prepared tins and bake for 25 mins, until risen, golden and springy to the touch.

3. Leave the cakes to cool in the tin for 10 mins, then turn out onto a cooling rack to cool completely.

4. Whip the cream until soft peaks form. Spread the lime curd onto the flat side of one cake, then top with whipped cream. Sandwich with the other cake, then dust with the icing sugar, to serve.

Each serving (91g) provides:

ENERGY	FAT	SATURATES	SUGARS	SALT
1640kJ 393kcal	24.1g	14.6g	25.2g	0.4g
20%	34%	73%	28%	6%

% of the Reference Intakes
Typical values per 100g: Energy 1802kJ/432kcal
Each serving provides:
38.9g carbohydrate | 1.2g fibre | 4.5g protein

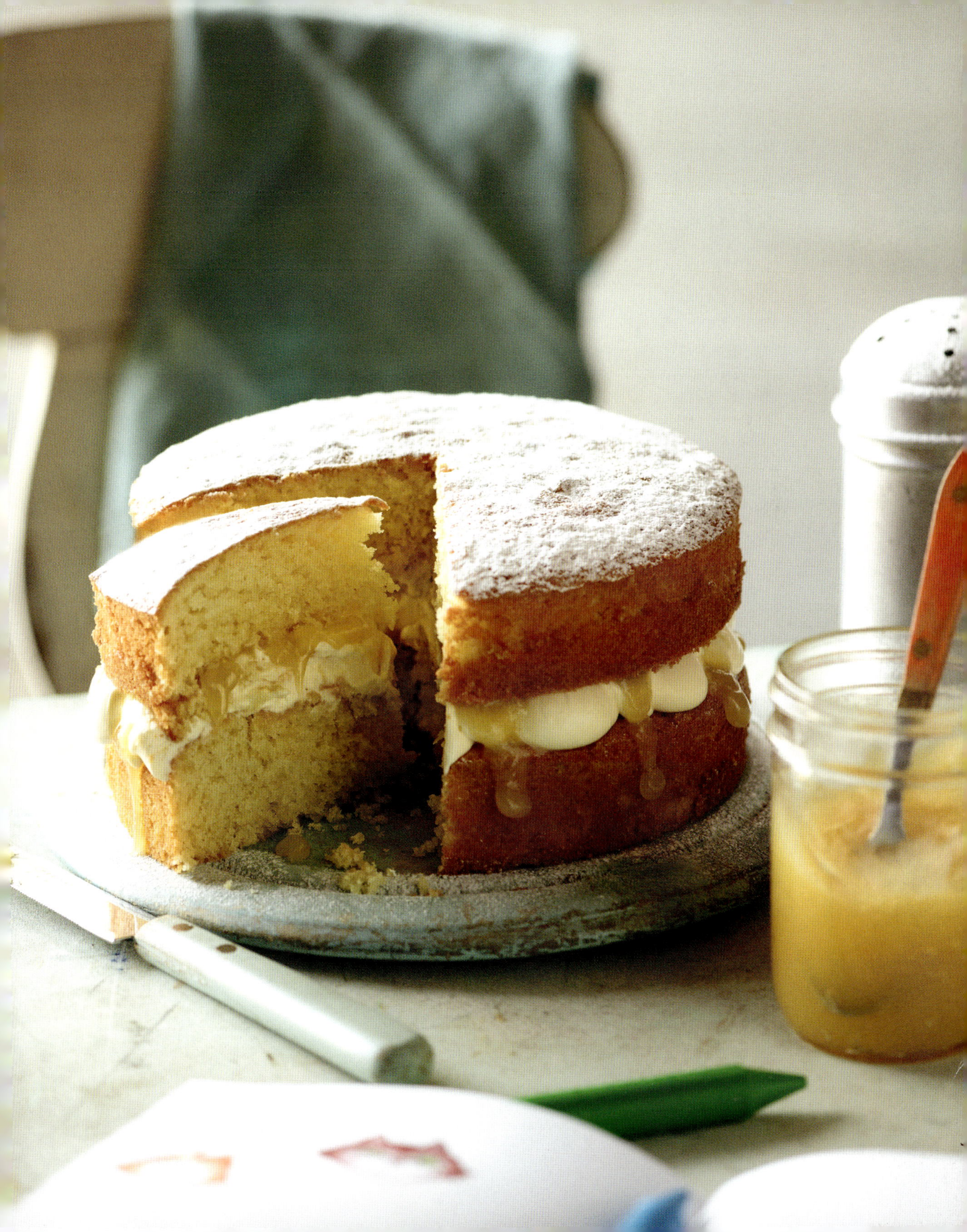

family weekends

SERVES 12
PREP TIME 20 mins, plus chilling
COOK TIME 55 mins-1 hour

Blackcurrant Bakewell tart

This recipe uses blackcurrant jam to create a twist on the British classic

Icing sugar, for dusting
375g ready rolled lighter shortcrust pastry by Sainsbury's
150g unsalted butter
150g caster sugar
150g ground almonds
$^{1}/_{2}$ tsp Taste the Difference French almond extract
2 eggs, lightly beaten
Zest of $^{1}/_{2}$ lemon
4 tbsp Taste the Difference blackcurrant conserve
25g flaked almonds

1. Lightly dust a work surface with icing sugar and unroll the pastry. Use a rolling pin to further roll out the pastry until it's about the thickness of a pound coin, then use it to line a 23cm loose-bottomed fluted flan tin. Rest the case in the fridge for 30 mins, then trim the edges and prick the base all over with a fork.

2. Preheat the oven to 200°C, fan 180°C, gas 6, along with a baking sheet. Line the pastry case with baking paper and fill with baking beans or rice. Put on the pre-heated baking sheet and blind-bake for 15 mins, then remove the beans/rice and paper. Cook for a further 5 mins until golden.

3. Meanwhile, make the filling. Melt the butter in a small pan over a low heat. Remove from the heat, then stir in the sugar, ground almonds and almond extract. Mix in the eggs and lemon zest.

4. Spread the jam evenly across the base of the pastry case, then spoon over the almond mixture, levelling the surface. Scatter over the flaked almonds and bake for 30-35 mins until golden, risen and just set in the middle. If the almonds start to colour too much during baking, cover the tart loosely with foil.

5. Leave to cool in the tin for 5 mins, then transfer to a cooling rack to cool completely. Dust with icing sugar to serve.

Each serving (76g) provides:

ENERGY	FAT	SATURATES	SUGARS	SALT
1670kJ 401kcal	26.1g	9.5g	19.3g	0.2g
20%	37%	48%	21%	3%

% of the Reference Intakes
Typical values per 100g: Energy 2197kJ/527kcal
Each serving provides:
33.9g carbohydrate | 2.2g fibre | 6.6g protein

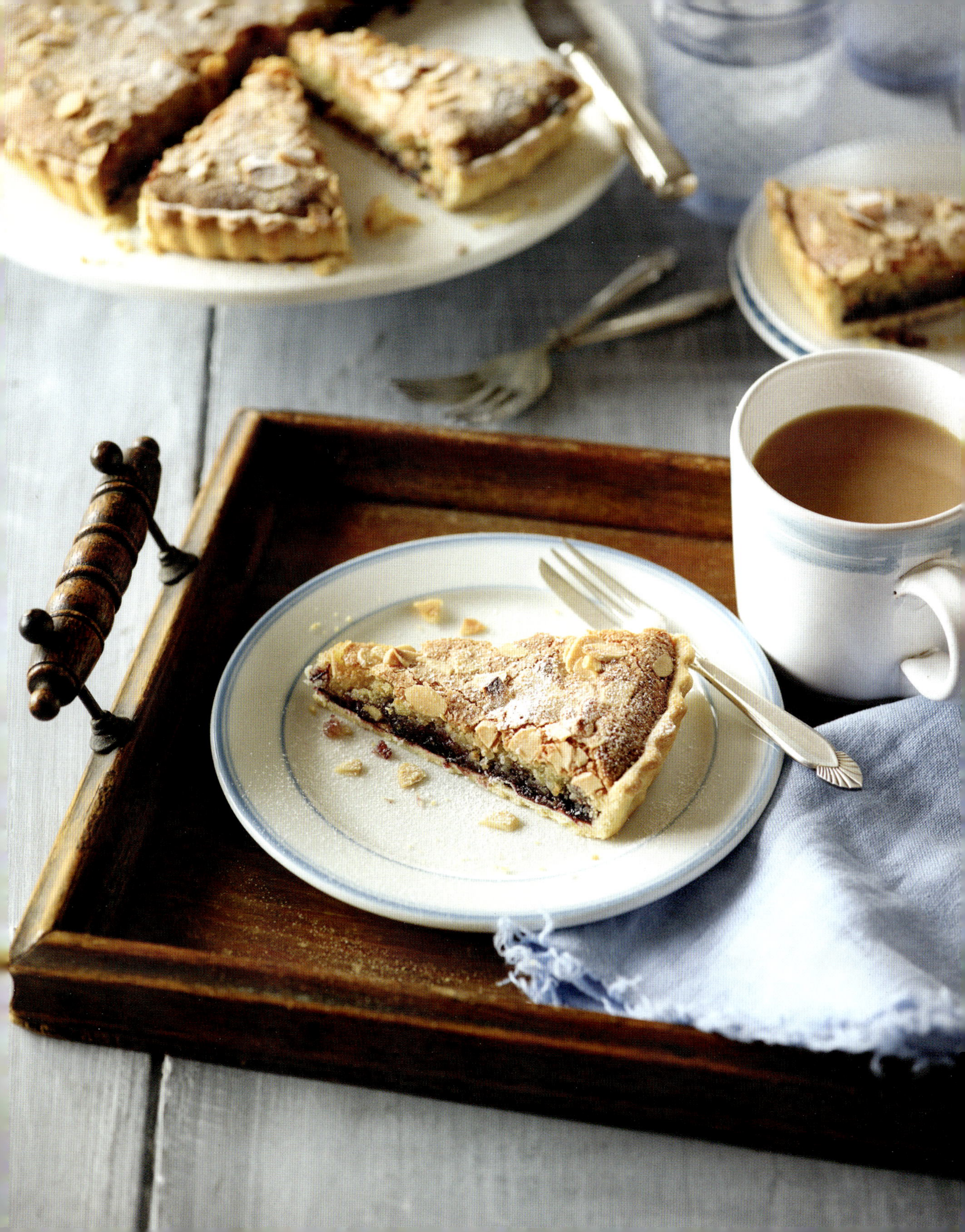

family weekends

MAKES 10
PREP TIME 20 mins
COOK TIME 30 mins

Salted caramel, banana & pecan muffins

Delicious tea-time treats, these are super-easy to bake and a great way to use up any overripe bananas you have

---

100g pecans by Sainsbury's
2 very ripe bananas (175g total peeled weight)
75g unsalted butter, softened
25g light brown soft sugar
260g jar Taste the Difference salted caramel sauce

2 large eggs
300g self-raising flour

YOU WILL ALSO NEED
10 paper Tulip muffin cases by Sainsbury's

---

1. Preheat the oven to 180°C, fan 160°C, gas 4. Arrange the paper muffin cases on a large baking tray.

2. Put the nuts on a separate baking tray and cook in the oven for 5 mins or until lightly toasted. Chop roughly and set aside.

3. In a small bowl, mash the bananas with a fork. In a separate, large bowl, beat together the butter and sugar until pale and fluffy, then add most of the caramel sauce (reserve 1-2 tablespoons for drizzling later), the eggs, mashed banana and flour. Beat until evenly mixed, then fold in three-quarters of the chopped pecans.

4. Divide the mixture between the paper muffin cases, then scatter over the remaining pecans. Bake for 25-30 mins or until risen and golden, and a skewer inserted in the middle of a muffin comes out clean.

5. Transfer to a cooling rack and serve warm or cold, drizzled with the reserved caramel sauce.

Cook's tip
To make a large cake, follow the recipe above but use a 900g (2lb) loaf tin, lined with a loaf tin cake liner by Sainsbury's. Bake for 1 hour or until a skewer inserted in the middle comes out clean.

Each muffin (91g) provides:

ENERGY	FAT	SATURATES	SUGARS	SALT
1544kJ 370kcal	20.9g	8.9g	17.9g	0.5g
18%	30%	45%	20%	8%

% of the Reference Intakes

Typical values per 100g: Energy 1697kJ/406kcal
Each serving provides:
38.6g carbohydrate | 1.6g fibre | 6g protein

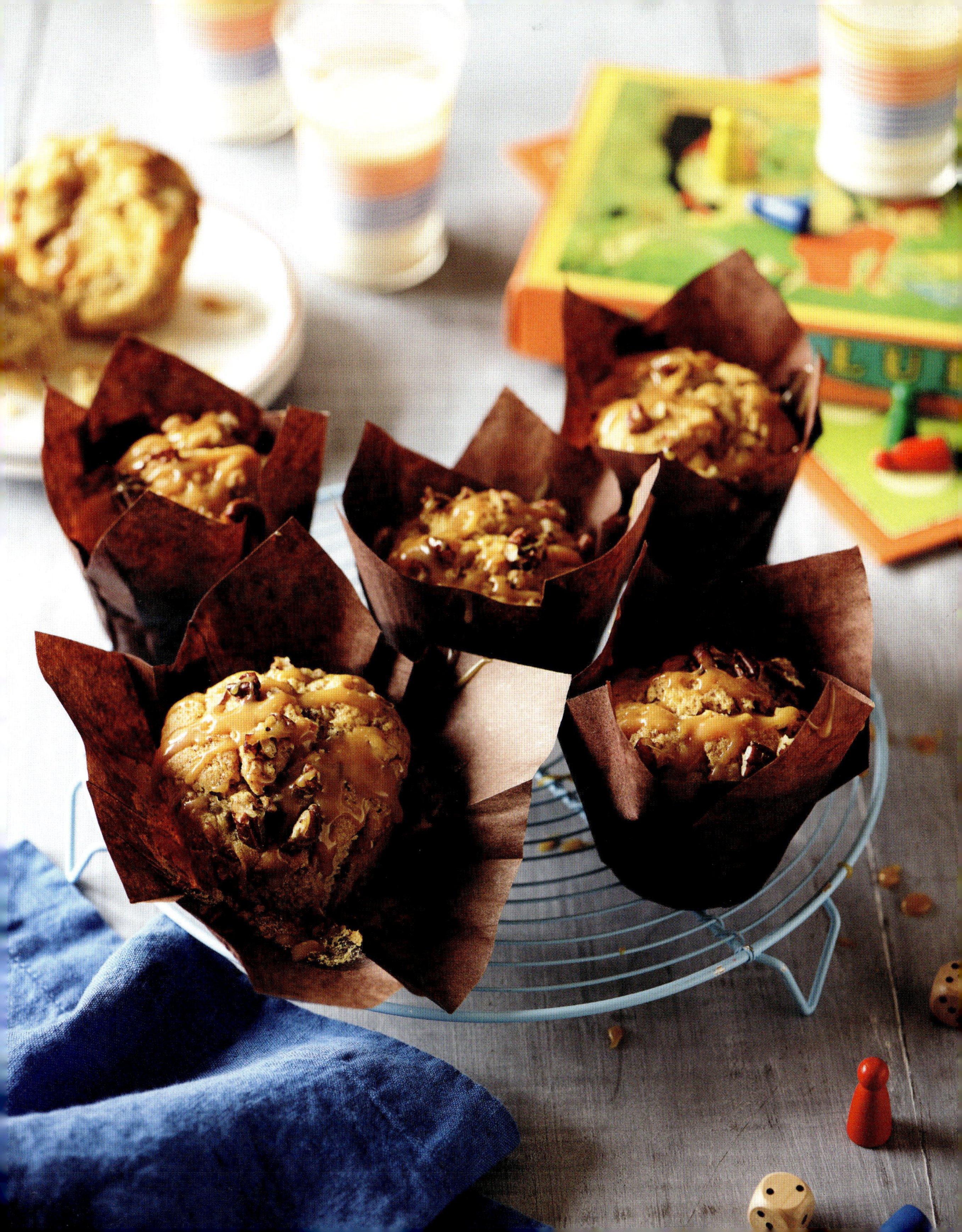

SERVES 12
PREP TIME 30 mins
COOK TIME 15 mins

Fig & nut roll

A nutty sponge Swiss roll filled with fig purée and vanilla mascarpone

---

Vegetable oil, for greasing
4 large eggs, separated
115g caster sugar
100g ground roasted hazelnuts by Sainsbury's
40g flaked almonds
300g dried figs
250ml apple juice
1 tbsp clear honey
250g tub lighter Italian mascarpone by Sainsbury's
2 tbsp icing sugar
Few drops Taste the Difference Madagascan vanilla extract

---

1. Preheat the oven to 190°C, fan 170°C, gas 5. Grease a 25cm x 35cm Swiss roll tin or roasting tin and line with baking paper. In a large bowl, whisk the egg whites using a hand-held electric whisk until stiff peaks form (see p7). Add 2 tbsp of the caster sugar and whisk again until the mixture is stiff and glossy.

2. In a separate bowl, add the yolks and remaining caster sugar and whisk until the mixture is pale and thick. Stir the hazelnuts into the yolk mixture, then stir in 1 heaped tbsp of the egg whites – this will loosen the mixture so that you can fold the rest in easily. Fold in the remaining egg whites.

3. Spoon the mixture into the prepared tin, gently levelling it and making sure it goes right into the corners of the tin. Sprinkle the almonds evenly on top.

4. Bake for 12-15 mins or until the cake is pale golden and the top springs back when lightly pressed. Carefully lift out of the tin, still in the paper lining, and cool on a cooling rack.

5. Meanwhile, put the figs, apple juice and honey in a pan, cover and simmer over a low heat for 15 mins until the figs are tender. Purée with a hand-held blender or in a food processor, then set aside to cool. In a bowl, mix the mascarpone with 2 tsp of the icing sugar and the vanilla, and set aside.

6. To assemble, sprinkle a sheet of baking paper with the remaining icing sugar, turn the cake out onto it and peel off the baking paper you used to line the tin. Trim off any hard edges to make rolling the cake easier. Spread first with the mascarpone, then with the fig mixture, leaving a border of clear sponge all around. Roll the sponge up from one long side. Put the roll seam-side down on a platter to serve.

Each serving (88g) provides:

ENERGY	FAT	SATURATES	SUGARS	SALT
1123kJ 269kcal	13.6g	3.5g	27.1g	0.1g
13%	19%	18%	30%	2%

% of the Reference Intakes
Typical values per 100g: Energy 1276kJ/305kcal
Each serving provides:
27.6g carbohydrate | 2.9g fibre | 7.5g protein

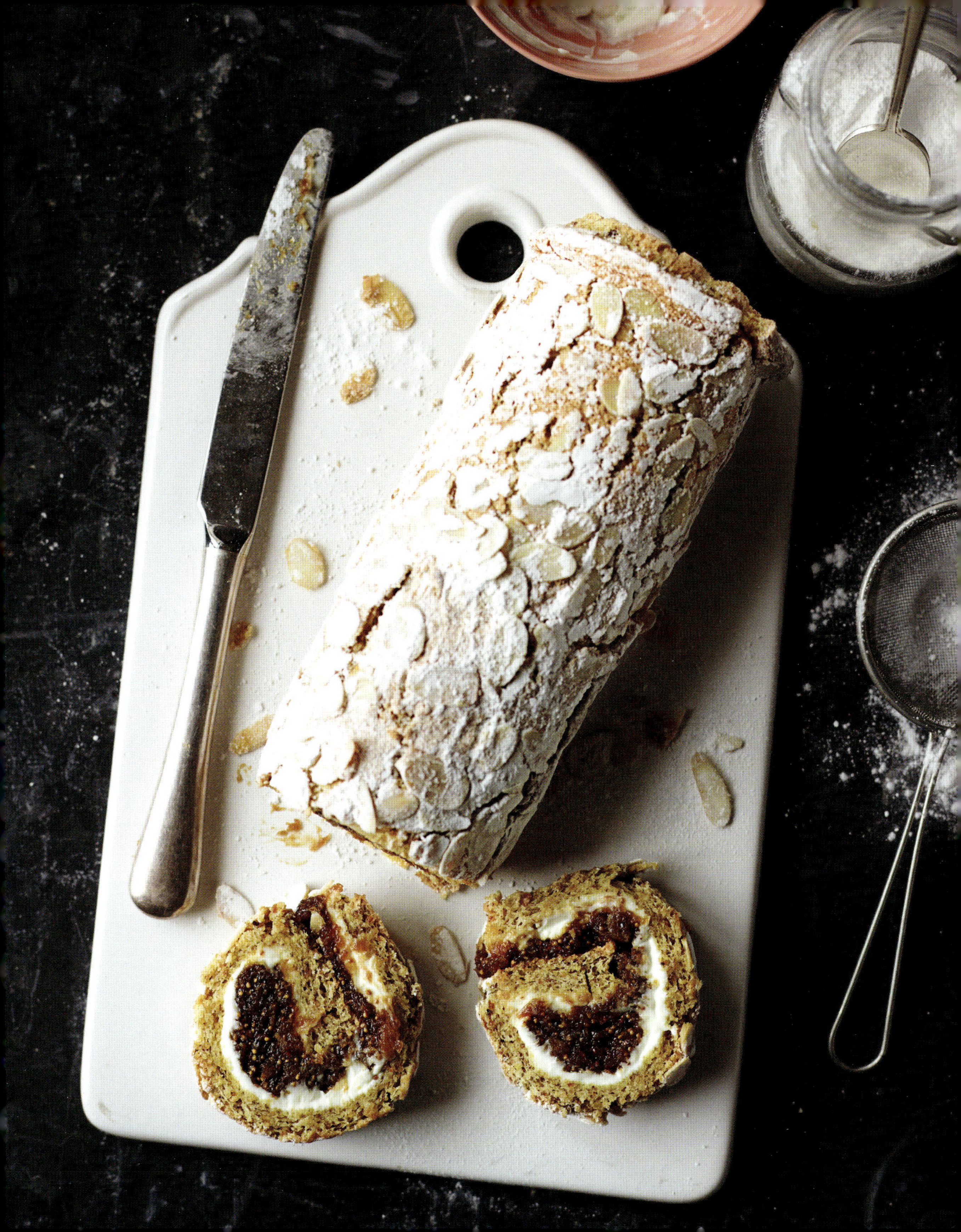

SERVES 16
PREP TIME 25 mins
COOK TIME 35 mins

Carrot & ginger cake

Everyone's favourite tea-time cake, with a delicious ginger and pecan twist

125ml sunflower oil, plus extra for greasing
200g self-raising flour
1 tsp bicarbonate of soda
2 tsp ground ginger
50g desiccated coconut
50g pecans, chopped
2 large eggs
175g light brown soft sugar
200g carrots, trimmed, peeled and coarsely grated

3 pieces stem ginger in sugar syrup by Sainsbury's, drained and chopped

FOR THE FROSTING
50g unsalted butter, softened
50g icing sugar, sifted
1 tsp freshly squeezed lemon juice
Few drops of Taste the Difference Madagascan vanilla extract
150g full-fat soft cheese

1 Preheat the oven to 180°C, fan 160°C, gas 4. Grease a 20cm square cake tin and line with baking paper.

2 In a large bowl, sift together the flour, bicarbonate of soda and ground ginger. Stir in the coconut and pecans.

3 Put the eggs, brown sugar and sunflower oil in another large bowl and whisk with a hand-held electric whisk for about 3 mins until the sugar has dissolved and the mixture looks pale and slightly thickened. Stir in the carrots, flour mixture and two-thirds of the stem ginger, reserving the rest for decoration.

4 Pour the mixture into the prepared tin and bake for 30-35 mins or until a skewer inserted in the centre of the cake comes out clean. Leave to cool in the tin for 5 mins, then turn out onto a cooling rack and leave to cool completely.

5 Make the frosting. Beat together the butter, icing sugar, lemon juice and vanilla extract until smooth and creamy. Stir in the soft cheese until evenly mixed. Spread over the top of the cooked cake and use a fork to make a wave pattern across the top, then decorate with the reserved stem ginger.

Cook's tip
For the frosting, it's essential to use full-fat soft cheese – reduced-fat soft cheese will make it too thin to spread.

Each serving (65g) provides:

ENERGY	FAT	SATURATES	SUGARS	SALT
1098kJ 263kcal	16.7g	5.8g	15.8g	0.4g
13%	24%	29%	18%	7%

% of the Reference Intakes
Typical values per 100g: Energy 1689kJ/404kcal
Each serving provides:
24.5g carbohydrate | 1.5g fibre | 3.2g protein

family weekends

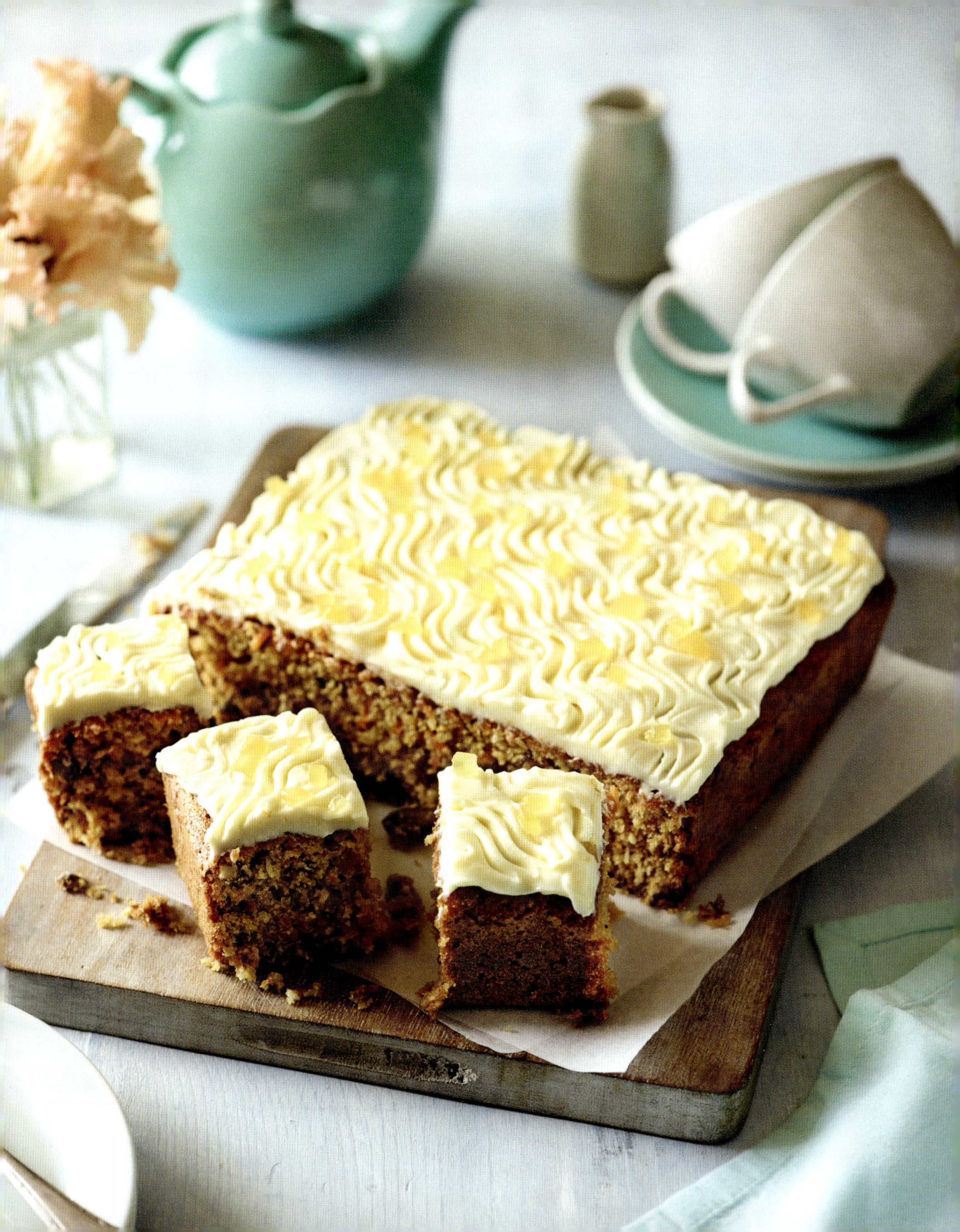

family weekends

MAKES 8
PREP TIME 40 mins plus rising time
COOK TIME 35-40 mins

Rhubarb & custard baked doughnuts

Soft, sugary baked doughnuts filled with tart rhubarb and smooth custard

25g unsalted butter, plus extra for greasing
300g strong white bread flour by Sainsbury's, plus extra for dusting
150g caster sugar
1 tsp fast-action dried yeast
1 large egg

150ml semi-skimmed milk, warmed in a small pan until hand-hot
225g rhubarb, cut into 2cm pieces
50g unsalted butter
125g lighter Italian mascarpone by Sainsbury's
½ x 300g tub be good to yourself custard

1. In a bowl, rub the butter into the flour using your fingertips (see p7), then add 50g of the sugar, the yeast and a pinch of salt. Lightly beat the egg with the milk and stir into the flour mixture to make a soft, quite sticky dough.

2. Knead the dough on a lightly floured surface for 10 mins (see p7), then shape it into 8 equal balls and put on a greased baking tray. Cover loosely with a piece of greased cling film and leave in a warm, hygienic place until the dough has risen and is almost double in size – this will take about 40 mins.

3. Preheat the oven to 200°C, fan 180°C, gas 6. Put the rhubarb in an ovenproof dish and sprinkle over 50g of the sugar. Cover with foil and roast for 15 mins. Remove the foil and stir gently. Return to the oven, uncovered, for another 5 mins, or until tender. Cool, then drain off any juices. Chill in the fridge while you bake the doughnuts.

4. Remove the cling film from the risen dough and bake at 180°C, fan 160°C, gas 4. for 10-15 mins until golden. To test if they're cooked, tap the base – they should sound hollow.

5. Melt the butter and transfer to a shallow bowl. Put the remaining caster sugar in another bowl. While the doughnuts are still hot, quickly brush them all over with the melted butter, then roll them in the sugar. Cool on a cooling rack. Put the mascarpone in a bowl and stir in the custard, then fold in the chilled rhubarb.

6. Cut the doughnuts almost all the way through and fill with the rhubarb and custard, then serve.

Each doughnut (135g) provides:

ENERGY	FAT	SATURATES	SUGARS	SALT
1329kJ 316kcal	11.4g	5.9g	18.5g	0.2g
16%	16%	30%	21%	3%

% of the Reference Intakes
Typical values per 100g: Energy 985kJ/234kcal
Each doughnut provides:
42.9g carbohydrate | 1.9g fibre | 9.6g protein

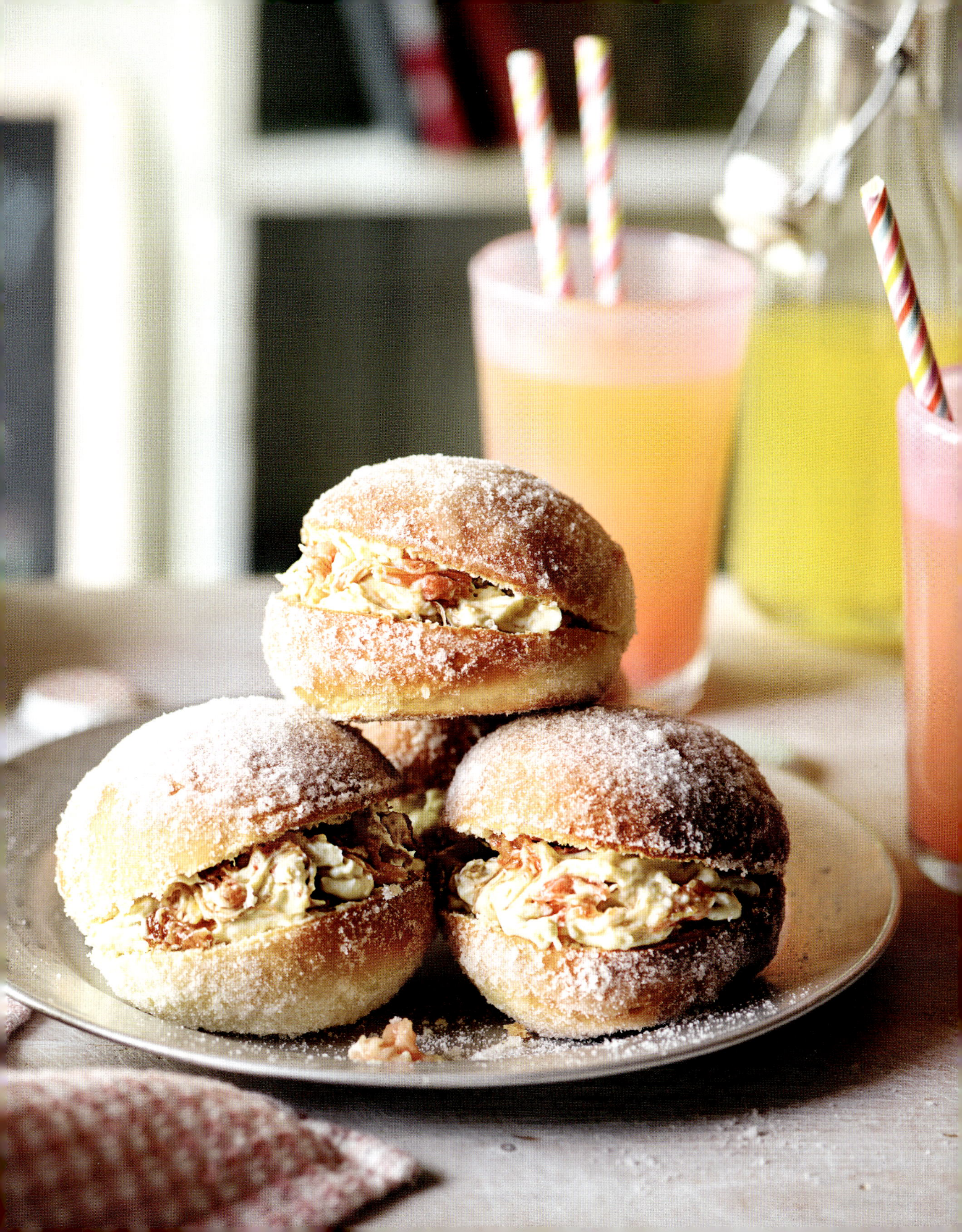

SERVES 16
PREP TIME 35 mins, plus chilling
COOK TIME 45 mins, plus 1 hour 30 mins (for biscuits),

Lemon fridge cake

A fun take on a cheesecake, this makes a great dessert for a special family meal, and is really easy to put together

400ml fresh double cream
250g tub lighter Italian mascarpone by Sainsbury's
30g icing sugar, plus 1 tsp extra for dusting
½ tsp Taste the Difference Madagascan vanilla extract
320g jar Taste the Difference lemon curd

48 lemon and almond butter biscuits (see recipe on page 46)

FOR THE CANDIED LEMON
1 lemon, cut into very thin slices
150g caster sugar

1 In a bowl, beat together the cream, mascarpone, icing sugar and vanilla until it just holds soft peaks. Add a quarter of this cream mixture to the lemon curd and gently fold through. Keep adding the cream mixture to the curd, bit by bit, until it's all combined.

2 On a large serving plate or cake stand, arrange seven of the biscuits in a circle, making sure they touch, then put one in the middle. Using a spatula or palette knife, spread a layer of the filling across the top, leaving the edges of the biscuits visible. This will be tricky at first, but hold the biscuits in place and it will get easier as you go along. Repeat so you have six layers, finishing with a final layer of the curd cream. Refrigerate for 3-4 hours to set.

3 Meanwhile, make the candied lemon decoration. Heat the sugar and 300ml water in a large, deep frying pan over a medium heat. Stir until the sugar is completely dissolved, then lower the heat. Add the lemon slices in a single layer and simmer for 40 mins until the rinds are translucent. Transfer to a baking sheet lined with baking paper and leave to cool completely.

4 Remove the cake from the fridge, dust with the extra icing sugar and decorate with the candied lemon. Cut into thin slices to serve.

Cook's tip
If you want to save time making this cake, you could use shop-bought biscuits, such as Taste the Difference lemon shortbread thins.

Each serving (105g) provides:

ENERGY	FAT	SATURATES	SUGARS	SALT
1779kJ / 427kcal	27.7g	15.2g	30.2g	0.1g
21%	40%	76%	34%	2%

% of the Reference Intakes
Typical values per 100g: Energy 1695kJ/407kcal
Each serving provides:
38.2g carbohydrate | 2.1g fibre | 5.1g protein

family weekends

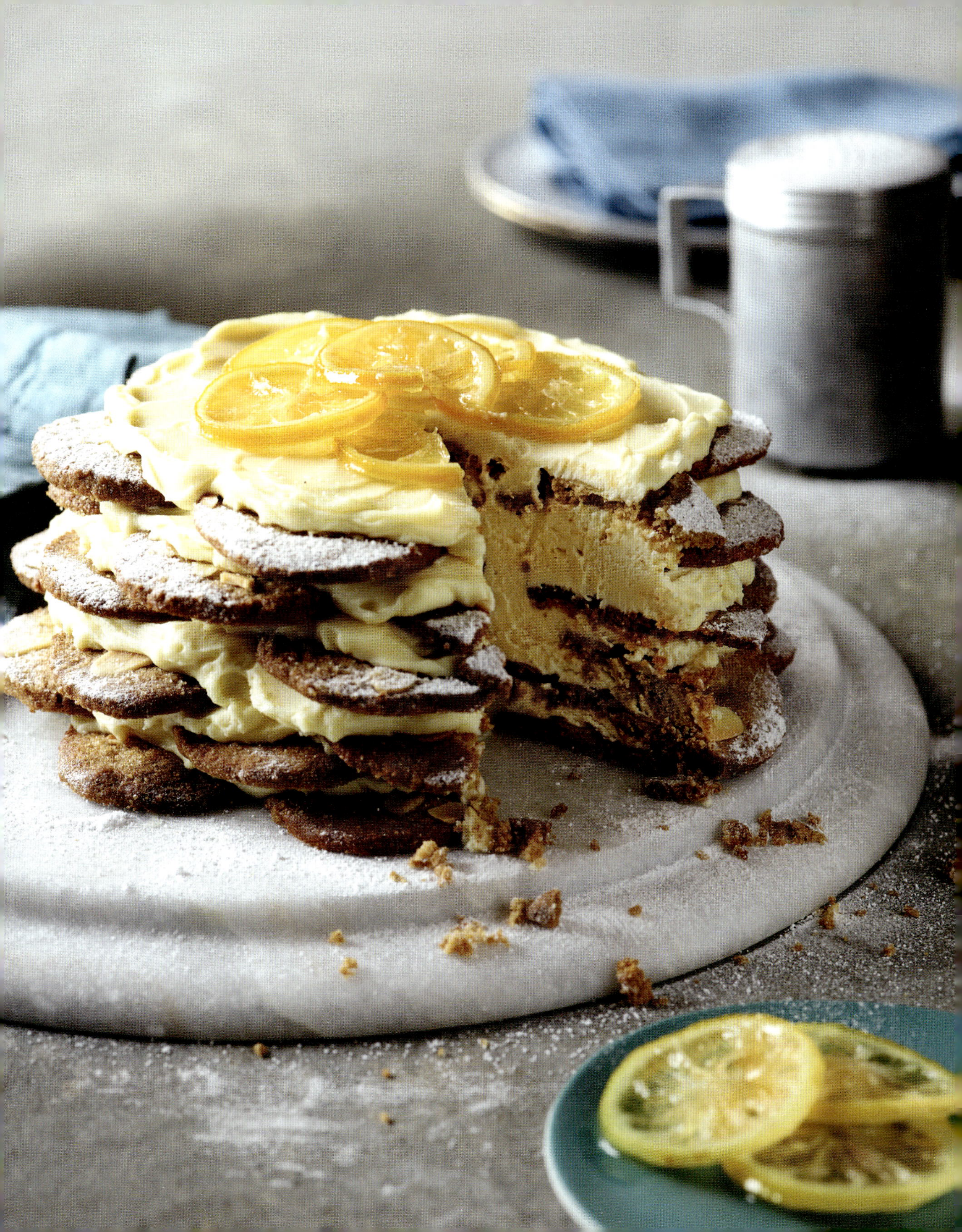

family weekends

SERVES 10
PREP TIME 15 mins
COOK TIME 45 mins

Red pepper cornbread

This easy loaf is a favourite with kids. Serve a slice with a tasty soup, or try it instead of rice with a chilli for an easy meal

50g unsalted butter, melted, plus extra for greasing
150g self-raising flour
2 tsp baking powder
½ tsp salt
½ tsp freshly ground black pepper

150g polenta
2 eggs, lightly beaten
300ml buttermilk by Sainsbury's
1 small red pepper, de-seeded and finely chopped

1. Preheat the oven to 180°C, fan 160°C, gas 4. Grease and line a 900g (2lb) loaf tin with baking paper.

2. Put the flour, baking powder, salt, pepper and polenta in a large mixing bowl. Make a well in the centre and stir in the eggs, butter and buttermilk. Add the chopped pepper and mix until everything is well combined.

3. Pour the mixture into the prepared tin and bake for 45 mins, until golden and a skewer inserted into the centre of the loaf comes out clean.

4. Allow to cool in the tin for 10 mins, then turn out onto a cooling rack. Serve warm or cold, cut into slices.

Cook's tip
You can add other flavours to this basic cornbread mixture. Instead of red pepper, use the same quantity of chopped crispy bacon, chopped spring onions or grated Cheddar cheese.

Each serving (84g) provides:

ENERGY	FAT	SATURATES	SUGARS	SALT
717kJ 170kcal	5.9g	3.1g	2.7g	0.8g
9%	8%	16%	3%	13%

% of the Reference Intakes
Typical values per 100g: Energy 853kJ/203kcal
Each serving provides:
23.7g carbohydrate | 0.8g fibre | 5.2g protein

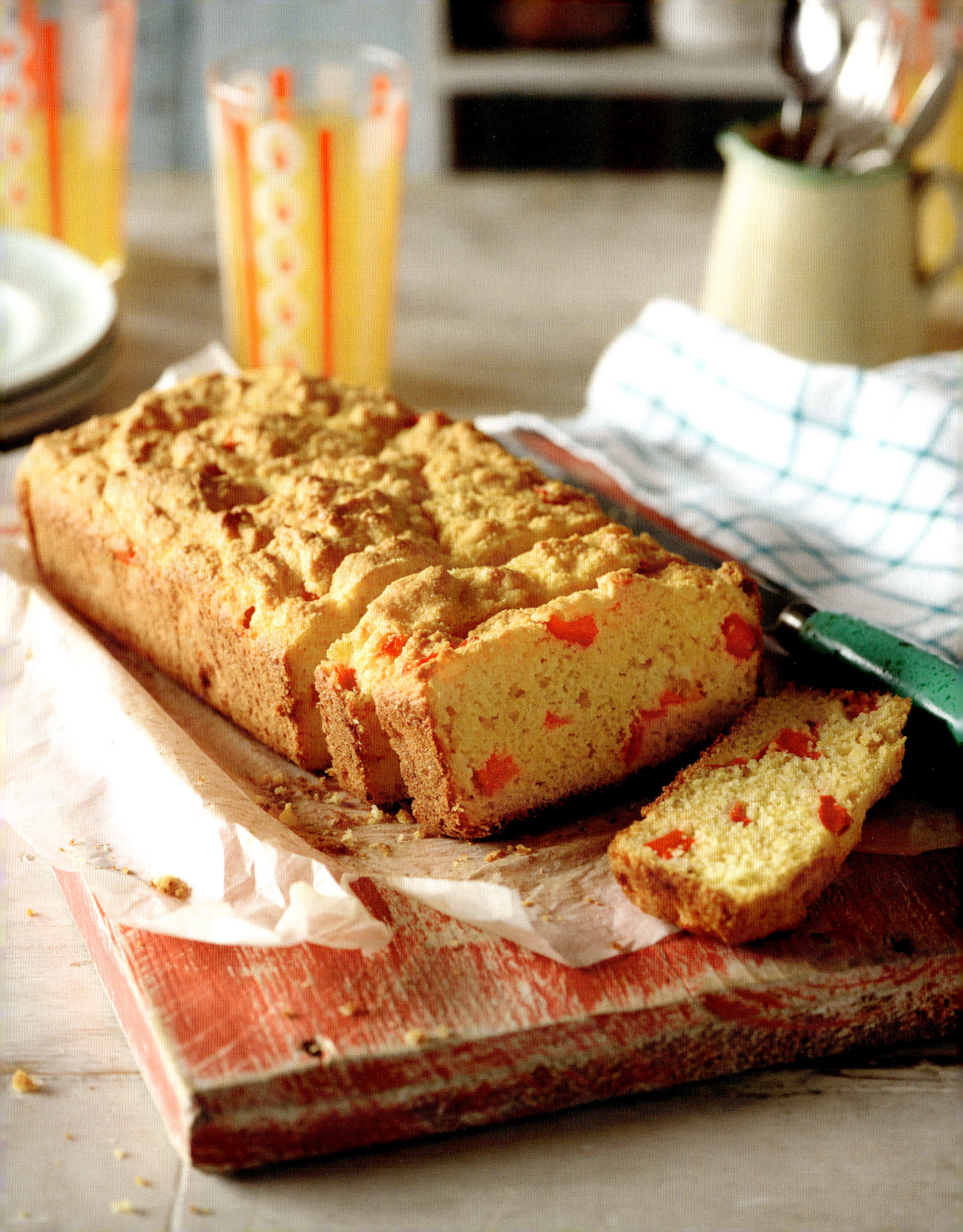

SERVES 4
PREP TIME 20 mins, plus 30 mins soaking and chilling
COOK TIME 40 mins

Bacon, broccoli & cheese bake

Bread pudding is a classic British recipe and this savoury version makes a great last-minute meal. Plus, it's perfect for using up stale bread

3 rashers reduced salt Danish back bacon by Sainsbury's, roughly chopped
15g unsalted butter, plus extra for greasing
3 spring onions, trimmed and chopped
125g Tenderstem broccoli, cut into 2cm pieces
140g day-old ciabatta, baguette or pain de campagne bread, cut in 3cm cubes
75g extra mature Cheddar, grated
4 large eggs
1 tsp Dijon mustard
Good pinch of cayenne pepper
300ml semi-skimmed milk

1. Dry-fry the bacon in a non-stick frying pan over a high heat until the fat starts to run and the bacon is golden. Add the butter and spring onions, and cook for another 2-3 mins.

2. Meanwhile, cook the broccoli in a pan of boiling water for 3 mins. Drain and run under cold running water to stop the cooking process.

3. Grease a 1-litre ovenproof dish with butter and layer about two-thirds of the bread in it with the broccoli, half the bacon and spring onion, and two-thirds of the cheese. Scatter the remaining bread cubes over, then top with the remaining bacon, spring onion and cheese.

4. In a large jug, lightly beat the eggs with the mustard and cayenne, and season with freshly ground black pepper. Beat in the milk until just blended. Pour over the bread. Refrigerate for at least 30 mins to allow the milk mixture to soak into the bread. You could leave it overnight if you want to get ahead.

5. Preheat the oven to 180°C, fan 160°C fan, gas 4. Bake the pudding for 30-40 mins or until the bread on top is golden at the edges and the savoury custard mixture is just set. Remove from the oven and let stand for 5-10 mins, then serve.

Each serving (216g) provides:

ENERGY	FAT	SATURATES	SUGARS	SALT
1585kJ 379kcal	20.7g	9.6g	5.4g	1.6g
19%	30%	48%	6%	27%

% of the Reference Intakes
Typical values per 100g: Energy 734kJ/176kcal
Each serving provides:
21.2g carbohydrate | 2.5g fibre | 25.7g protein

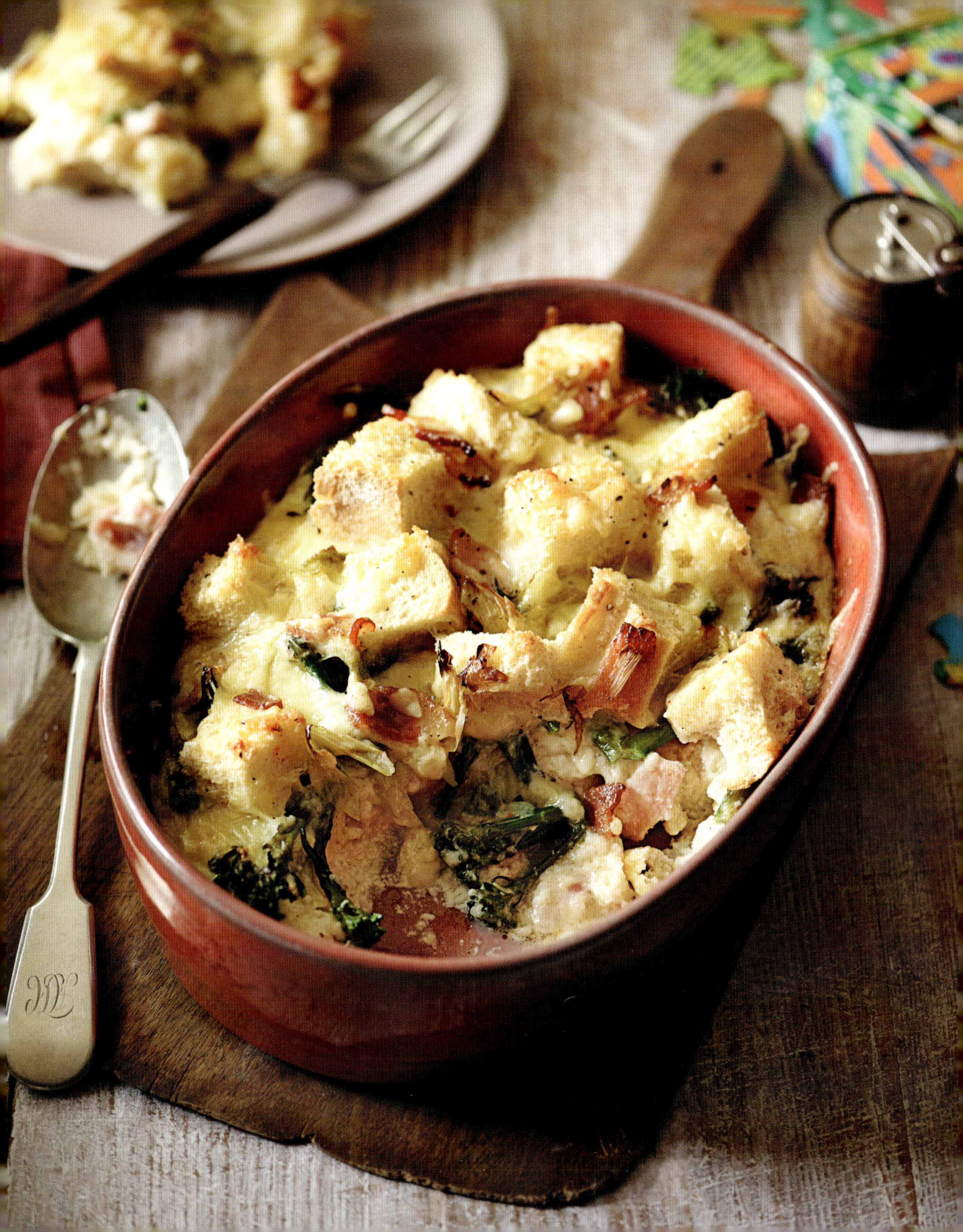

family weekends

SERVES 12
PREP TIME 50 mins, plus proving
COOK TIME 40 mins

Courgette & oregano bread

A deliciously different accompaniment for soups and salads

400g courgettes, trimmed and grated
1 tsp salt
4 spring onions, trimmed and chopped
2 tbsp olive oil
500g pack crusty white bread mix by Sainsbury's
1 tsp mustard powder
½ tsp cayenne pepper
2 tsp dried oregano
100g parmesan, grated
Plain flour for dusting
Vegetable oil, for greasing

1. Put the grated courgettes in a colander in the sink and sprinkle over the salt. Leave for 30 mins, stirring after 15 mins – the salt helps draw out the liquid. Wrap the courgettes in a clean tea towel and squeeze out as much liquid as possible.

2. Heat 1 tbsp of the oil in a large frying pan and cook the spring onions for 2-3 mins until soft. Add the rest of the oil and the courgettes and cook, stirring often, over a low heat, for another 5 mins. Transfer to a colander to cool, pressing the courgettes with the back of a spoon to drain off any excess liquid.

3. Tip the bread mix into a large bowl and stir in the mustard powder, cayenne and oregano until evenly mixed. Add the courgettes and spring onions, parmesan and about 310ml tepid water, and mix to make a soft dough. Don't add all the water at once, as you may not need it all. The dough should be soft, but not too sticky.

4. Knead the dough on a lightly floured work surface for 10 mins until it feels smooth and elastic (see p7).

5. Shape the dough into a ball and put on a lightly greased baking tray. Make 3 parallel cuts in the top with a sharp knife. Cover the loaf with a loose piece of lightly oiled cling film and leave in a warm place until doubled in size – this should take about an hour.

6. Preheat the oven to 220°C, fan 200°C, gas 7. Remove the cling film, dust the top of the bread with a little flour and bake for 30 mins until golden and crusty. The cooked loaf should sound hollow when tapped on the bottom.

Each serving (98g) provides:

ENERGY	FAT	SATURATES	SUGARS	SALT
664kJ 158kcal	6g	2.2g	1.6g	0.8g
8%	9%	11%	2%	13%

% of the Reference Intakes

Typical values per 100g: Energy 677kJ/161kcal
Each serving provides:
17.8g carbohydrate | 1.4g fibre | 7.6g protein

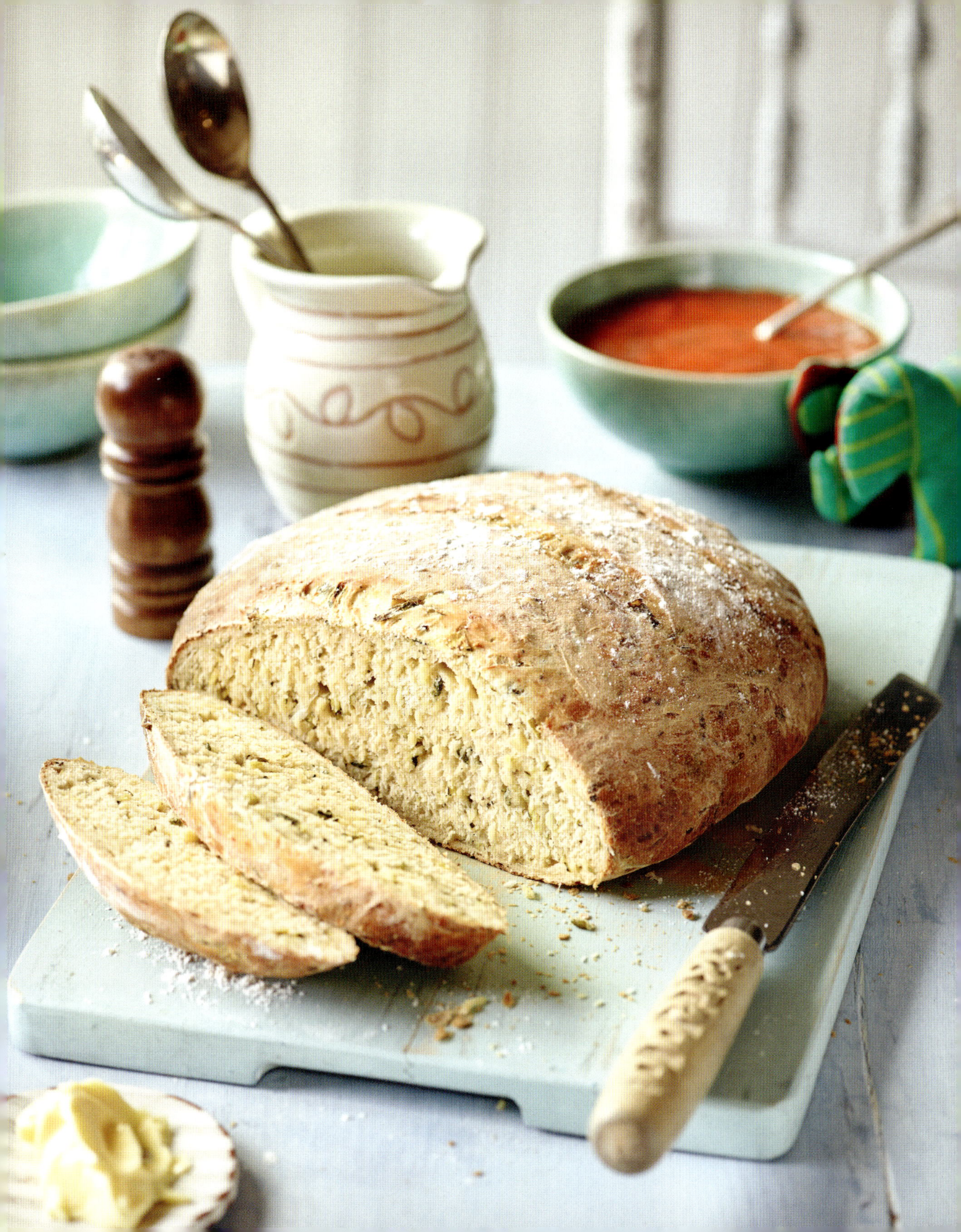

Best sellers

These pretty cupcakes are the perfect idea for bake sales. Decorate them with sprinkles and sparkles, then package them in egg cartons for easy transportation. Find the recipe on p58.

bakes for on the move

take-anywhere treats for picnics, bake sales and more

Raspberry & ricotta muffins	42
Banana blondies	44
Lemon & almond butter biscuits	46
Portuguese custard tarts	48
Pear & almond turnovers	50
Pistachio & apricot financiers	52
Chocolate-dipped Madeleines	54
Blueberry crumble squares	56
Mini cupcakes	58
Black bean brownies	60
Townies	62
Cheese & mustard gougères	64
Butternut filo parcels	66
Soft pretzels	68

on the move

MAKES 12
PREP TIME 15 mins
COOK TIME
30-35 mins

Raspberry & ricotta muffins

Perfect for a picnic, these easy-to-make fruity muffins are just the right combination of sweet and tart. The ricotta makes them nice and moist

250g self-raising flour
200g golden caster sugar
100g ground almonds
125g unsalted butter, melted and cooled slightly

250g tub ricotta by Sainsbury's
1 large egg
Finely grated zest of 1 lemon
150g fresh raspberries
25g flaked almonds

1. Preheat the oven to 180°C, fan 160°C, gas 4 and line a 12-hole muffin tin with paper cases.

2. Mix the flour, sugar and ground almonds together in a large bowl. In a separate bowl or jug, whisk together the melted butter, ricotta, egg and lemon zest. Pour the wet ingredients into the dry ingredients, and use an electric hand-held whisk to mix together until just combined (see Cook's tip, below).

3. Spoon half of the mixture into the muffin cases, then top with two-thirds of the raspberries. Spoon over the remaining muffin mixture and top with the remaining raspberries and the flaked almonds. Bake for 30-35 mins until a skewer inserted into the centre of a muffin comes out with just a few crumbs clinging to it. Transfer to a cooling rack to cool.

Cook's tip
If you don't have an electric whisk, use a wooden spoon – this mixture is too thick for a balloon whisk.

Each muffin (84g) provides:

ENERGY	FAT	SATURATES	SUGARS	SALT
1306kJ 313kcal	17.2g	7.1g	17.6g	0.3g
16%	25%	36%	20%	4%

% of the Reference Intakes
Typical values per 100g: Energy 1555kJ/372kcal
Each muffin provides:
31.8g carbohydrate | 1.7g fibre | 6.7g protein

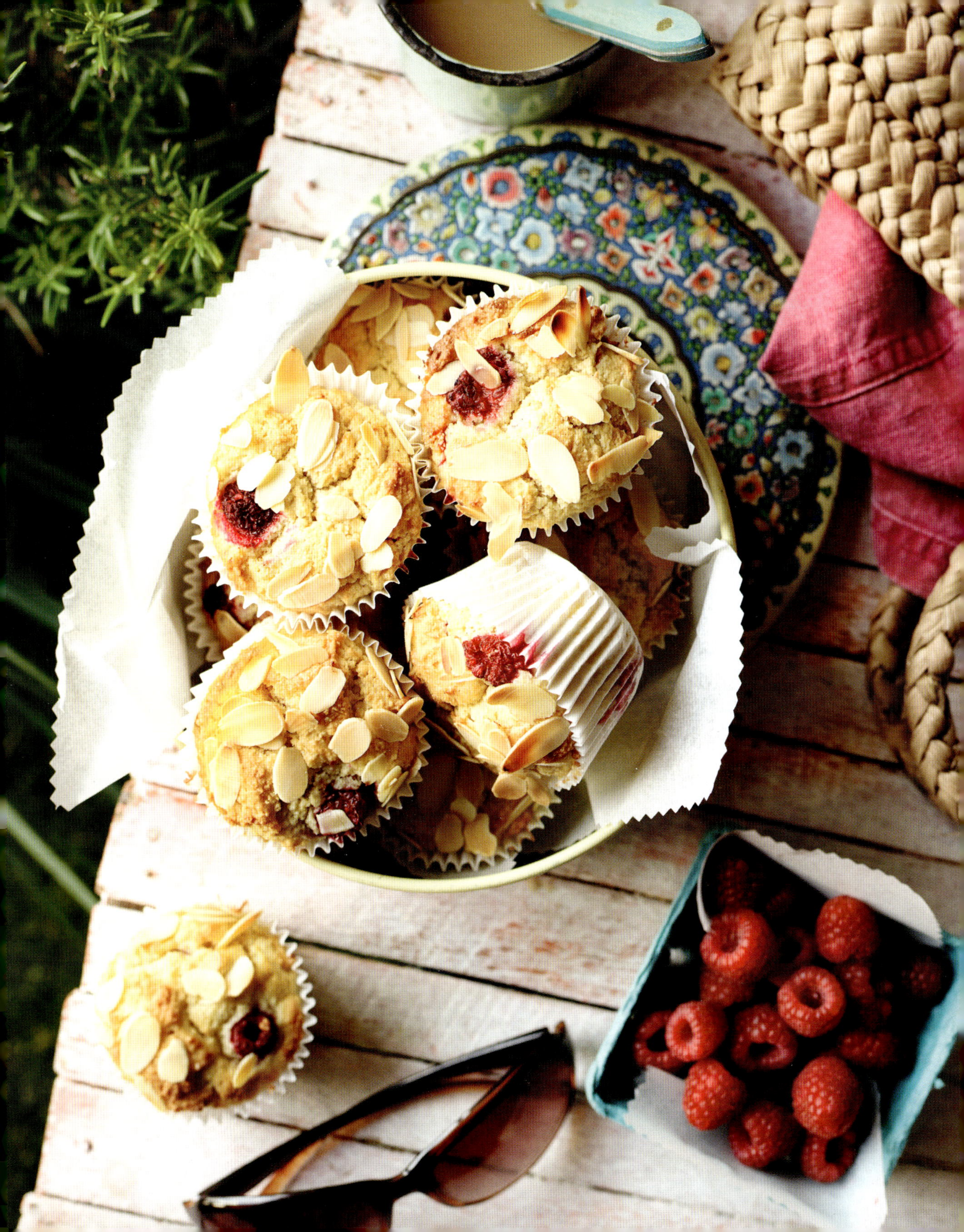

on the move

MAKES 16
PREP TIME
20 mins
COOK TIME
30-35 mins

Banana blondies

Blondies are the white chocolate version of brownies – and they couldn't be easier to make. This recipe uses bananas and pecan nuts

---

100g unsalted butter, plus extra for greasing
200g smooth white chocolate by Sainsbury's, roughly chopped
150g plain flour
½ tsp baking powder
¼ tsp table salt

2 eggs, lightly beaten
150g light brown soft sugar
1 tsp Taste the Difference Madagascan vanilla extract
2 very ripe bananas (175g total peeled weight)
100g pecan nut halves by Sainsbury's

---

1. Preheat the oven to 180°C, fan 160°C, gas mark 4. Lightly grease and line a 20cm square cake or tray-bake tin.

2. Melt 100g of the chocolate and half of the butter in a heatproof bowl set over a pan of simmering water, making sure that the base of the bowl doesn't touch the water. Remove the bowl from the pan and set aside to cool slightly.

3. Meanwhile, sift the flour, baking powder and salt into a separate large bowl. Whisk the eggs, sugar and vanilla into the cooled butter mixture, then add it to the dry ingredients and slowly whisk to combine.

4. Peel and mash the bananas until smooth, and fold into the mixture, along with half of the pecans and the remaining chopped white chocolate.

5. Pour the mixture into the prepared tin, levelling out the top, then scatter over the remaining pecans. Bake for 25-30 mins until golden and just firm to the touch.

6. Leave to cool for a few mins in the tin, then turn out onto a cooling rack to cool completely. Cut into 16 pieces.

Each blondie (50g) provides:

ENERGY	FAT	SATURATES	SUGARS	SALT
1032kJ 248kcal	15.2g	6.7g	16.8g	0.2g
12%	22%	34%	19%	4%

% of the Reference Intakes

Typical values per 100g: Energy 2065kJ/495kcal
Each blondie provides:
23.7g carbohydrate | 0.8g fibre | 3.5g protein

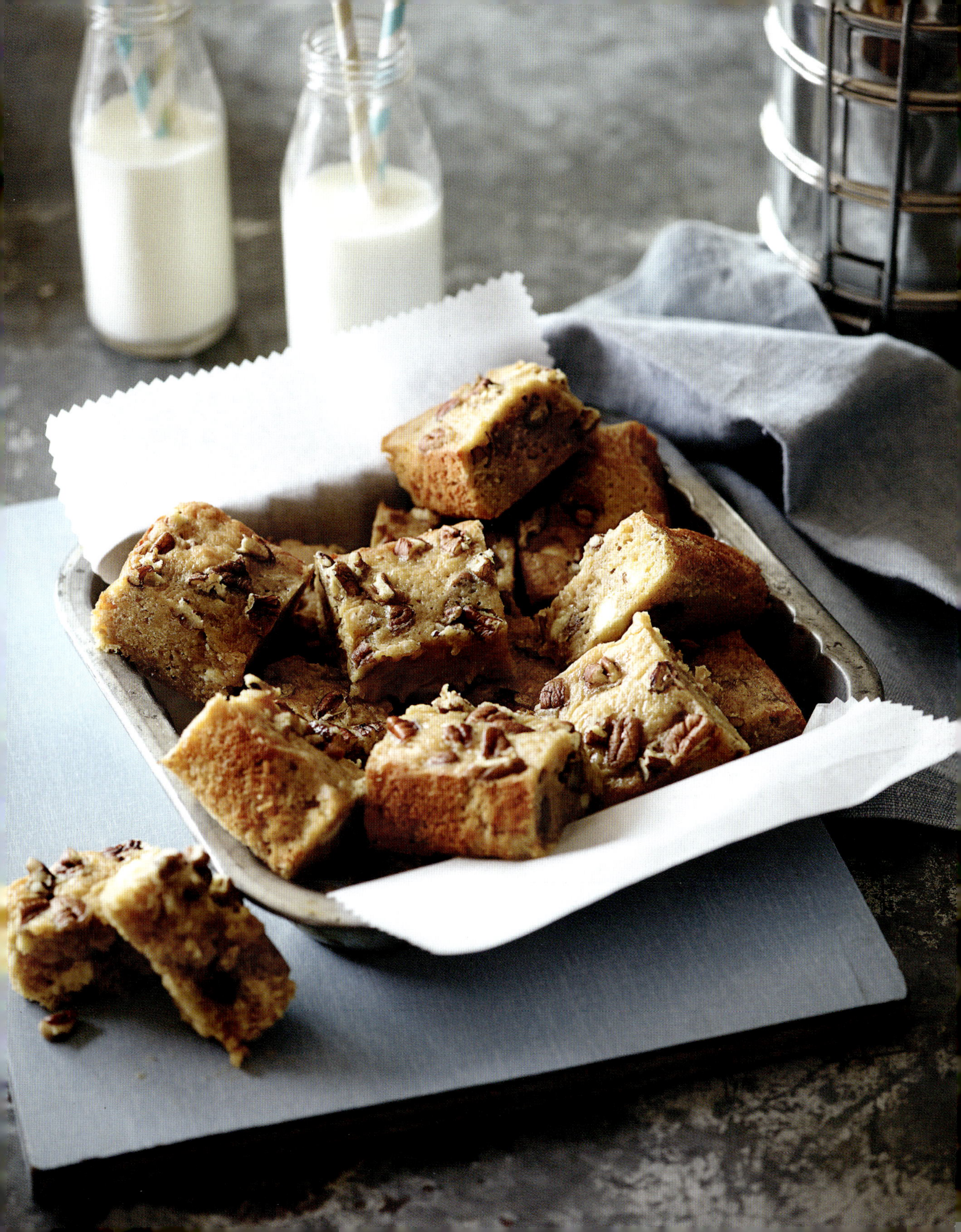

on the move

MAKES 48
PREP TIME 15 mins, plus freezing
COOK TIME 14 mins

Lemon & almond butter biscuits

Melt-in-the-mouth biscuits with a classic lemon and almond flavour combination. Try making a batch for your school fête

150g unsalted butter, chilled and cut into cubes
175g rye flour, plus extra for dusting
50g ground almonds by Sainsbury's
100g caster sugar
Finely grated zest of 2 lemons
1 egg, beaten
1 tbsp demerara sugar
2 tbsp flaked almonds

1 In a food processor or hand blender, process the butter, flour and ground almonds until the mixture looks sandy with some small lumps of butter. Add the caster sugar and lemon zest, and pulse briefly until combined. Gradually pour in the beaten egg and continue to pulse until the mixture just comes together to form a soft dough. Tip onto a well-floured surface and, using floured hands, knead briefly. The mixture will be quite sticky, but don't add more flour.

2 Shape the dough into a 24cm-long log, wrap tightly in cling film, then chill in the freezer for 1 hour.

3 Preheat the oven to 180°C, fan 160°C, gas 4. Line 2 baking sheets with baking paper. Remove the cling film from the dough and use a serrated knife to slice 48 rounds from the log, each one about 5mm thick. Arrange the biscuits on the prepared baking sheets, then sprinkle over the demerara sugar and almonds. Bake for 13-14 mins, or until just golden at the edges. You may need to bake the biscuits in batches.

4 Remove from the oven and let cool on the tray for a couple of mins, then transfer to a cooling rack to cool completely.

Cook's tip
These can be kept for up to a week in an airtight container. For a showstopping dessert for a special occasion, try using these biscuits to make the Lemon fridge cake on p32.

Each biscuit (11g) provides:

ENERGY	FAT	SATURATES	SUGARS	SALT
233kJ 56kcal	3.6g	1.7g	2.4g	trace
3%	5%	9%	3%	<1%

% of the Reference Intakes
Typical values per 100g: Energy 2118kJ/509kcal
Each biscuit provides:
4.6g carbohydrate | 0.7g fibre | 0.8g protein

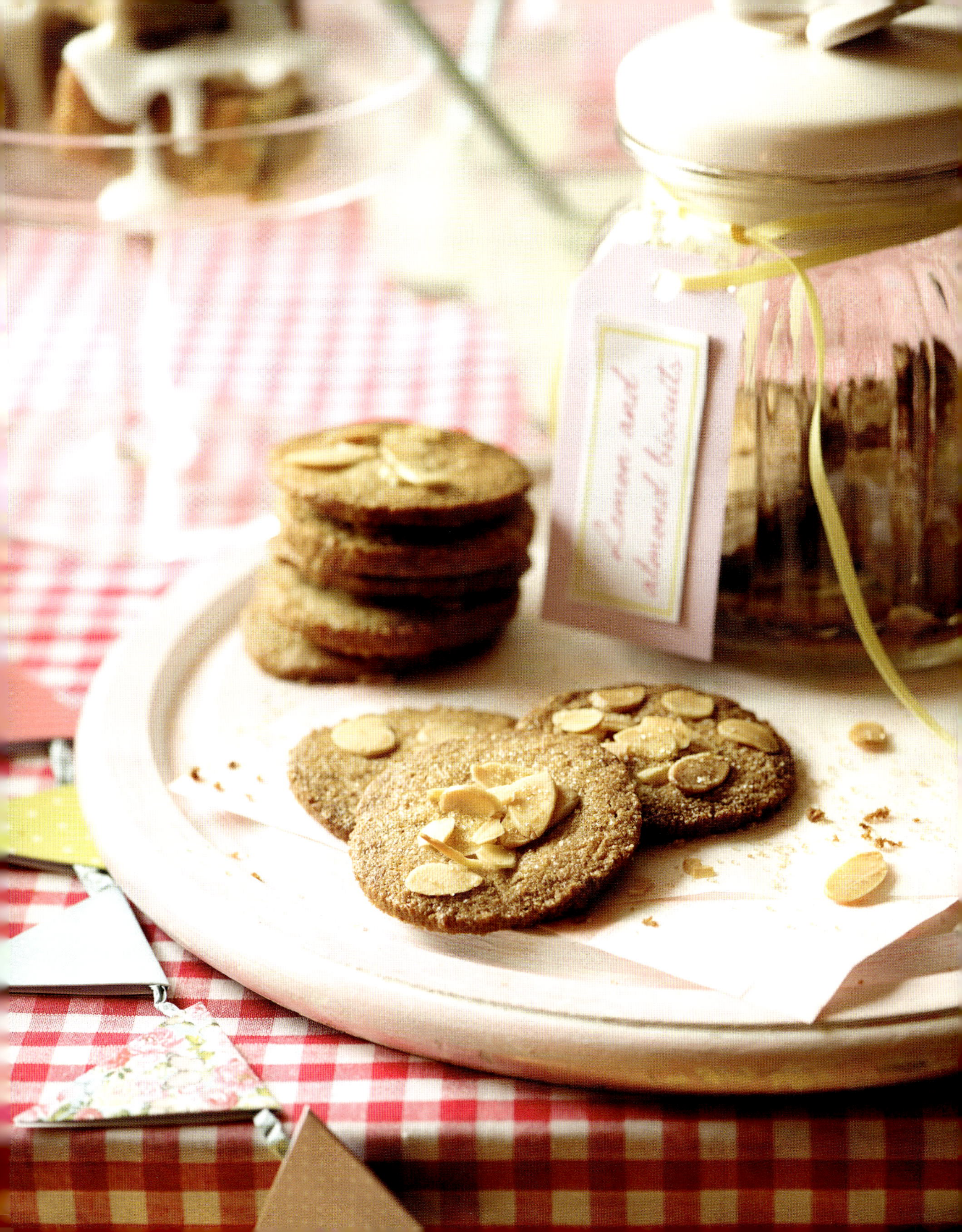

on the move

MAKES 12
PREP TIME 20 mins, plus cooling and chilling
COOK TIME 35 mins

Portuguese custard tarts

These little flaky pastry treats are known as *pastel de nata* in Portugal, where they were originally made in convents and monasteries

---

75g caster sugar
3 egg yolks
2 tbsp cornflour
1 tsp vanilla extract
350ml semi-skimmed milk

5g unsalted butter, softened
375g pack ready rolled puff pastry by Sainsbury's
Plain flour for dusting

---

1 Put the sugar in a small pan with 100ml cold water. Heat gently, stirring, until the sugar has dissolved. Bring to the boil and boil for 3-4 mins, without stirring, until the liquid is syrupy. Leave to cool for 20 mins.

2 To make the custard, whisk together the egg yolks*, cornflour and vanilla extract in a large pan and gradually whisk in the milk and cold sugar syrup. Bring to the boil over a medium heat, whisking all the time until you have a smooth, thick custard. Simmer for 2 mins, then transfer to a heatproof bowl and cover the surface with cling film to prevent a skin forming. Leave to cool completely.

3 Grease a 12-hole muffin tray with the softened butter. Preheat the oven to 220°C, fan 200°C, gas 7. Unroll the pastry sheet with one long side facing you and cut the sheet in half. Sit one piece on top of the other. With the longest side facing you, roll up tightly to make a log. Trim both ends of the log with a serrated knife.

4 Cut the log into 12 even rounds. Lay each round, cut side up, on a lightly floured surface and roll out to a 10cm circle. Gently press the pastry rounds into the holes of the prepared muffin tray.

5 Divide the custard evenly between the pastry cups. Bake for about 25 mins or until the pastry is crisp and golden and the custard has browned in places. If some of the custard has spilled out of the pastry cases, gently ease it back inside with a small palette knife. Cool in the tin for 5 mins, then transfer to a cooling rack. Serve warm or cold.

*See p191 for a list of recipes to use leftover egg whites.

Each tart (68g) provides:

ENERGY	FAT	SATURATES	SUGARS	SALT
822kJ 197kcal	10.3g	4.4g	8.3g	0.2g
10%	15%	22%	9%	3%

% of the Reference Intakes
Typical values per 100g: Energy 1209kJ/289kcal
Each tart provides:
21g carbohydrate | 1.3g fibre | 4.4g protein

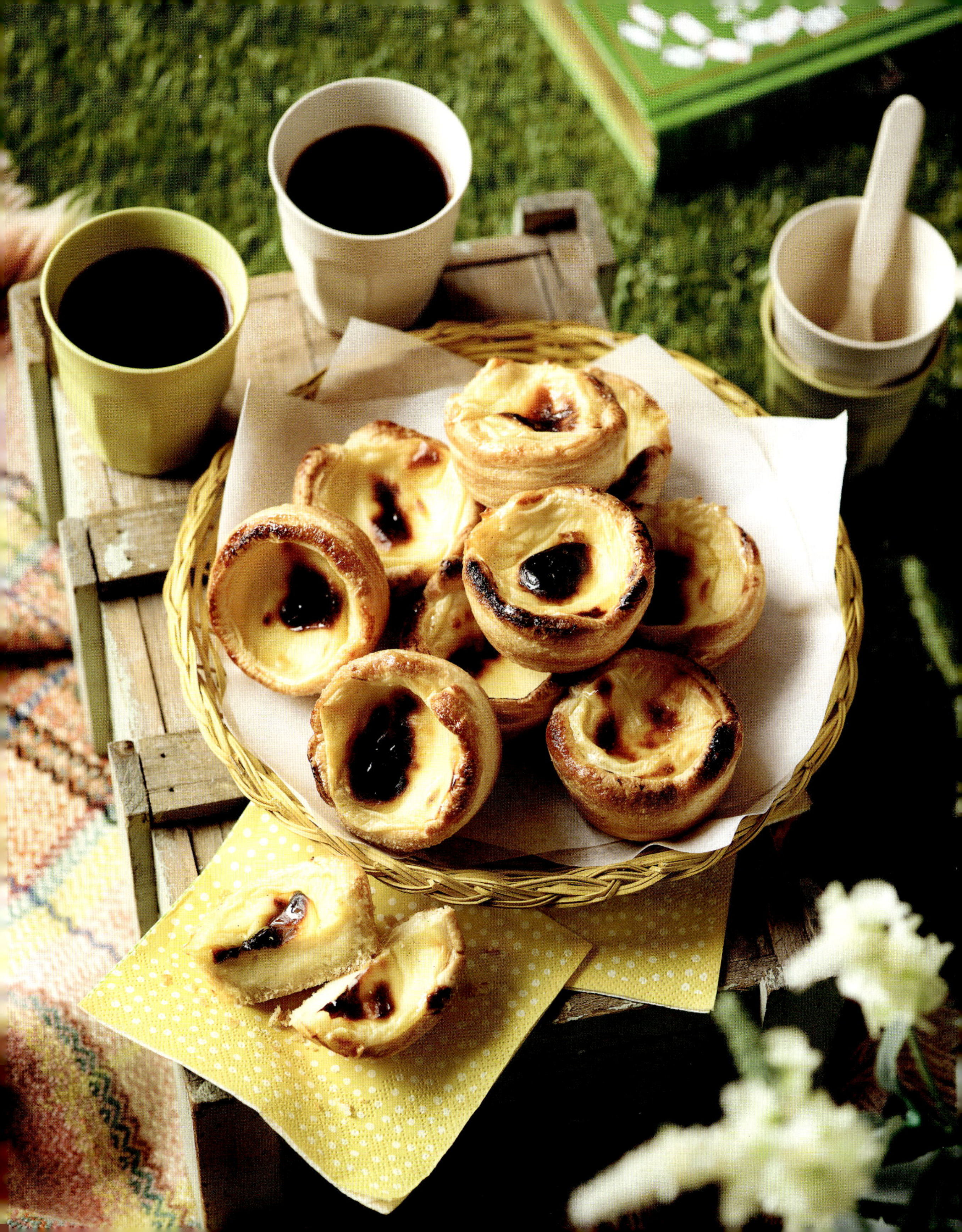

on the move

MAKES 9
PREP TIME 30 mins
COOK TIME 18-20 mins

Pear & almond turnovers

Crispy puff pastry parcels filled with a tasty mix of pear and marzipan

Plain flour, for dusting
375g pack ready rolled lighter puff pastry by Sainsbury's
2 firm but ripe pears (about 175g prepared weight)
Finely grated zest of 1 lemon, plus 1 tbsp lemon juice
2 tbsp ground almonds
50g golden marzipan by Sainsbury's, cut into ½-1cm cubes
1 egg, beaten
2 tbsp flaked almonds
1 tsp demerara sugar

1. Preheat the oven to 200°C, fan 180°C, gas 6. On a clean, lightly floured work surface, unroll the pastry sheet then use a rolling pin to roll it out a little further to form a 30cm square. Cut the pastry into 9 x 10cm squares. Transfer to 2 baking trays lined with baking paper and chill in the fridge while you prepare the filling.

2. Peel, core and cut the pears into 1cm cubes. Transfer to a bowl, add the lemon zest and juice, ground almonds and marzipan, and toss together.

3. Remove the pastry from the fridge. Spoon 1 tbsp of the pear mixture into the centre of each square. Brush the pastry edges with a little beaten egg, then take one corner and fold over to the opposite corner to make a triangle. Gently press the edges together, using a fork to seal. Repeat with the remaining turnovers.

4. Brush the tops of the turnovers with the remaining egg, then use a sharp knife to cut a couple of small incisions into the top of each one. Sprinkle with the flaked almonds and demerara sugar.

5. Bake for 18-20 mins until crisp and golden. Leave to cool for a few mins and serve warm, or leave to cool completely on a cooling rack.

Each turnover (76g) provides:

ENERGY	FAT	SATURATES	SUGARS	SALT
862kJ 206kcal	10.3g	3.5g	7g	0.3g
15%	15%	18%	8%	4%

% of the Reference Intakes
Typical values per 100g: Energy 1135kJ/271kcal
Each turnover provides:
22.1g carbohydrate | 1.8g fibre | 5.4g protein

Park Fm
Church
Itteringham
He.
Ford
Blickling Mill
Mill
Church
Itteringham

MAKES 10
PREP TIME 15 mins, plus chilling
COOK TIME 30 mins

on the move

Pistachio & apricot financiers

These little French cakes were traditionally made to look like gold bars, which it's believed is how they got their name

150g unsalted butter, plus extra for greasing
2 x 100g packs pistachio kernels by Sainsbury's
200g icing sugar
50g plain flour
1 tsp baking powder
Pinch of salt

4 large egg whites
1 tsp Taste the Difference Madagascan vanilla extract
100g dried apricots, finely chopped

YOU WILL ALSO NEED
Pack of 10 mini loaf cases by Sainsbury's

1. Melt the butter in a small pan over a medium heat, then continue to heat for about 5 mins until it has turned golden brown. Remove from the heat and set aside to cool.

2. In a food processor or hand blender, whizz the pistachios until roughly chopped, remove 2 tablespoons and reserve. Continue to pulse until the pistachios are finely chopped. Add the icing sugar and pulse until the mixture is finely ground. Transfer to a large bowl and stir in the flour, baking powder and salt.

3. Gradually add the egg whites*, whisking to combine after each addition. Pour the cooled melted butter and vanilla onto the mixture and whisk until combined. Fold in the apricots and chill the mixture in the fridge for 30 mins.

4. Grease the mini loaf cases with a little butter and arrange on a baking tray. Preheat the oven to 190°C, fan 170°C, gas 5. Divide the chilled cake mixture equally between the prepared loaf cases. Scatter over the reserved chopped pistachios and bake for 20-22 mins until the financiers are risen and golden and a skewer inserted into the centre comes out clean.

*See p191 for a list of recipes to use leftover egg yolks.

Each financier (75g) provides:

ENERGY	FAT	SATURATES	SUGARS	SALT
1448kJ 348kcal	22.4g	8.7g	23.5g	0.3g
17%	32%	44%	26%	5%

% of the Reference Intakes
Typical values per 100g: Energy 1931kJ/463kcal
Each financier provides:
28.1g carbohydrate | 1.9g fibre | 7.5g protein

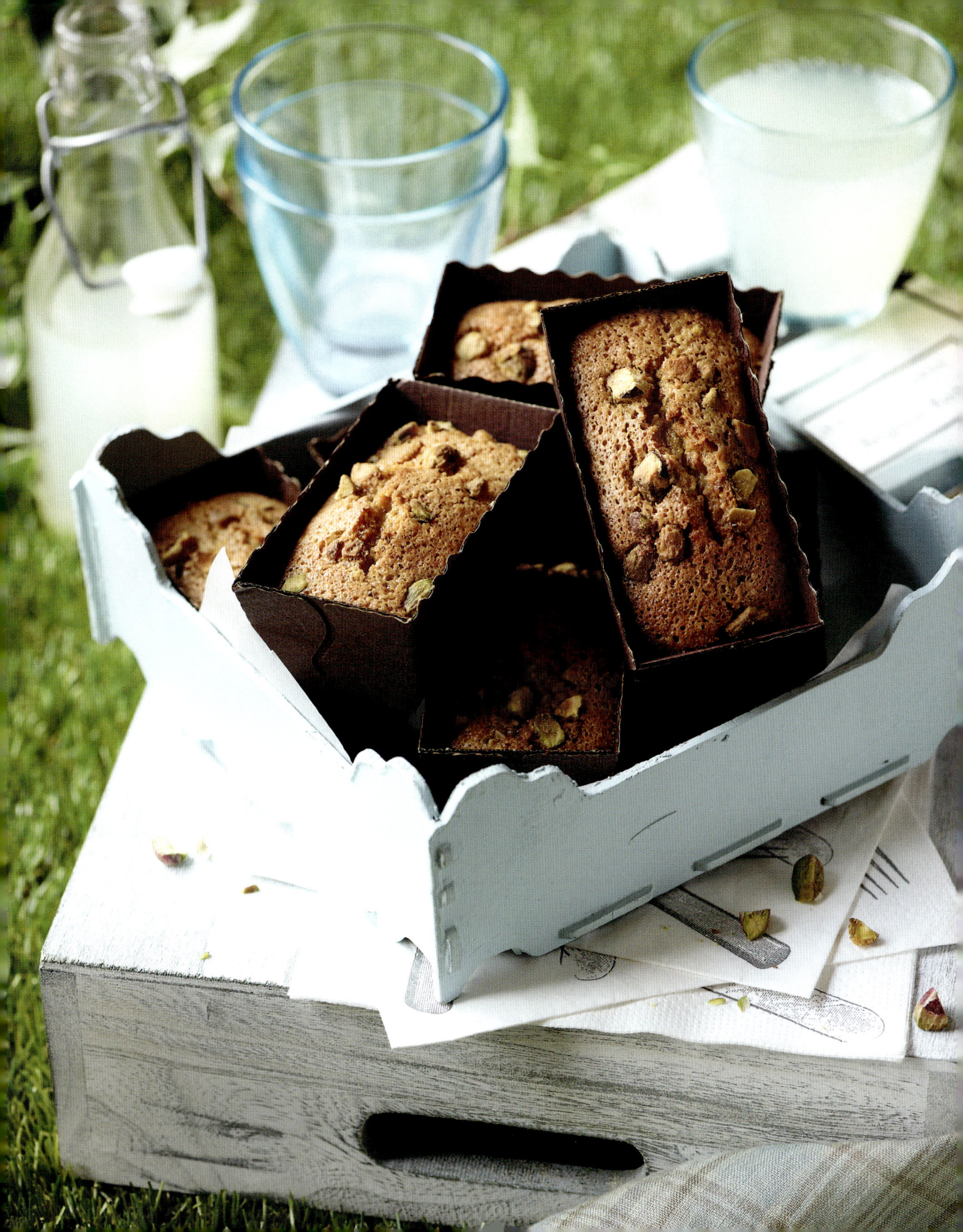

MAKES 12
PREP TIME 15 mins plus resting and setting time
COOK TIME 25 mins

Chocolate-dipped Madeleines

Take a batch of these to the office and watch them disappear!

60g unsalted butter, cut into small cubes, plus extra, melted, for greasing
60g self-raising flour, sifted, plus extra for dusting
50g caster sugar
2 eggs, at room temperature
½ tsp Taste the Difference Madagascan vanilla extract
100g Taste the Difference Belgian 72% dark chocolate, chopped

YOU WILL ALSO NEED
1 x 12-hole Madeleine tin

1. Brush the Madeleine tin generously with the extra melted butter and dust with a little flour.

2. Put the 60g butter in a small pan set over a low heat. Slowly melt until it starts to turn a deep, brown colour and gives off a nutty aroma. Keep an eye on the pan – you want the butter to be browned but not burnt. Remove from the heat and set aside to cool.

3. In a large bowl, beat together the sugar, eggs and vanilla using an electric hand-held whisk until the mixture is very thick and pale – this will take about 5 mins. Fold in one-third of the flour until combined, then add another third of flour and fold again. Finally, fold in the remaining flour and half of the melted butter until combined, then fold in the remaining butter. Cover with cling film so that it's touching the mixture, then set aside to rest for 10 mins.

4. Preheat the oven to 180°C, fan 160°C, gas 4. Divide the mixture equally between the holes in the prepared tin. Bake for 12 mins until the Madeleines are puffed up and turning slightly golden on the edges. Carefully remove from the tins and cool on a cooling rack.

5. Line a baking sheet with baking paper and sit a cooling rack on top. Melt the chocolate in a small heatproof bowl (see p7). Dip the top of each Madeleine into the chocolate, then put on the cooling rack and set aside in a cool place (not the fridge) for 30-40 mins until the chocolate is set.

Each Madeleine (31g) provides:

ENERGY	FAT	SATURATES	SUGARS	SALT
558kJ 134kcal	9.1g	5.3g	6.1g	0.1g
7%	13%	27%	7%	1%

% of the Reference Intakes
Typical values per 100g: Energy 1799kJ/432kcal
Each Madeleine provides:
10.2g carbohydrate | 1g fibre | 2.2g protein

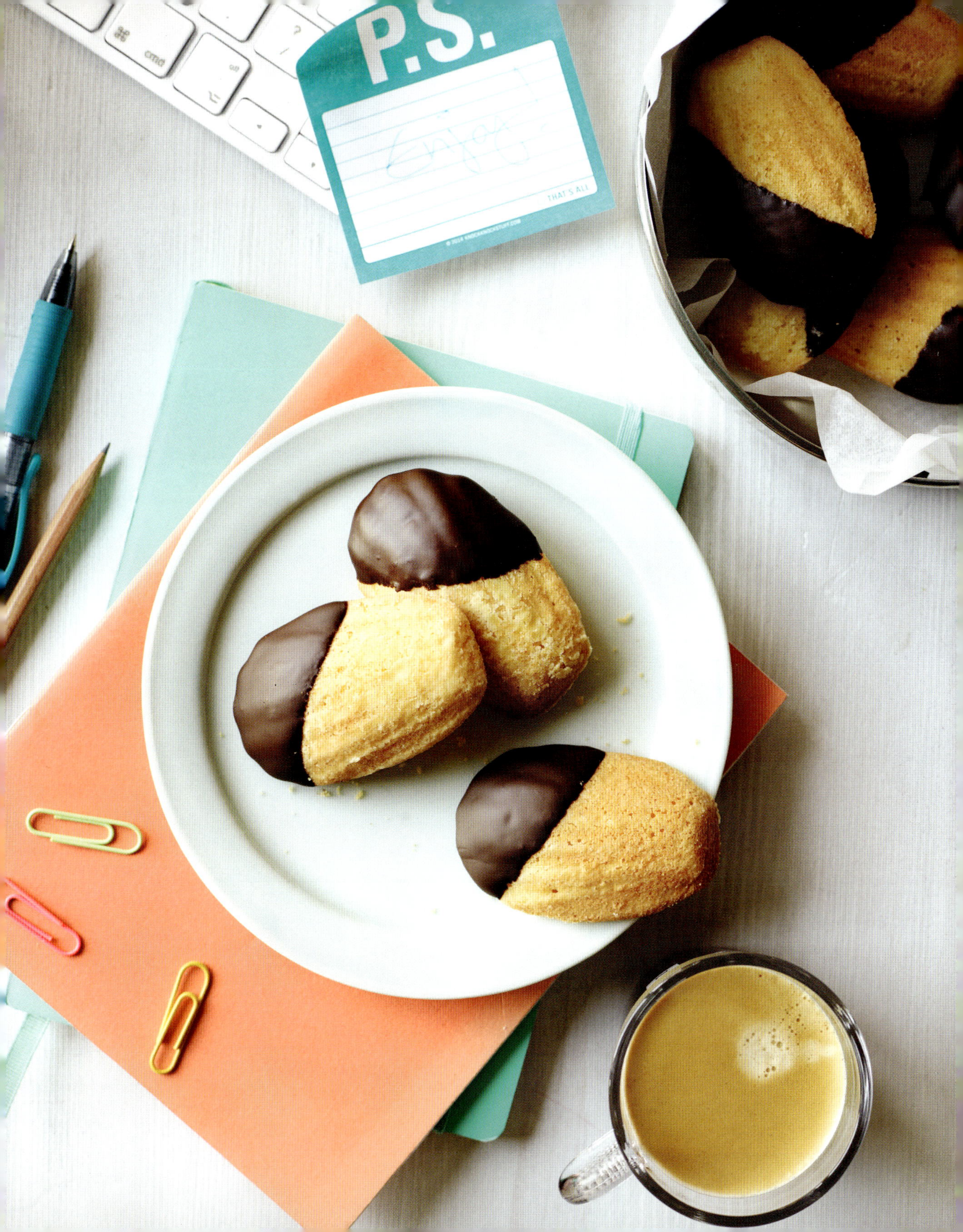
P.S.
THAT'S ALL

on the move

MAKES 16
PREP TIME 20 mins
COOK TIME 40-45 mins

Blueberry crumble squares

A buttery, fruity, crumbly traybake that's a guaranteed crowd-pleaser

FOR THE BASE
100g unsalted butter, chilled and cut into cubes, plus extra for greasing
100g ground almonds by Sainsbury's
100g plain flour
100g caster sugar
Finely grated zest of 1 lemon
Pinch of salt

FOR THE TOPPING
100g blanched almonds by Sainsbury's
50g plain flour
75g unsalted butter, chilled
50g demerara sugar
25g whole rolled oats
250g blueberries
2 tsp cornflour
2 tbsp lemon juice

1 Preheat the oven to 180°C, fan 160°C, gas 4. Grease and line the base and sides of a 20cm square cake or traybake tin with baking paper.

2 Make the base. In a food processor, whizz together the butter, ground almonds, flour, sugar, half the lemon zest and a pinch of salt until it comes together as a dough. Press into the base of the prepared tin and chill in the fridge while you make the topping.

3 Whizz the blanched almonds in the food processor until roughly chopped, remove about half and set aside. Continue to whizz the remaining almonds until finely ground, then add the flour, butter and sugar and pulse until the mixture forms rough breadcrumbs. Transfer to a bowl and stir in the oats, reserved chopped almonds and remaining lemon zest.

4 Mix the blueberries with the cornflour and lemon juice until coated, then spoon half over the chilled base. Scatter over half of the crumble topping, then repeat with the remaining blueberries and topping. Bake for 40-45 mins until the crumble is crisp and golden.

5 Leave to cool completely in the tin. Use the lining paper to lift the cake out the tin, then cut into 16 squares.

Each square (57g) provides:

ENERGY	FAT	SATURATES	SUGARS	SALT
1019kJ 245kcal	16.4g	6g	11.1g	0.1g
12%	23%	30%	12%	1%

% of the Reference Intakes
Typical values per 100g: Energy 1787kJ/429kcal
Each square provides:
19g carbohydrate | 1.6g fibre | 4.5g protein

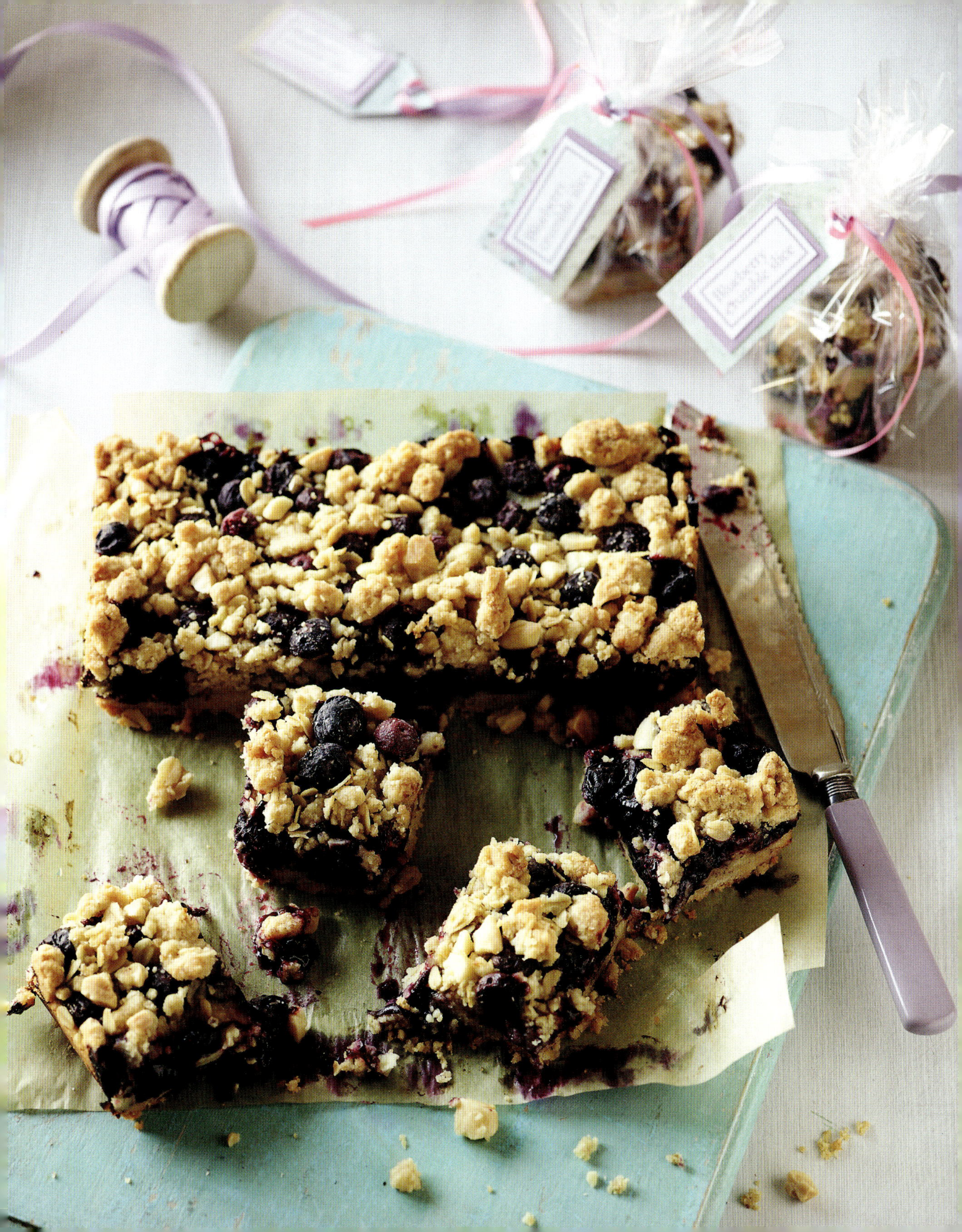

on the move

MAKES 24
PREP TIME 25 mins
COOK TIME
10-12 mins

Mini cupcakes

Box up these pretty cakes in egg cartons for the perfect bake sale treats

55g unsalted butter, softened
55g caster sugar
Few drops Taste the Difference Madagascan vanilla extract
1 large egg, beaten
55g self-raising flour

FOR THE BUTTERCREAM
90g unsalted butter, softened
180g icing sugar, sifted
Yellow food colouring by Sainsbury's
Multi coloured 100s and 1000s by Sainsbury's, to decorate
Mini blossom and wild rose cake decorations by Sainsbury's, to decorate

YOU WILL ALSO NEED
24 petits fours cases by Sainsbury's

1. Preheat the oven to 200°C, fan 180°C, gas 6. Line 2 x 12-hole mini muffin tins with the petits fours cases.

2. In a small bowl, beat the butter and sugar together using a hand-held electric whisk until pale and fluffy. Beat in the vanilla extract and egg, then sift over the flour and fold in with a metal spoon.

3. Use a teaspoon to spoon the mixture evenly between the petits fours cases. Bake for 10-12 mins until the cupcakes are risen, golden and just firm to the touch. Cool for 5 mins, then transfer to a cooling rack and leave to cool completely.

4. To make the buttercream, put the butter in a mixing bowl and gradually beat in the icing sugar until very smooth and creamy.

5. Decorate the cupcakes. Spoon half the buttercream into a piping bag fitted with a plain round nozzle. Pipe a round on top of 12 of the cupcakes. Beat a little yellow food colouring into the rest of the buttercream. Spoon into a second piping bag and pipe rounds on the rest of the cupcakes. Alternatively, use a small angled palette knife to swirl the buttercream on the top of each cupcake. Decorate each cake with the 100s and 1000s, blossom and wild rose decorations.

Cook's tip
For Easter cupcakes, top with a mini sugar-coated chocolate egg or for Christmas, use red icing and top with chocolate stars, edible gold pearls or silver balls. You can find decorative egg boxes for sale online.

Each cupcake (22g) provides:

ENERGY	FAT	SATURATES	SUGARS	SALT
411kJ 98kcal	5.2g	3g	10.5g	trace
5%	7%	15%	12%	<1%

% of the Reference Intakes
Typical values per 100g: Energy 1956kJ/467kcal
Each cupcake provides:
12.2g carbohydrate | 0.1g fibre | 0.6g protein

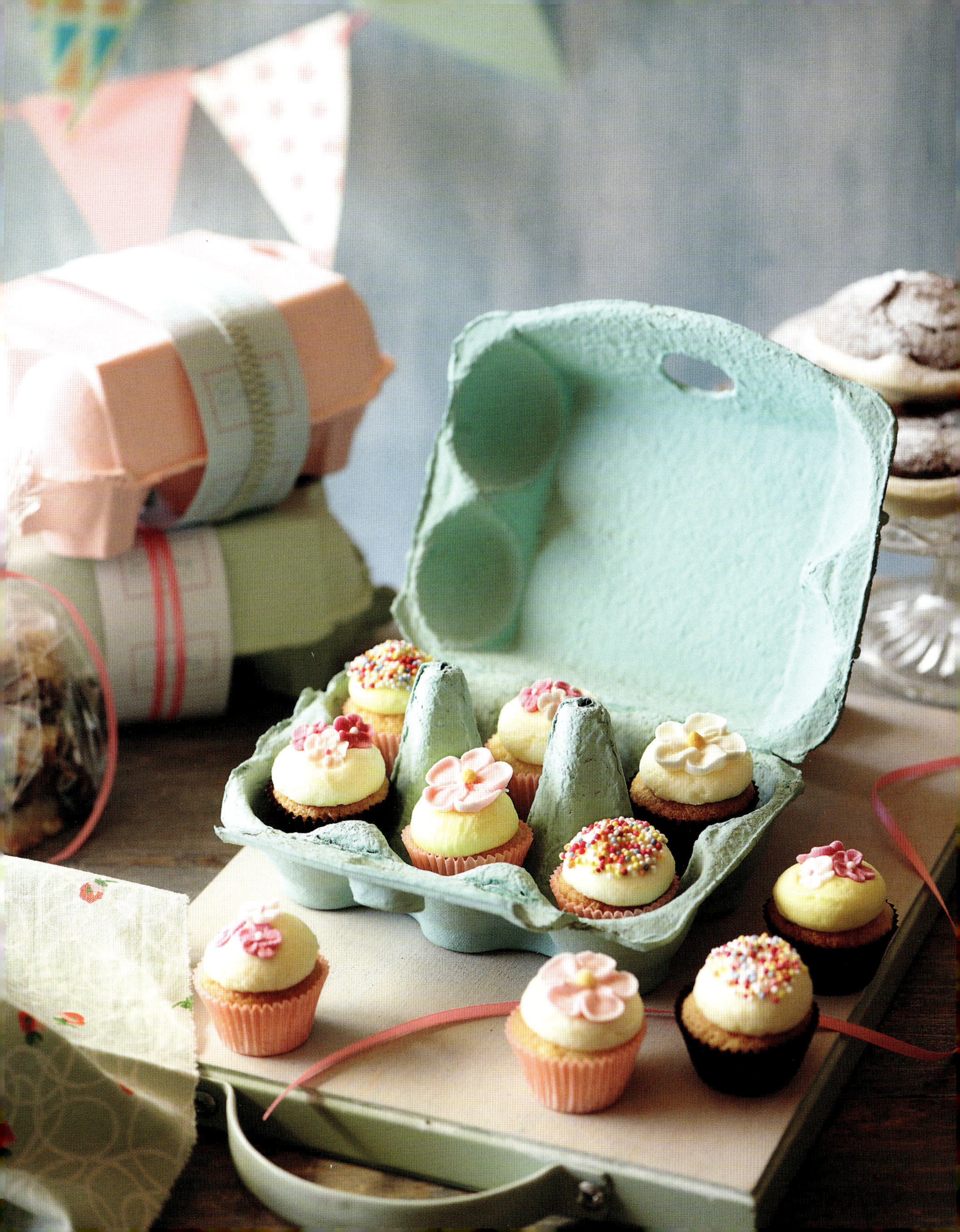

MAKES 18
PREP TIME 15 mins
COOK TIME 30 mins

Black bean brownies

These fudgy brownies are made with black beans instead of flour – but are still full of intense, chocolately flavour

200g unsalted butter, plus extra for greasing
200g Taste the Difference Belgian dark chocolate, broken into chunks
380g carton Sainsbury's SO organic black beans in water, drained and rinsed
50g cocoa by Sainsbury's
250g light muscovado sugar
3 large eggs
2 tsp Taste the Difference Madagascan vanilla extract
1½ tsp baking powder
100g smooth white chocolate by Sainsbury's, roughly chopped

1. Preheat the oven to 180°C, fan 160°C, gas 4. Grease and line a 30cm x 20cm baking tin with baking paper. Melt the butter and chocolate together in a heatproof bowl set over a pan of simmering water, making sure that the bottom of the bowl doesn't touch the water. Remove the bowl from the pan and set aside to cool slightly.

2. Put the black beans in a food processor or hand blender, together with the butter and chocolate mixture, and process until smooth. Add all the other ingredients except the white chocolate, and process until smooth and combined, scraping the sides of the bowl a few times using a spatula.

3. Pour the mixture into the prepared tin and smooth gently with the spatula. Sprinkle over the white chocolate and bake for 20-25 mins until the top has risen slightly and the cake looks slightly softer in the middle than around the edges.

4. Remove from the oven and let cool in the tin, then turn out onto a cooling rack. Let cool completely before cutting into 18 pieces.

Each brownie (55g) provides:

ENERGY	FAT	SATURATES	SUGARS	SALT
1101kJ 265kcal	18.3g	10.8g	18.4g	0.2g
13%	26%	54%	20%	4%

% of the Reference Intakes
Typical values per 100g: Energy 2001kJ/481kcal
Each brownie provides:
20.1g carbohydrate | 2g fibre | 4g protein

on the move

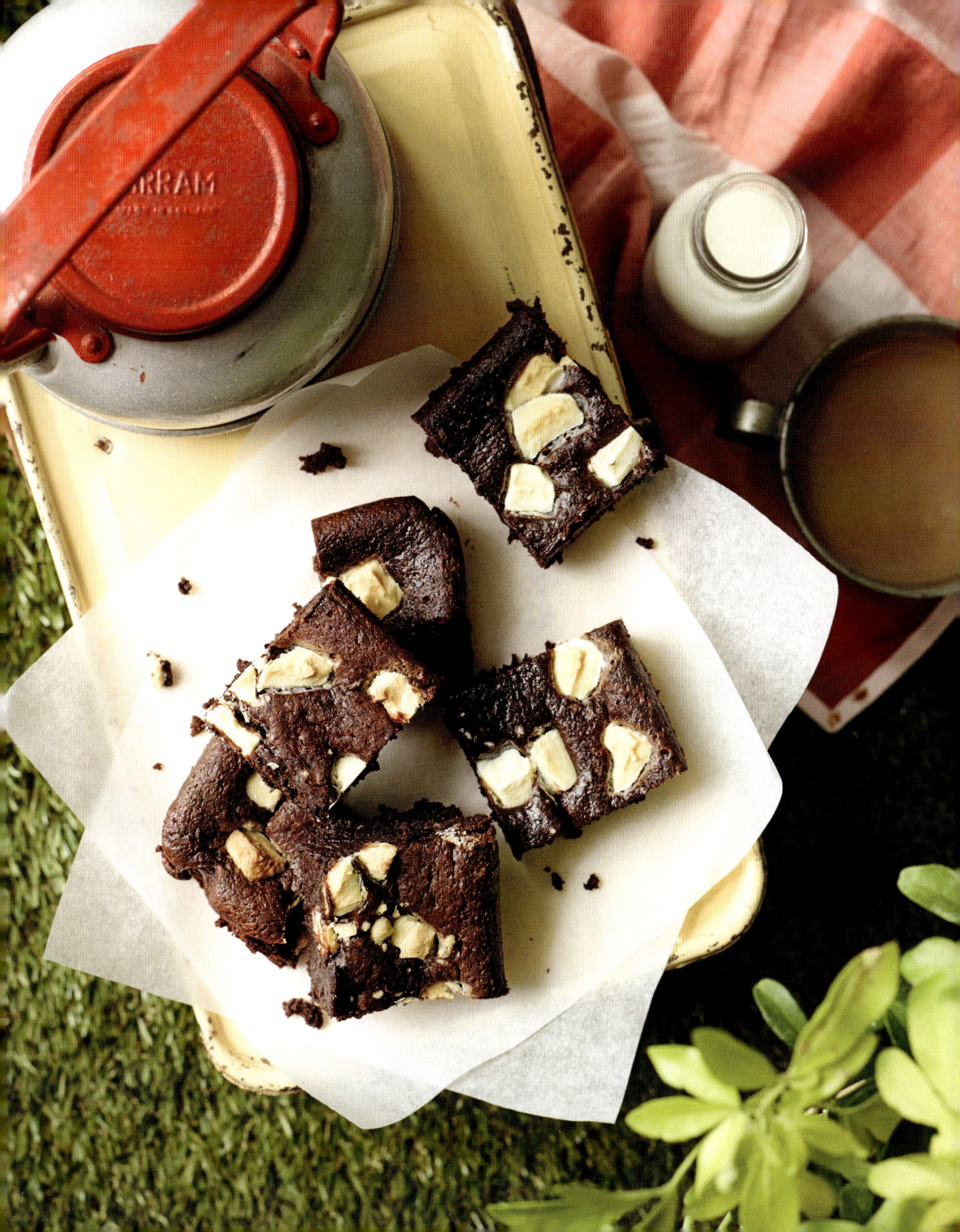

on the move

MAKES 18
PREP TIME 30 mins
COOK TIME 20 mins

Townies

Jam tarts meet brownies in these delicious hybrids – townies! Take a few on a train journey to help the time pass more deliciously

---

375g dessert pastry by Sainsbury's (from 500g block)
75g self-raising flour, plus extra for dusting
175g orange curd by Sainsbury's
115g unsalted butter
50g cocoa

2 large eggs
225g caster sugar
¼ tsp Taste the Difference Madagascan vanilla extract
50g pecans, roughly chopped

---

1 Preheat the oven to 180°C, fan 160°C, gas 4. Roll out the pastry on a lightly floured surface and stamp out as many 8cm rounds as possible. Gather up the pastry scraps, knead lightly, then roll and stamp out more rounds – you'll need 18 altogether. Use to line 18 holes in 2 x 12-hole bun trays. Spoon the orange curd over each pastry base.

2 Melt the butter in a small pan over a low heat, then stir in the cocoa until evenly combined. Set aside to cool slightly.

3 Whisk the eggs, sugar and vanilla extract together in a large bowl until pale, foamy and starting to thicken. Stir in the cocoa and butter mixture, flour and pecans until just evenly mixed.

4 Divide the brownie mixture equally between the tarts and bake for 20-23 mins until the pastry is golden and the brownie is slightly risen and cracked. Remove from the oven and cool on a cooling rack.

Each townie (56g) provides:

ENERGY	FAT	SATURATES	SUGARS	SALT
1137kJ 272kcal	14.5g	6.2g	19.5g	0.2g
14%	21%	31%	22%	3%

% of the Reference Intakes

Typical values per 100g: **Energy** 2030kJ/485kcal
Each townie provides:
31.3g carbohydrate | 1.3g fibre | 3.3g protein

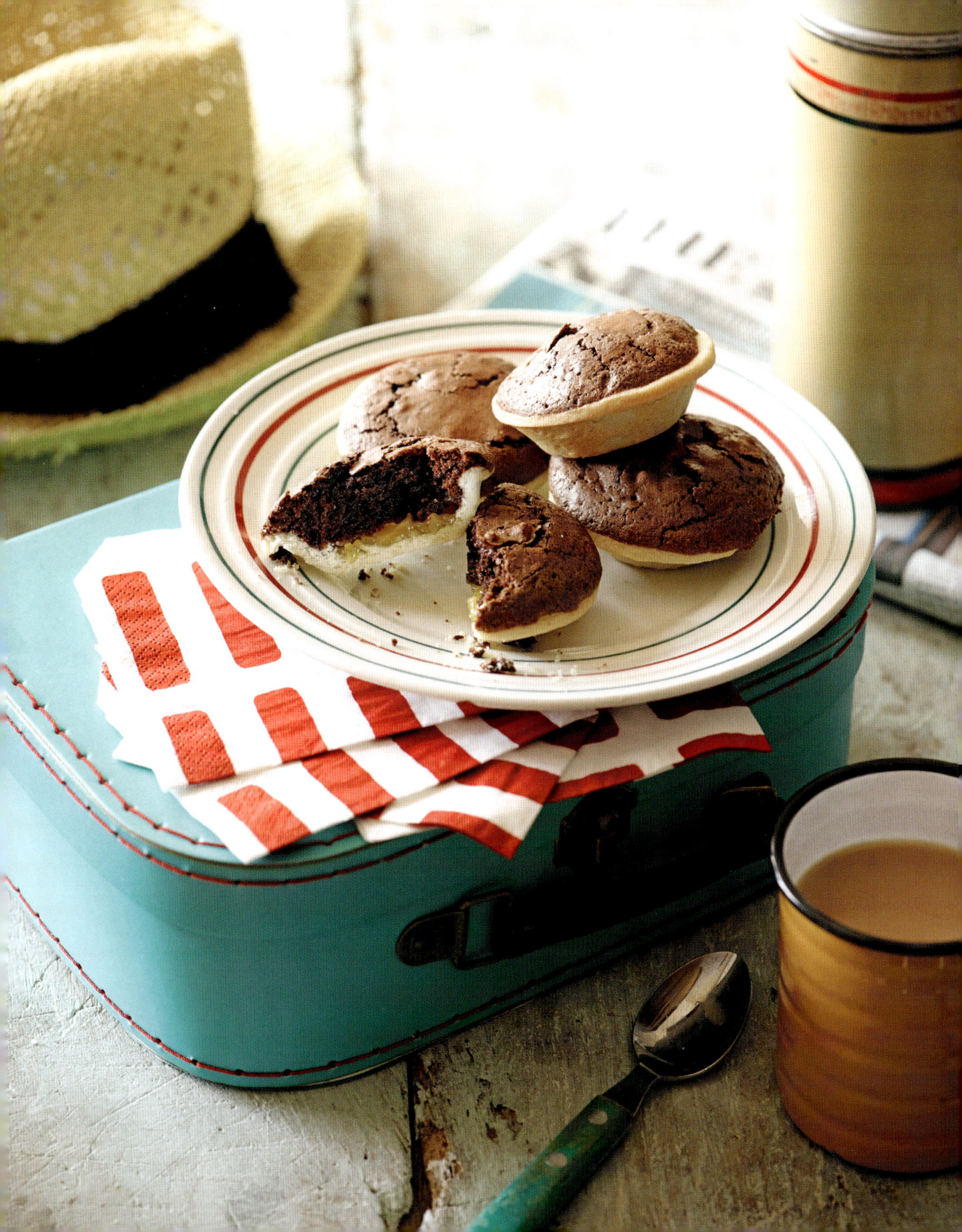

on the move

MAKES 24
PREP TIME 15 mins
COOK TIME 35-40 mins

Cheese & mustard gougères

Perfect for picnics, these moreish bite-size cheese puffs are made using a savoury choux pastry flavoured with cheese and mustard

125g plain flour, sifted
1/2 tsp paprika
3 eggs
80g salted butter, cubed

75g Swiss Gruyère by Sainsbury's, grated
2 tsp English mustard powder
1 tsp finely chopped fresh chives, to serve

1. Put the flour and paprika in a large jug, season with freshly ground black pepper and mix to combine. In a separate jug, lightly beat the eggs together with a fork.

2. Put the butter and 220ml cold water in a large pan over a medium heat. Bring to a rolling boil and, when it's boiling vigorously, remove the pan from the heat.

3. Add the flour mixture to the pan all at once, and beat with a wooden spoon for about 1 min - it will become thick and pull away from the sides of the pan, forming a ball shape.

4. Take the pan off the heat and let the mixture cool for a few mins, then slowly beat in the eggs, a little at a time, with a wooden spoon until the mixture is stiff and shiny with a dropping consistency. You may not need to use all of the eggs. Fold in the grated cheese and mustard.

5. Preheat the oven to 220°C, fan 200°C, gas 7. Line 2 baking trays with baking paper and spoon walnut-size balls of the dough onto the trays - you should have enough mixture to make about 24. Bake for 25-30 mins until puffed and golden. Tap the base of the gougères - they should sound hollow when tapped.

6. Cool on a cooling rack, then sprinkle with the chives to serve.

Each gougère (20g) provides:

ENERGY	FAT	SATURATES	SUGARS	SALT
258kJ 62kcal	4.3g	2.3g	0.1g	0.1g
3%	6%	12%	<1%	2%

% of the Reference Intakes
Typical values per 100g: Energy 1289kJ/310kcal
Each gougère provides:
3.6g carbohydrate | 0.2g fibre | 2.2g protein

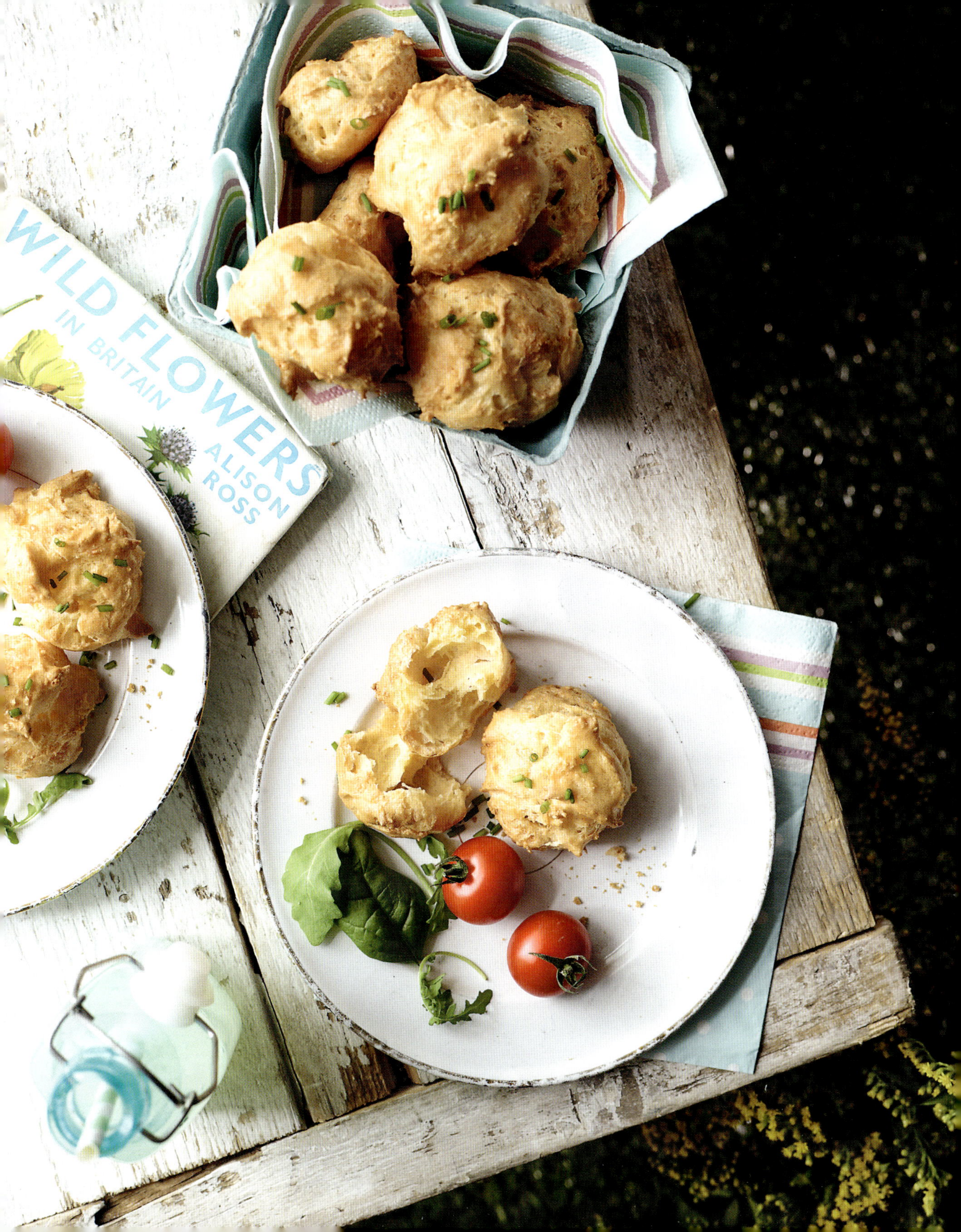
WILD FLOWERS
IN BRITAIN
ALISON
ROSS

on the move

MAKES 12
PREP TIME 40 mins
COOK TIME 35 mins

Butternut filo parcels

These little parcels make great finger food and are so simple to make. The sweetness of the squash goes perfectly with the savoury feta

1 tbsp olive oil, plus extra for brushing
1 small red onion, finely chopped
1 clove garlic, crushed
1 red chilli, deseeded and finely chopped
350g peeled and deseeded butternut squash, cut into 1.5cm cubes
100g Greek feta by Sainsbury's, crumbled
1 tbsp chopped fresh dill
Finely grated zest of 1 lemon
220g packet filo pastry by Sainsbury's

1. Heat the oil in a large frying pan over a medium heat, add the onion and cook for 2 mins, then add the garlic and chilli, and fry for a further 2-3 mins. Add the butternut squash and a splash of water, reduce the heat, then cover and cook for 8-10 mins or until the butternut squash is soft. Add a splash more water if it's starting to stick. Remove from the heat and set aside to cool.

2. Preheat the oven to 200°C, fan 180°C, gas 6. Tip the cooled squash mixture into a large bowl, add the feta, dill and lemon zest, then mash together with a fork.

3. Unroll the filo and peel off one sheet. Cover the remaining filo with cling film so it doesn't dry out. Lay the pastry on a flat surface and lightly brush all over with olive oil. Fold in one third of the pastry lengthways towards the middle. Brush again with the olive oil and fold in the other side to make a triple-layered strip.

4. Put 1 heaped tablespoon of the filling in the middle of the pastry at one end, then fold a corner of the pastry over to make a triangle. Fold over again in the opposite direction and continue folding in alternate directions until you have a neat, triangle-shaped parcel. Repeat until you have 12 parcels.

5. Put the parcels on a baking tray, seam-side down and brush lightly with more oil. Bake for 20 mins or until the pastry is golden and crisp.

Each parcel (58g) provides:

ENERGY	FAT	SATURATES	SUGARS	SALT
534kJ 127kcal	5.5g	1.9g	2g	0.2g
6%	8%	10%	2%	4%

% of the Reference Intakes
Typical values per 100g: Energy 921kJ/220kcal
Each parcel provides:
15g carbohydrate | 0.7g fibre | 4.2g protein

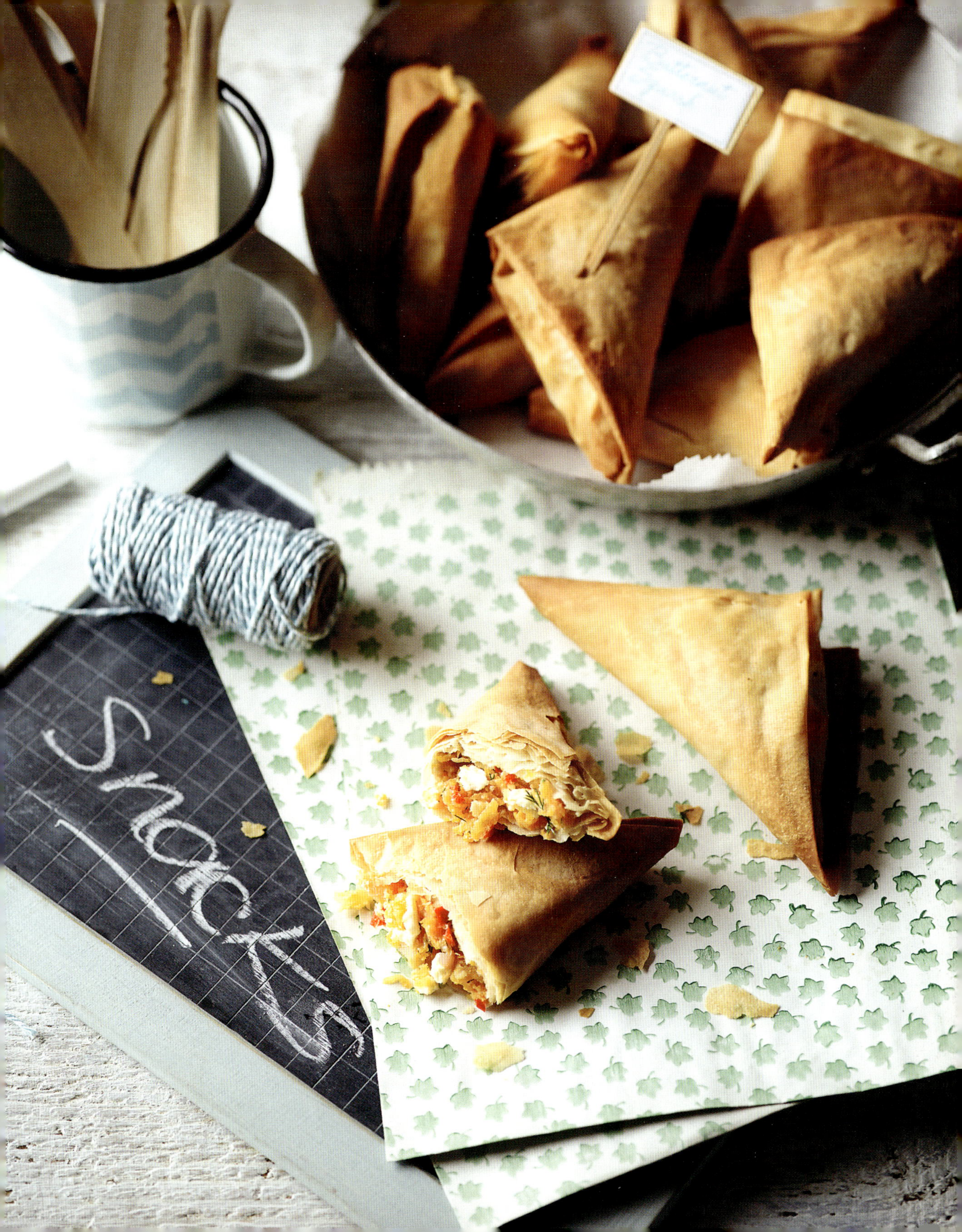
Snacks

on the move

MAKES 12
PREP TIME 45 mins, plus proving
COOK TIME 25 mins

Soft pretzels

Once you've got the hang of these, you can try all sorts of flavours

500g strong white bread flour by Sainsbury's, plus extra for dusting
7g sachet fast action dried yeast by Sainsbury's
1 tsp table salt
1 tbsp caster sugar

30g unsalted butter, melted and cooled
Vegetable oil, for greasing
30g bicarbonate of soda
1 egg yolk, beaten with 1 tbsp of water
2 tsp rock salt

1. Put the flour, yeast, salt, sugar into a mixing bowl and make a well in the centre. In a small jug, mix the melted butter with 350ml warm water, then gradually pour it into the dry ingredients, mixing it with your hands until a soft dough forms. You may not need to add all the liquid. Turn out onto a lightly floured surface and knead for 10 mins until smooth and elastic. Transfer to a lightly oiled large bowl, cover with cling film and set aside in a warm place for 1 hour until doubled in size.

2. Turn the dough out onto a lightly oiled work surface and divide into 12 equal pieces. Roll each piece into a 43cm-long 'rope' then make a U-shape with each rope. Hold each end and cross them over each other, then press onto the bottom of the U to form the shape of a pretzel, using a drop of water to make it stick. Transfer to two baking trays lined with baking paper, cover loosely with lightly oiled cling film and leave in a warm place for 20 mins until puffed up.

3. In a large pan, bring 2.5 litres of water to the boil. Preheat the oven to 220°C, fan 200°C, gas 7. Once the water is boiling, add the bicarbonate of soda then gently lower the pretzels, two at a time, into the boiling water. Leave for 30 seconds then carefully flip them and leave for another 30 seconds. Remove from the water, drain and return to the baking tray. Repeat with the remaining pretzels.

4. Brush the tops of the pretzels with the beaten egg yolk* and sprinkle with the rock salt. Bake for 12-15 mins until golden.

*See p191 for a list of recipes to use leftover egg yolks.

> **Cook's tip**
> For cinnamon pretzels, omit the egg wash and, after baking, brush with melted butter, then toss in 175g caster sugar combined with 2 tsp ground cinnamon.

Each pretzel (77g) provides:

ENERGY	FAT	SATURATES	SUGARS	SALT
711kJ 169kcal	3.8g	1.5g	1.6g	1.9g
8%	5%	8%	2%	32%

% of the Reference Intakes
Typical values per 100g: Energy 923kJ/219kcal
Each pretzel provides:
26.9g carbohydrate | 1.4g fibre | 6.1g protein

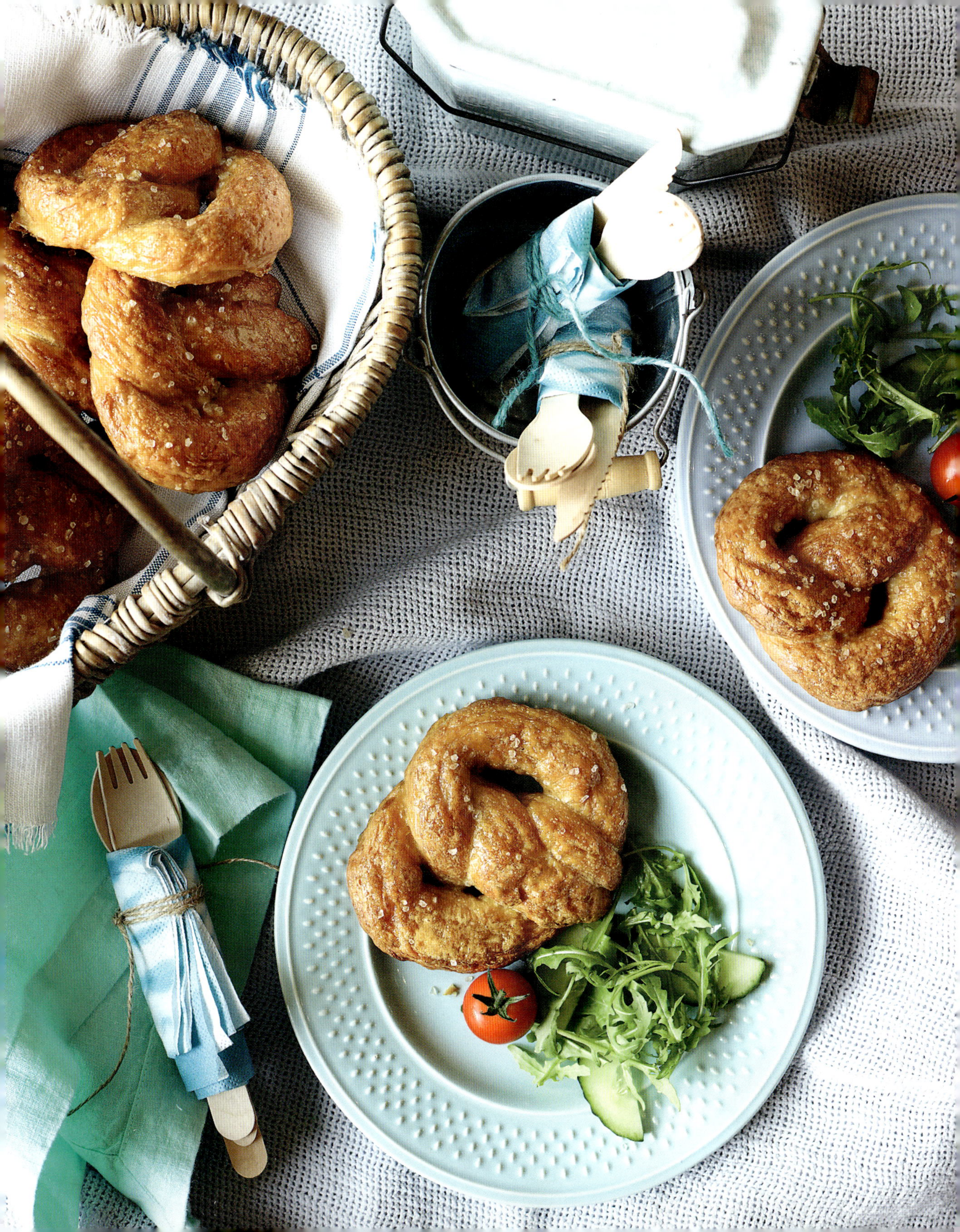

On a roll

Why settle for an everyday Swiss roll when you can have this fun polka dot version? Simple to make and tasty to eat, it's a great bake for creative young cooks. Find the recipe on p88.

bakes to make with kids

fun recipes young bakers will love to help make - and eat

Rainbow cupcakes	72
Popcorn cookies	74
Zebra cake	76
Ice cream sandwiches	78
No-bake fruity flapjacks	80
Rice pop cake	82
Marshmallow fudge bites	84
Cookie pizza	86
Chocolate dotty roll	88
Puzzle biscuits	90
Chocolate bark	92
Iced jewels	94
Pinwheel scones	96
Tomato & mozzarella hand pies	98
Ham & pineapple muffins	100

baking with kids

MAKES 12
PREP TIME 25 mins
COOK TIME
12-15 mins

Rainbow cupcakes

Get colourful and creative with your little ones by making these amazing technicolour cupcakes

125g unsalted butter
125g granulated sugar
1 tsp Taste the Difference Madagascan vanilla extract
2 eggs
125g self-raising flour
2-3 tsp semi-skimmed milk

Blue, green, yellow and pink food colouring
Multi-coloured confetti by Sainsbury's, to decorate

FOR THE ICING
150g icing sugar
Juice of ½ lemon

1. Preheat the oven to 180°C, fan 160°C, gas 4. Line a 12-hole cupcake tin with paper cases.

2. In a medium bowl, use a hand-held electric whisk to beat together the butter, sugar and vanilla for 3-4 mins until pale and fluffy. Add the eggs, one at a time, beating well after each addition. Sift over half the flour and mix well to combine. Pour in half the milk and mix well. Repeat with the remaining flour and milk until you have a smooth mixture. Divide the mixture between four smaller bowls.

3. Add a few drops of the blue food colouring to the first bowl, stirring until combined. Repeat with the remaining food colours and mixtures so you have four separate coloured mixtures. Drop a teaspoonful or so of each mixture into each of the prepared cases so you have a mix of the four colours.

4. Bake for 12-15 mins until the cakes spring back when lightly pressed. Transfer to a cooling rack to cool completely.

5. Make the icing. Sift the icing sugar into a bowl and mix in the lemon juice to make a smooth, thick icing, adding a few drops of water if necessary. Spread the icing over the cupcakes and decorate with the multi-coloured confetti.

Each cupcake (53g) provides:

ENERGY	FAT	SATURATES	SUGARS	SALT
937kJ 223kcal	9.6g	5.4g	25.1g	0.1g

Typical values per 100g: Energy 1768kJ/421kcal
Each cupcake provides:
31.9g carbohydrate | 0.3g fibre | 2.1g protein

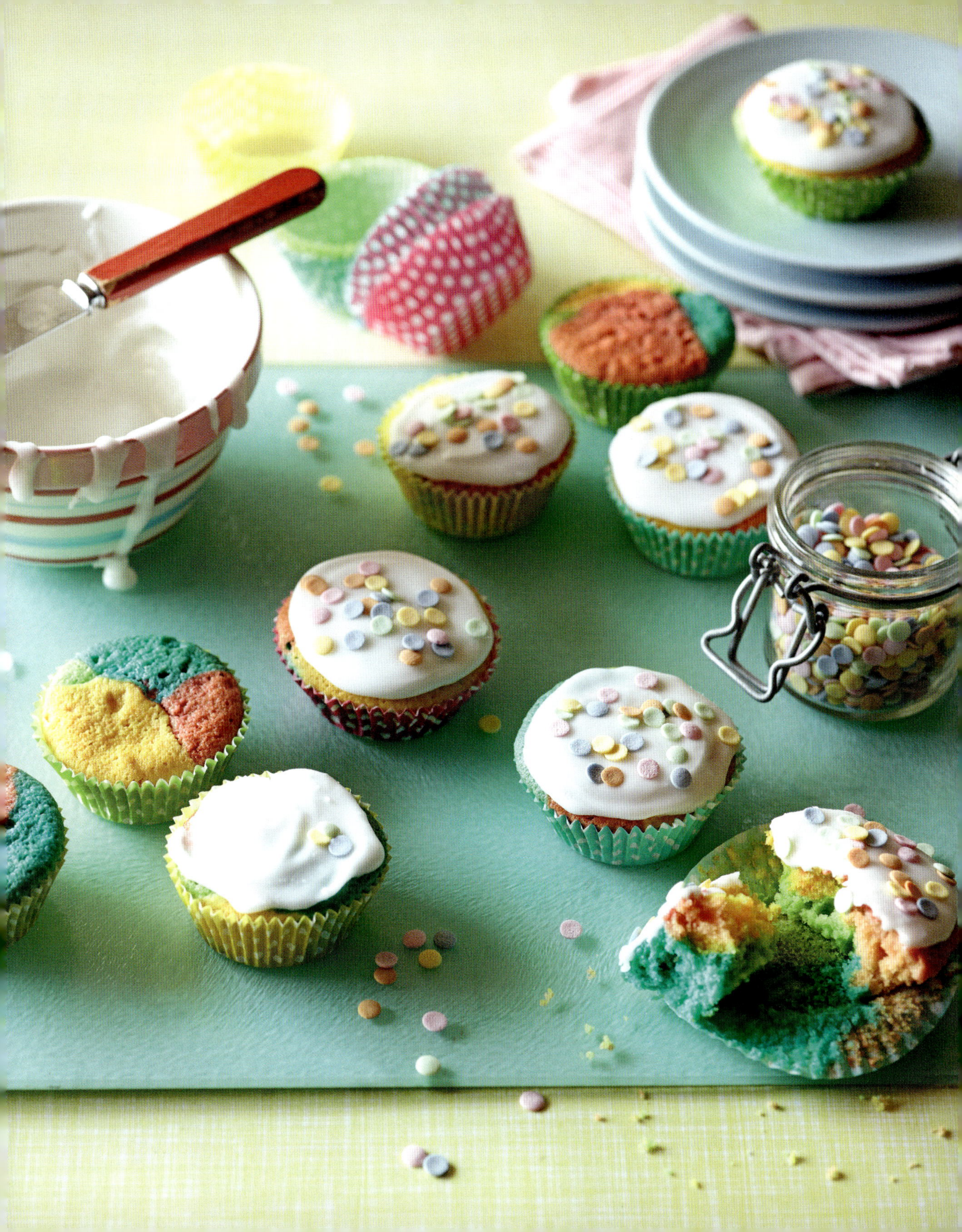

MAKES 12
PREP TIME 15 mins
COOK TIME 10-12 mins

Popcorn cookies

Everyone loves biscuits and everyone loves popcorn. Combine the two and you got a delicious treat that's easy to make

100g unsalted butter, cubed
140g plain flour
1 egg yolk
50g caster sugar
¼ tsp Taste the Difference Madagascan vanilla extract

50g sweet and salty popcorn by Sainsbury's
50g glacé cherries by Sainsbury's, roughly chopped

1. Preheat the oven to 180°C, fan 160°C, gas 4. Line a large baking sheet with baking paper.

2. In a large bowl, rub the butter and flour together until the mixture resembles breadcrumbs. Stir in the egg yolk*, sugar and vanilla extract, and gather the mixture together to form a soft dough. Add the popcorn and chopped cherries to the bowl and gently press into the dough.

3. Break off small pieces of the dough and form into walnut-sized balls. Arrange them on the prepared baking sheet and press each dough ball down slightly with the palm of your hand. Bake for 10-12 minutes until crisp and golden.

4. Cool on a cooling rack, then store in an airtight container until ready to eat. They will keep in the container for up to a week.

*See p191 for a list of recipes to use leftover egg whites.

> **Cook's tip**
> For a less sweet cookie, try swapping the glacé cherries with the same quantity of roughly chopped dried apricots or dried mango.

Each cookie (32g) provides:

ENERGY	FAT	SATURATES	SUGARS	SALT
647kJ 155kcal	8.6g	4.4g	7.8g	trace

Typical values per 100g: Energy 2021kJ/484kcal
Each cookie provides:
17.3g carbohydrate | 0.7g fibre | 1.6g protein

baking with kids

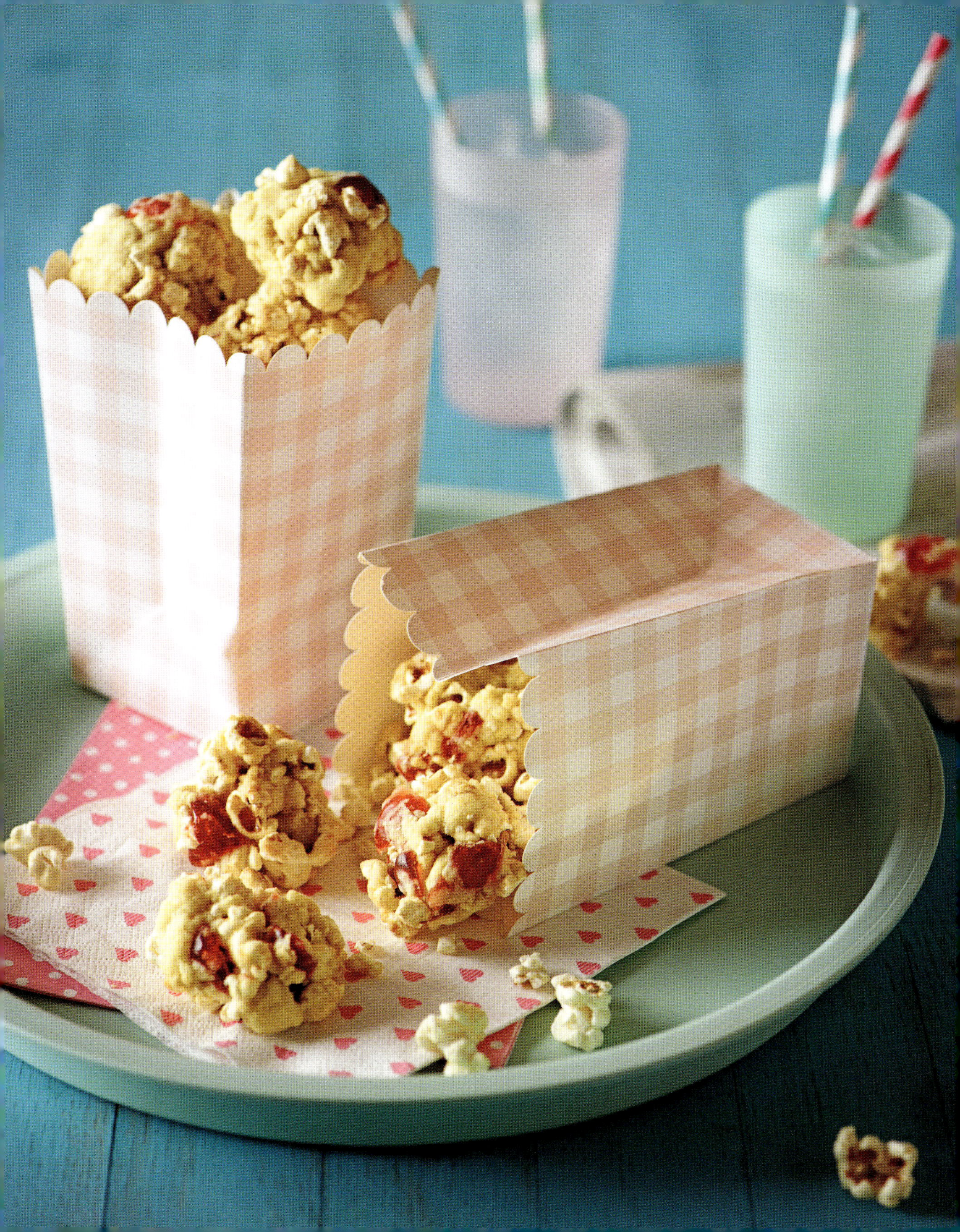

SERVES 12
PREP TIME
40 mins
COOK TIME
45-55 mins

Zebra cake

An eye-catching cake that's perfect for parties – the stripes might look tricky, but getting the look is easy once you know how

250g caster sugar
4 large eggs, beaten
150ml semi-skimmed milk
200ml vegetable oil, plus extra for greasing
350g self-raising flour
½ tsp baking powder

2 tbsp cocoa powder
Juice and finely grated zest of ½ orange, plus extra zest for decorating
1 tsp Taste the Difference Valencian orange extract
150g icing sugar

1. Preheat the oven to 180°C, fan 160°C, gas 4. Grease a 23cm springform cake tin and lined the base and sides with baking paper.

2. Put the sugar and eggs in a large bowl and beat for 1 min with a hand-held electric whisk. Gradually whisk in the milk and oil. Sift over the flour and baking powder and whisk until smooth – don't over-mix at this stage or the baked cake will have lots of air bubbles.

3. Transfer half the mixture to another bowl. Whisk the cocoa into one bowl of mixture and the orange zest and orange extract into the second bowl. Both mixtures should be the same runny consistency – add a little more milk to the chocolate mixture if it's thicker than the orange one.

4. Using a dessertspoon, drop 2 heaped spoonfuls of the orange mixture into the centre of the base of the prepared tin. With a second dessertspoon, quickly drop 2 heaped spoonfuls of the chocolate mixture directly on top. Continue dropping alternate spoonfuls of the mixture into the tin until both mixtures have been used up. You should end up with lots of concentric circles of the two mixtures – don't worry if they are a little uneven.

5. Bake for 45-55 mins, or until a skewer inserted into the centre of the cake comes out clean. Cool in the tin for 10 mins then transfer to a cooling rack to cool completely.

6. Sift the icing sugar into a bowl and mix in the orange juice to make a smooth thick icing, adding a few drops of water if necessary. Spread the icing over the cake, letting it run down the sides. Decorate with the extra zest, then leave until the icing is set before serving.

Each serving (102g) provides:

ENERGY	FAT	SATURATES	SUGARS	SALT
1634kJ 390kcal	17.2g	2g	32.7g	0.4g

Typical values per 100g: Energy 1602kJ/382kcal
Each serving provides:
52.4g carbohydrate | 1g fibre | 5.9g protein

baking with kids

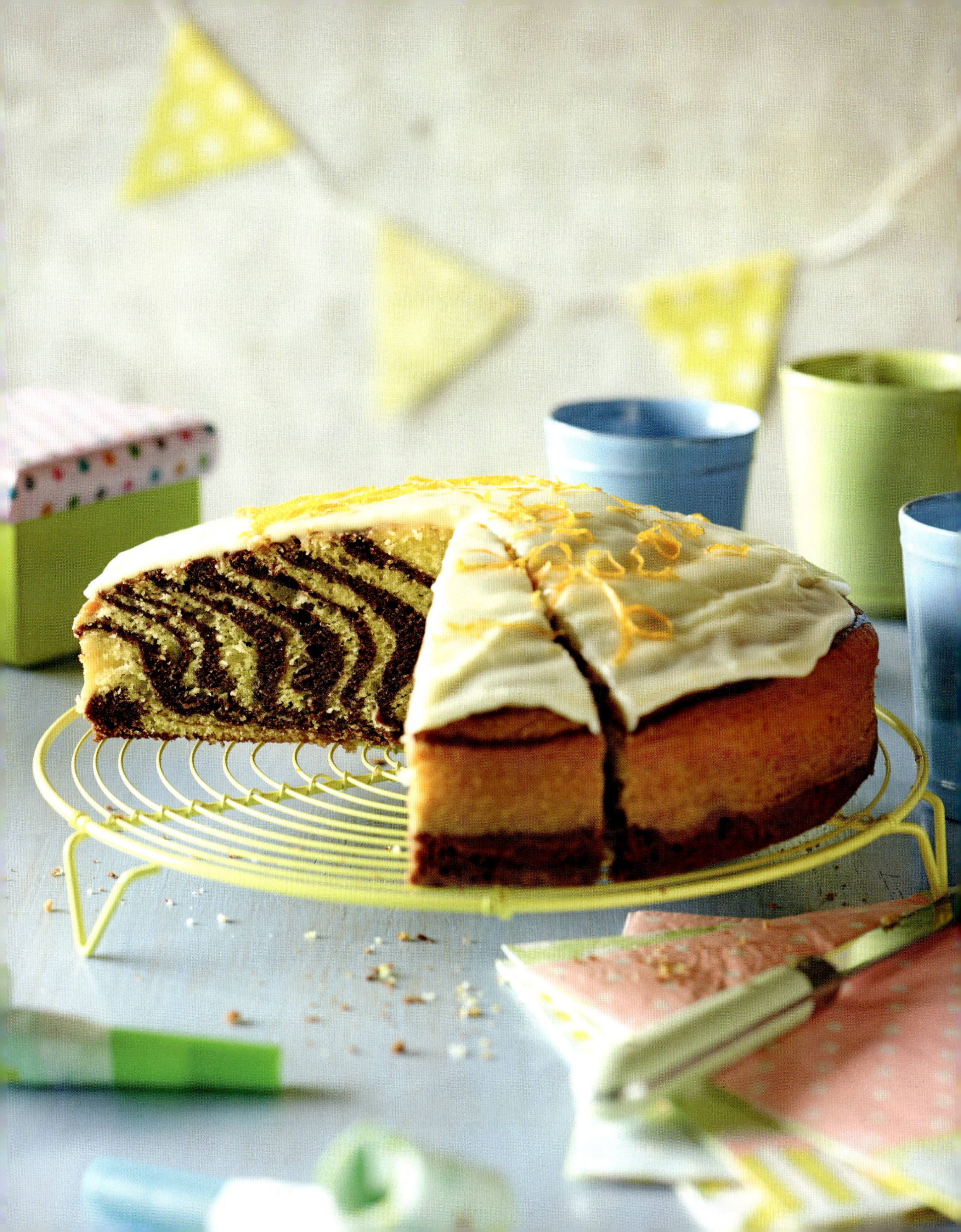

baking with kids

> **MAKES** 9
> **PREP TIME** 15 mins, plus freezing
> **COOK TIME** 15-18 mins

Ice cream sandwiches

A sunny-day sweet treat that's always a big hit for kids' parties. The choc-chip biscuits tastes great on their own, too

125g butter, softened
125g light brown soft sugar by Sainsbury's
75g caster sugar
1 tsp Taste the Difference Madagascan vanilla extract
1 large egg
150g plain flour
½ tsp baking powder
100g chocolate chips
500ml raspberry ripple soft scoop ice cream by Sainsbury's
Multicoloured 100s & 1000s by Sainsbury's, to decorate

1 Preheat the oven to 180°C, fan 160°C, gas 4. Line a large baking sheet with baking paper.

2 Put the butter, brown sugar and caster sugar in a large bowl and cream together using a hand-held electric whisk until pale and fluffy. Beat in the vanilla extract and the egg, then fold in the flour and baking powder.

3 Stir in the chocolate chips, then put heaped teaspoonfuls of the mixture onto the baking trays, leaving plenty of space for them to spread. You may need to do this in batches of depending on the size of your tray.

4 Bake in the oven for 15-18 minutes until golden but still soft. Leave on the trays to cool for a couple of minutes, then transfer to a cooling rack to cool completely.

5 Carefully lift the biscuits from the baking paper. Put a scoop of ice cream onto one of the biscuits, then top with another biscuit and squeeze gently until the ice cream is nearly squidging out at the sides. Roll in the sprinkles, return to the baking tray and repeat with the rest of the biscuits and ice cream. Discard any leftover sprinkles. Put in the freezer until ready to serve.

Cook's tip
Take a bit of time to make the biscuits as evenly sized as you can. Once they're cooked, sort them into matching pairs before sandwiching them together.

Each sandwich (96g) provides:

ENERGY	FAT	SATURATES	SUGARS	SALT
1513kJ / 361kcal	16.8g	10g	35.1g	0.2g

Typical values per 100g: Energy 1576kJ/376kcal
Each sandwich provides:
48g carbohydrate | 1g fibre | 4g protein

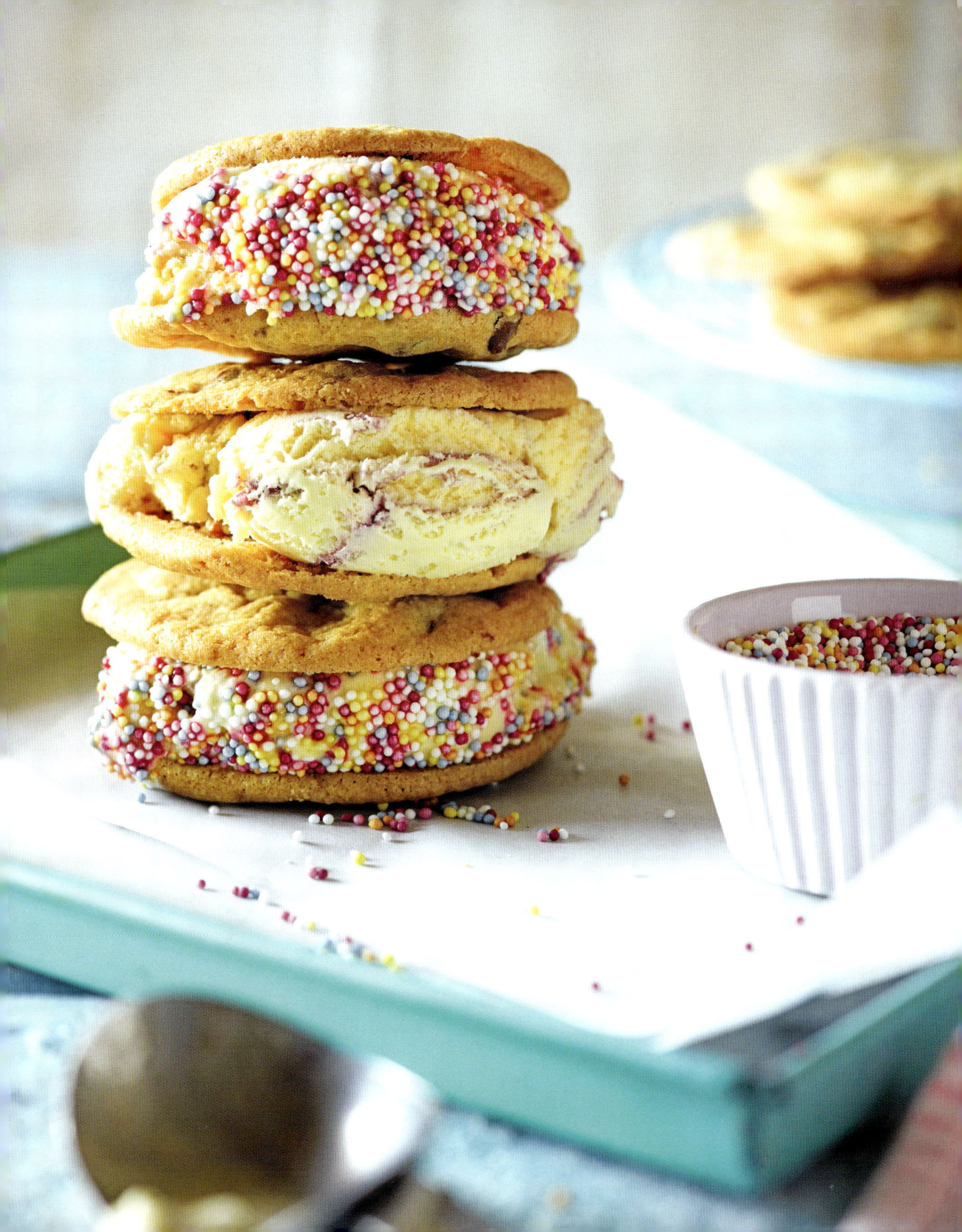

baking with kids

MAKES 24
PREP TIME 10 mins plus chilling
COOK TIME 5 mins

No bake fruity flapjacks

These easy-to-make oat and fruit squares are a great after-school treat, or just as nice served with an afternoon cup of tea

75g unsalted butter, plus extra for greasing
225g Scottish porridge oats by Sainsbury's
40g sunflower seeds
50g dried apricots, finely chopped
50g dried pitted dates, finely chopped
100g light brown soft sugar
75g golden syrup

1. Lightly grease a 20cm square shallow cake tin, and line the base and two sides with baking paper, making sure the paper hangs over the edges of the tin.

2. Mix together the porridge oats, sunflower seeds, apricots and dates in a large bowl. Make a well in the centre.

3. Put the butter, sugar and golden syrup in a pan set over a low heat and heat gently, stirring with a wooden spoon, until the sugar has dissolved. Let the mixture bubble gently for 1-2 mins.

4. Pour the melted mixture into the oats and mix thoroughly. Tip the mixture into the prepared tin and press down firmly with the back of a spoon.

5. Chill in the fridge for 1 hour 30 mins to 2 hours, until firm. Use the overhanging greaseproof paper to gently ease the flapjack slab from the tin. Cut into 24 pieces and store in an airtight container in the fridge for up to 4 days. Remove the flapjacks from the fridge about 30 mins before serving to allow them to soften a little.

Cook's tip
For a flavour change, replace the sunflower seeds with pumpkin seeds and use 100g dried mixed fruit instead of the apricots and dates. For chocolate flapjacks, swap the fruit for 100g milk chocolate chips.

Each flapjack (25g) provides:

ENERGY	FAT	SATURATES	SUGARS	SALT
421kJ 100kcal	4.2g	1.8g	8.4g	trace

Typical values per 100g: Energy 1684kJ/402kcal
Each flapjack provides:
13.6g carbohydrate | 1g fibre | 1.6g protein

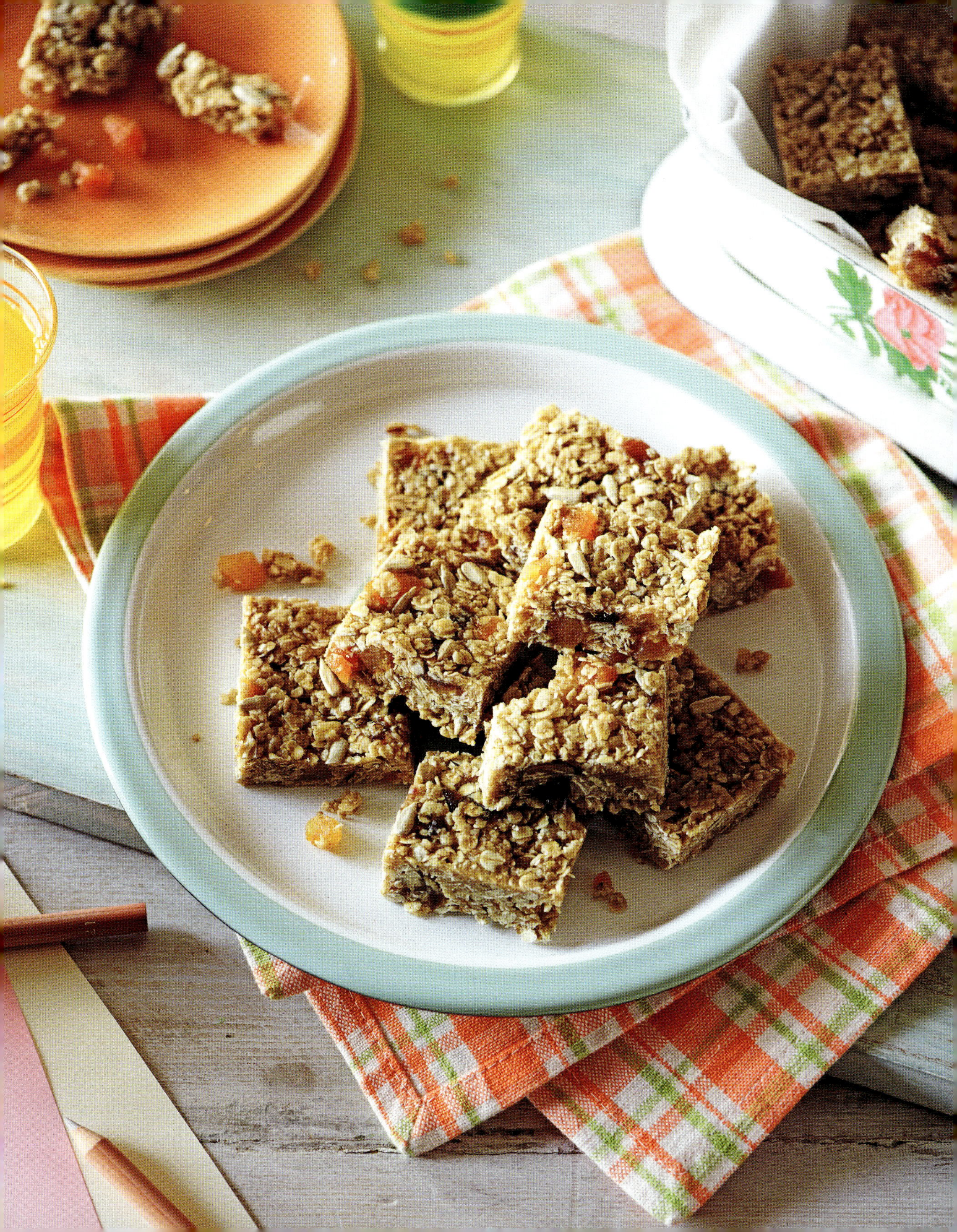

SERVES 12
PREP TIME 15 mins
plus chilling
COOK TIME
15 mins

Rice pop cake

This fuss-free, no-bake chocolate cake is a winner at birthday parties – and it couldn't be simpler to make

200g cook's Belgian dark chocolate by Sainsbury's, broken into pieces
100g cook's Belgian milk chocolate by Sainsbury's, broken into pieces
100g golden syrup
200g rice pops by Sainsbury's

TO DECORATE
75g cook's Belgian dark chocolate, melted (see p7)
75g cook's Belgian white chocolate, melted (see p7)
8 strawberries
Multicoloured 100s & 1000s by Sainsbury's

1. Line a deep 23cm round cake tin with greaseproof paper.

2. Put the dark chocolate, milk chocolate and golden syrup in a medium saucepan and gently melt over a low heat, stirring to combine. Remove from the heat and transfer to a large mixing bowl. Stir in the rice pops until they are fully coated then spoon press the mixture into the prepared tin, pressing it in lightly and levelling the surface. Put in the fridge to chill until firm.

3. When the cake is firm, remove it from the tin and put on a serving plate. Dip 4 of the strawberries in the melted dark chocolate, then sprinkle over the 100s & 1000s. Repeat with the remaining strawberries and white chocolate.

4. Drizzle the remaining melted dark and white chocolate over the cake, sprinkle with more 100s & 1000s, then top with the strawberries. Set aside in a cool place until the chocolate on the strawberries is set, then serve.

Each serving (71g) provides:

ENERGY	FAT	SATURATES	SUGARS	SALT
1245kJ 297kcal	14.1g	8.8g	26.1g	0.2g

Typical values per 100g: Energy 1754kJ/419kcal
Each serving provides:
38.2g carbohydrate | 2.4g fibre | 3.2g protein

baking with kids

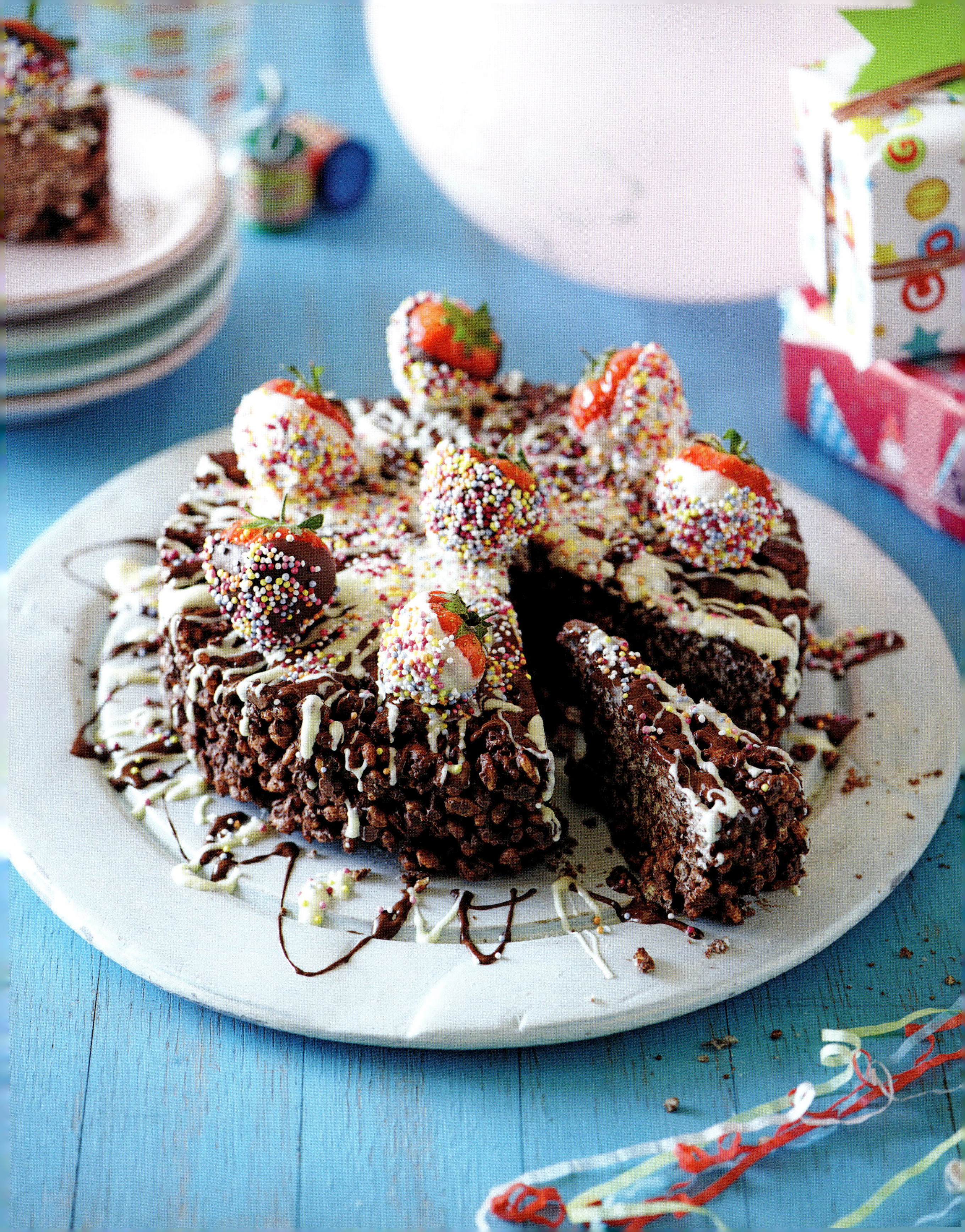

MAKES 50
PREP TIME 15 mins, plus chilling
COOK TIME 5 mins

Marshmallow fudge bites

These tasty little morsels are great to make with the kids. If you like, you can add nuts to the mixture, too

200g cook's Belgian dark chocolate by Sainsbury's, broken into pieces
100g cook's Belgian milk chocolate by Sainsbury's, broken into pieces
397g tin sweetened condensed milk
50g unsalted butter
180g pack vanilla pink and white mini marshmallows by Sainsbury's

1. Line a 23cm square traybake tin with baking paper.

2. Heat the chocolate, condensed milk and butter in a pan set over a medium heat for 3-4 mins, stirring constantly until melted and combined. Remove from the heat and set aside to cool.

3. Stir half of the marshmallows into the chocolate mixture, then pour into the prepared tin and level the surface. Scatter over the remaining marshmallows. Cover with cling film and chill in the fridge for 4 hours.

4. Remove from the fridge and cut into bite-size squares to serve.

Each bite (14g) provides:

ENERGY	FAT	SATURATES	SUGARS	SALT
316kJ 75kcal	3.6g	2.3g	8.6g	trace

Typical values per 100g: Energy 2258kJ/539kcal
Each bite provides:
9.4g carbohydrate | 0.4g fibre | 1.1g protein

baking with kids

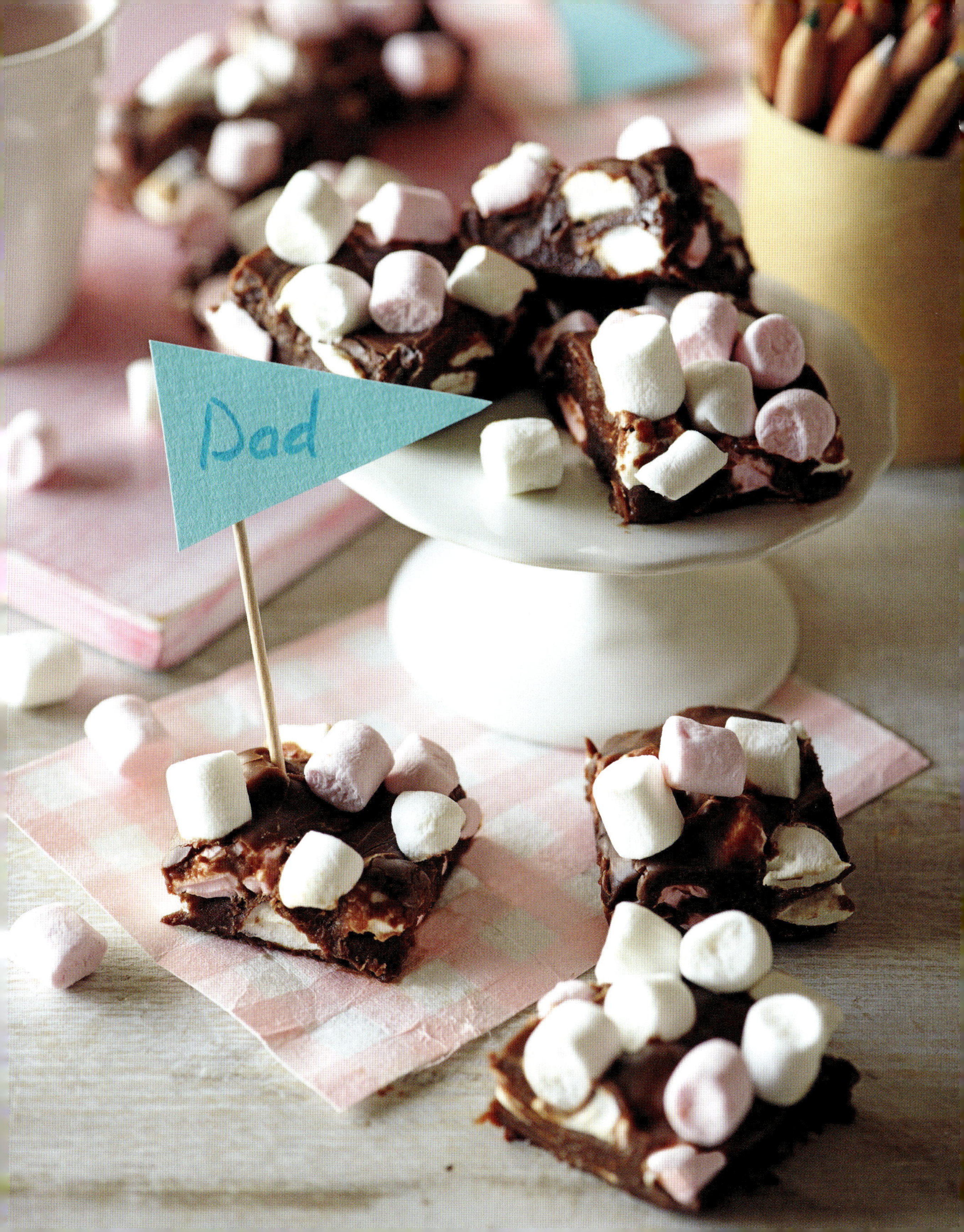
Dad

SERVES 8
PREP TIME 25 mins
COOK TIME 35 mins

Cookie pizza

Get the kids to help put the toppings on the cookie – they can come up with their own ideas to include their favourite things

200g plain flour
110g unsalted butter, cubed
50g caster sugar

FOR THE TOPPING
3 tbsp smooth peanut butter
3 tbsp hazelnut chocolate spread by Sainsbury's
1 banana, sliced
8 strawberries, sliced
50g white chocolate chips
50g milk chocolate chips

1. Put the flour into a medium bowl, stir through the sugar and add the butter. Rub the butter into the flour and sugar until the whole mixture comes together into a dough. Roll out the dough between 2 pieces of baking paper to a rough 30cm round. Transfer to a baking sheet and remove the top layer of baking paper. Prick all over with a fork and mark out 8 segments with a knife, but don't cut all the way through the dough. Chill for 30 minutes in the fridge.

2. Preheat the oven to 180°C, fan 160°C, gas 4. Bake the cookie for 12-15 minutes until pale golden. Remove from the oven and score through the segments again, but don't cut all the way through. Allow to cool completely.

3. Spread alternate segments with the peanut butter, then spread the remaining segments with the hazelnut spread. Top with the strawberries and banana, then sprinkle over the chocolate chips. Cut the segments all the way through to serve.

Cook's tips
Sprinkle a little lemon juice over the sliced banana to stop it from turning brown. For a less sweet treat, try swapping the chocolate chips for 50g dessicated coconut flakes.

Each serving (91g) provides:

ENERGY	FAT	SATURATES	SUGARS	SALT
1584kJ 379kcal	21.8g	9.9g	21.2g	0.1g

Typical values per 100g: Energy 1741kJ/417kcal
Each serving provides:
39g carbohydrate | 2.3g fibre | 5.8g protein

baking with kids

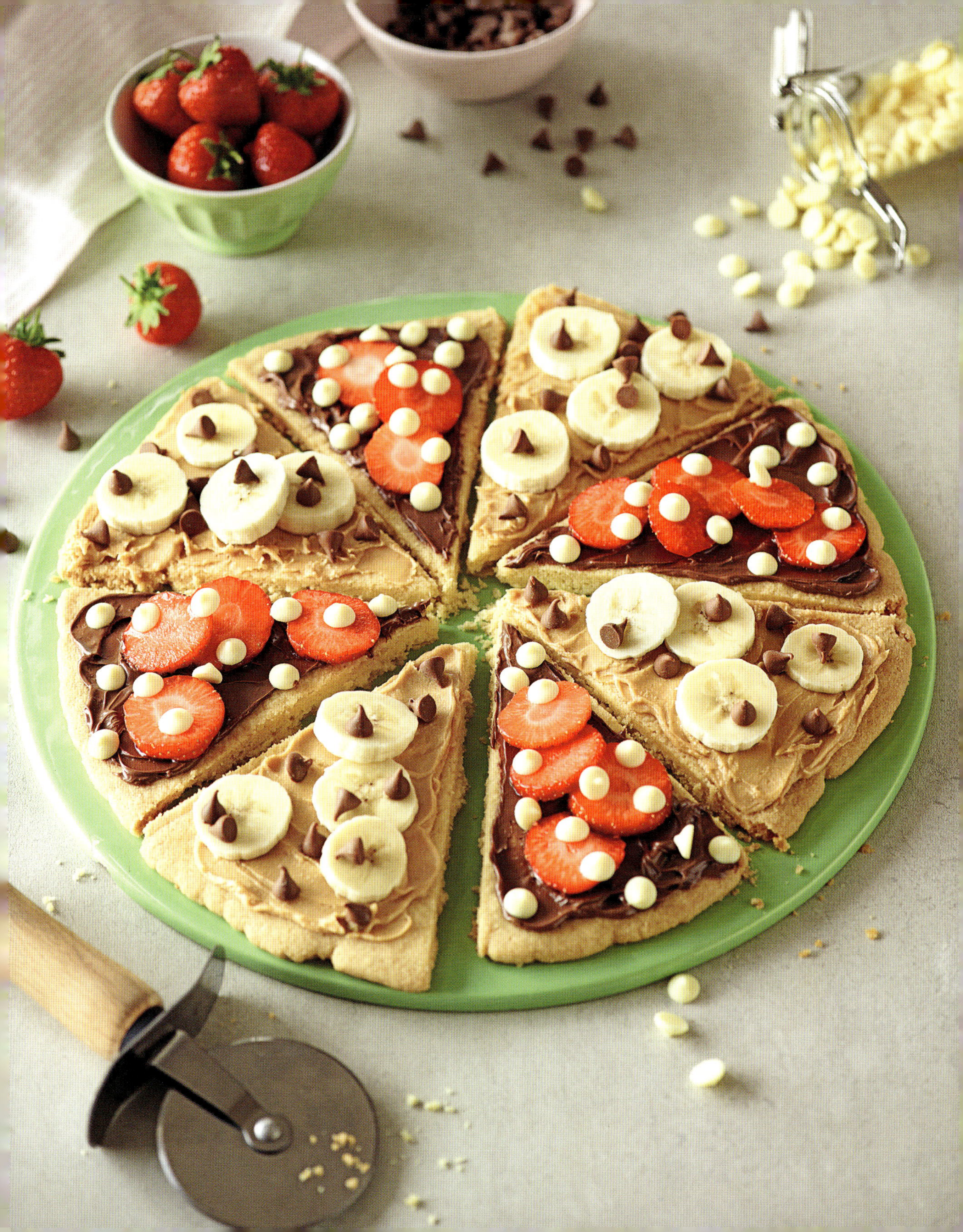

Chocolate dotty roll

Little ones will love a slice of this delicious patterned Swiss roll

SERVES 10
PREP TIME 30 mins
COOK TIME 10-12 mins

50g unsalted butter, softened, plus extra for greasing
4 eggs
100g caster sugar, plus an extra 1 tbsp for sprinkling
1 tsp Taste the Difference Madagascan vanilla extract
100g self-raising flour, sifted
1 tbsp cocoa powder
125g icing sugar
50g cook's Belgian dark chocolate by Sainsbury's, melted and cooled slightly (see p7)
25ml double fresh cream

1. Grease and line a 22cm x 32cm Swiss roll or traybake tin with baking paper. In a large bowl, cream together the eggs, sugar and vanilla extract using a hand-held electric whisk until pale and thickened. Gently fold in half the flour until fully combined, then fold in the remaining flour.

2. Preheat the oven to 200°C, fan 180°C, gas 6. Transfer 100g of the mixture to a small bowl and sift over the cocoa. Gently fold in until combined. Spoon the mixture into a piping bag fitted with a round nozzle and pipe rows of small circular shapes across the baking paper – they don't have to be too even. Bake for 1 min until just set. Pour over the remaining mixture, level the top, and bake for 8-10 mins until pale golden and the top springs back when lightly pressed.

3. Lay a damp, clean tea towel on your work surface and top with a large sheet of baking paper. Sprinkle over the 1 tbsp caster sugar. Turn the cake out onto the paper, peel the baking paper from the base the turn the cake over so the pattern is underneath. Trim the edges of the cake, then top with another sheet of baking paper. Carefully roll up the sponge, then wrap in the tea towel and set aside to cool on a cooling rack.

4. Put the butter and icing sugar in a medium bowl and beat together with an hand-held electric whisk for 2-3 mins until pale and soft. Gradually beat in the melted chocolate until smooth, then add the cream and continue to beat for 2 mins until the mixture is fluffy.

5. Assemble the cake. Gently unroll the sponge and spread the chocolate cream over the non-patterned side, leaving a little border of clear sponge all around. Carefully roll the sponge back up then put seam-side down on a platter to serve.

Each serving (62g) provides:
ENERGY	FAT	SATURATES	SUGARS	SALT
963kJ 230kcal	9.6g	5.2g	24.7g	0.2g

Typical values per 100g: Energy 1553kJ/370kcal
Each serving provides:
31.5g carbohydrate | 0.8g fibre | 3.9g protein

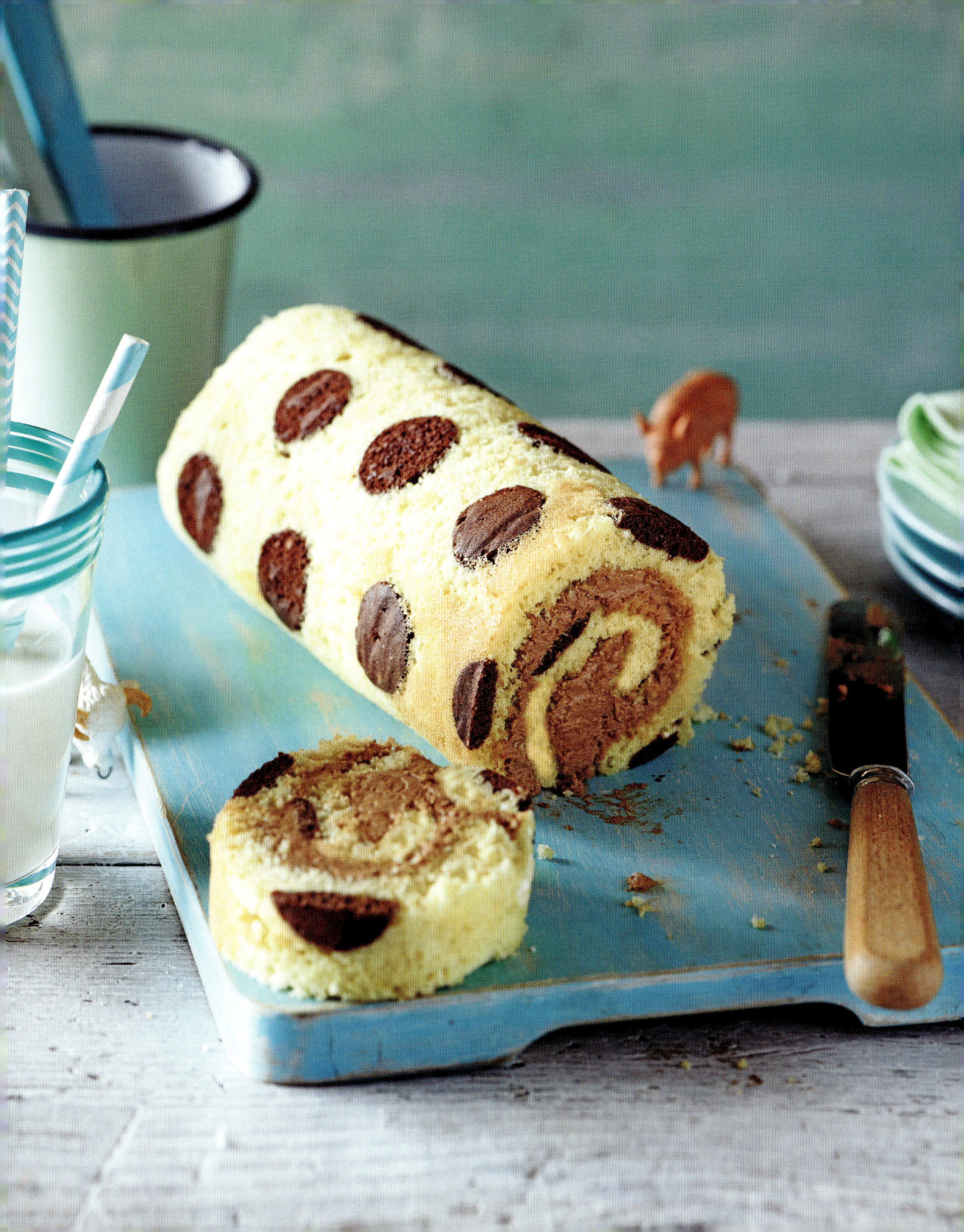

MAKES 18
PREP TIME
1 hour 30 mins, plus chilling
COOK TIME
20-25 mins

Puzzle biscuits

Serve these all jumbled up and let little ones put the shapes back together

115g unsalted butter, softened
115g caster sugar
1/2 tsp Taste the Difference Madagascan vanilla extract
1 large egg yolk
200g plain flour, plus extra for dusting

90g each yellow, orange and pink ready-to-roll icing by Sainsbury's
25g icing sugar, plus extra for dusting

YOU WILL ALSO NEED
7cm round, star and heart biscuit cutters (measured across the widest part)

1 Use a hand-held electric whisk to beat the butter and caster sugar in a bowl until pale and fluffy. Beat in the egg yolk* and vanilla extract, then gradually beat in the flour to form a crumbly dough. Gather the dough with your hands and knead lightly until smooth. Wrap in cling film and chill for 30 mins.

2 Line two baking sheets with baking paper. Roll the dough out on a lightly floured surface to a thickness of 3mm. Using the biscuit cutters, stamp out 6 of each shape, re-rolling the dough as necessary. Place on the baking sheets, then cut each shape into three pieces, but don't separate the pieces. Chill in the fridge for 15 mins. Preheat the oven to 190°C, fan 170°C, gas 5.

3 Bake the biscuits for 10-12 mins, or until pale golden. As soon as you take the baking sheets out of the oven, cut through the biscuits again to separate the pieces. Leave to cool completely on the baking sheets.

4 In a small bowl, mix the icing sugar with a few drops of water to make a thick glacé icing. Roll each of the three different coloured icings out on a surface dusted with icing sugar to about 2mm thick. Use each biscuit cutter to stamp out 2 shapes from each colour – you may need to re-roll the trimmings. Cut the icing shapes into pieces to match the biscuits. Spread the biscuit pieces with a little of the glacé icing and attach the matching pieces of coloured icing. Store in an airtight container for up to a week.

*See p191 for a list of recipes to use leftover egg whites.

Cook's tip
Leftover ready to roll icing can be wrapped in cling film and kept in a cool, dry place for up to 2 months.

Each biscuit (41g) provides:

ENERGY	FAT	SATURATES	SUGARS	SALT
753kJ 179kcal	6.7g	3.7g	20.3g	trace

Typical values per 100g: Energy 1836kJ/437kcal
Each biscuit provides:
28.2g carbohydrate | 0.4g fibre | 1.4g protein

baking with kids

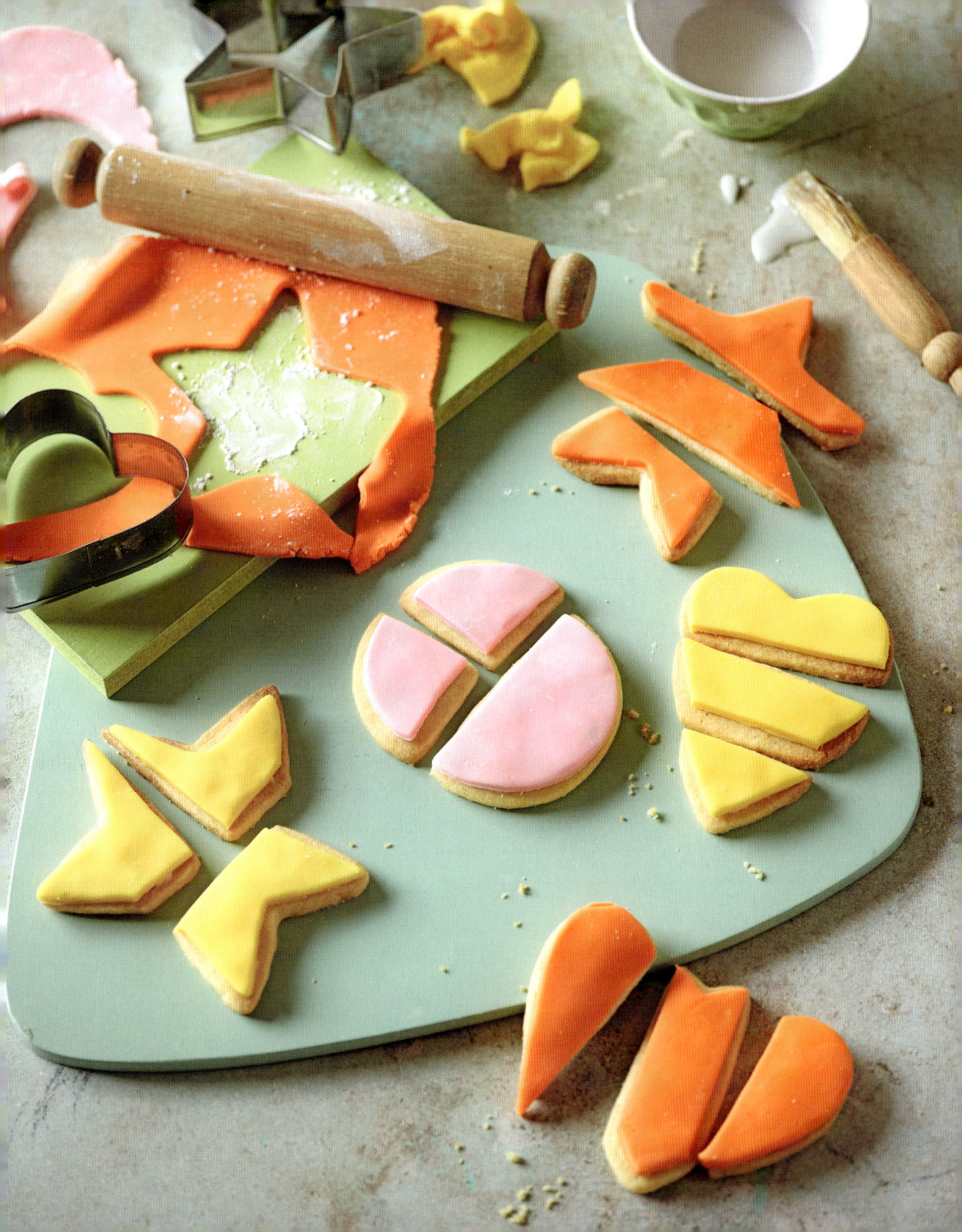

baking with kids

MAKES 12 pieces
PREP TIME 30 mins
COOK TIME 15 mins

Chocolate bark

This is an easy and fun recipe for kids to help make, and makes a great edible gift. Mix and match the toppings for a different look

200g cook's Belgian dark chocolate by Sainsbury's
100g cook's Belgian white chocolate by Sainsbury's

½ x 6g pack freeze dried strawberry pieces by Sainsbury's

1. Cover a large baking sheet with baking parchment.

2. Melt the dark and white chocolates in two separate heatproof bowls over a pan of boiling water (see p7). Remove the heat and pour the dark chocolate onto the baking sheet.

3. Pour over the white chocolate in small patches and use a skewer or cocktail stick to swirl the white and dark chocolates together to create a marbled pattern.

4. Sprinkle over the dried strawberry pieces, and leave the chocolate bark in a cool place (not the fridge) to set. Break into 12 even-sized pieces to serve.

Variations

Peanut butter & pretzels
Swirl a dollop of peanut butter into the melted chocolate, top with broken pretzels and leave to set.

Orange & raisins
Mix a few drops of Taste the Difference Valencian orange extract and some finely grated orange zest in with the melted chocolate, then decorate with raisins and leave to set.

Crunchy granola
Sprinkle a handful of your favourite crunchy breakfast granola over the top of the melted chocolate, then leave to set.

Each serving (25g) provides:
ENERGY	FAT	SATURATES	SUGARS	SALT
570kJ 137kcal	9.2g	5.7g	11.2g	trace

Typical values per 100g: Energy 2279kJ/548kcal
Each serving provides:
11.6g carbohydrate | 1.2g fibre | 1.4g protein

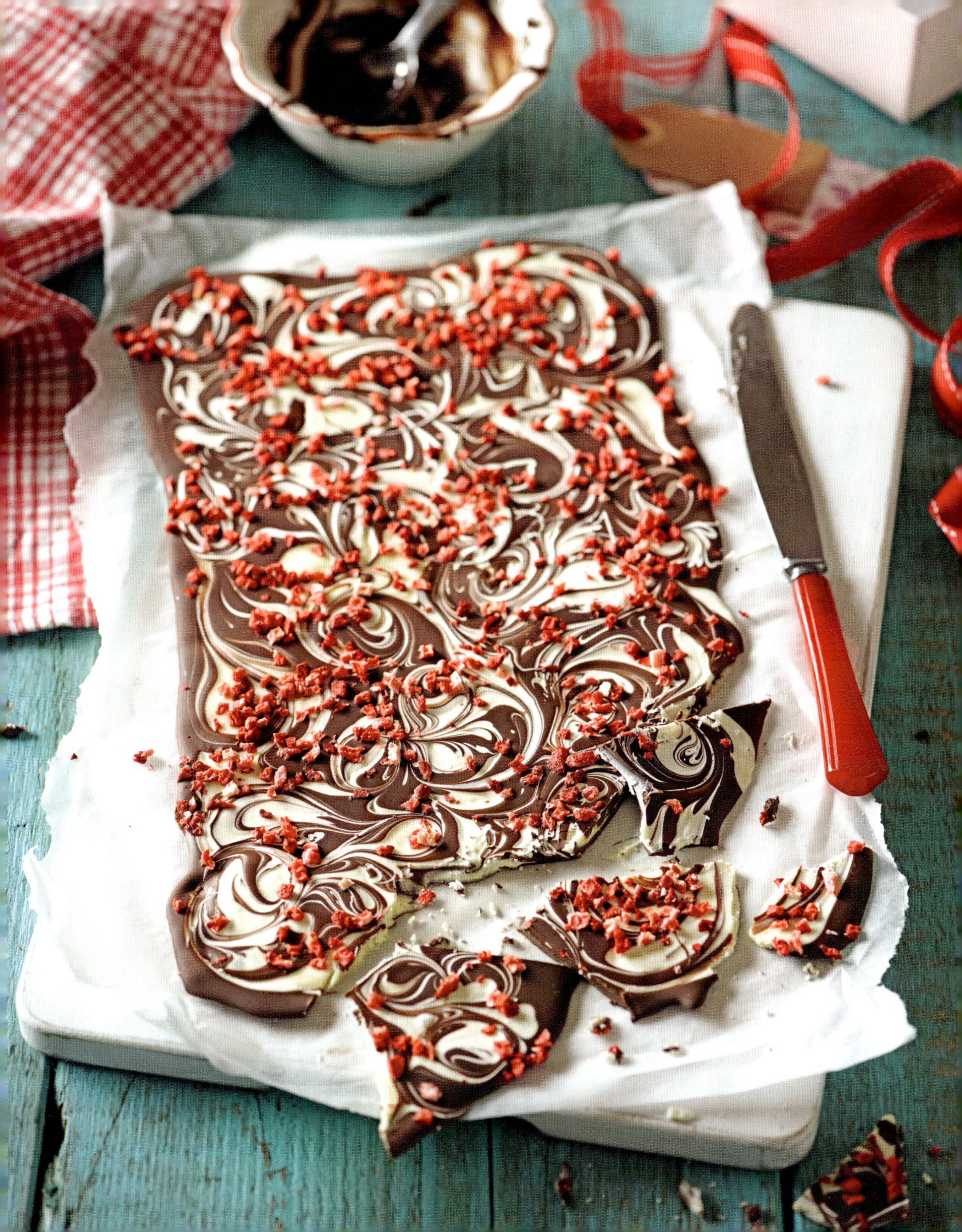

MAKES 80
PREP TIME 20 mins, plus chilling
COOK TIME 12-15 mins

Iced jewels

Everyone's favourite biscuit – these colourful little bite-size treats will be a hit at a child's birthday party

---

100g unsalted butter, softened
100g caster sugar
1 egg, beaten
225g plain flour, plus extra for dusting
1 tsp Taste the Difference Madagascan vanilla extract

FOR THE ICING
150g butter, softened
200g icing sugar
1-2 tsp semi-skimmed milk
Drops of blue, green, yellow and pink food colouring by Sainsbury's

---

1 Beat together the butter and sugar with a hand-held electric whisk. Stir in the egg, flour and vanilla extract, then gather the mixture together to form a soft dough. Wrap in cling film and chill in the fridge for 30 mins.

2 Preheat the oven to 180°C, fan 160°C, gas 4. Line two large baking sheets with baking paper.

3 Roll out the dough on a floured surface to the thickness of a £1 coin. Use a 3.5cm biscuit cutter to stamp out 80 rounds – you'll need to re-roll the trimmings. Place on the prepared baking sheets and chill in the fridge for 20 minutes.

4 Bake for 12-15 mins until just golden. Cool on a cooling rack.

5 To make the icing, beat the butter until soft and stir through the icing sugar. If the icing is a little stiff, soften with a drop of two of the milk. Divide between 4 bowls and add a few drops of different coloured food colouring to each bowl. Mix well until each icing has an even colour. Pipe the different coloured icings onto the biscuits using a piping bag fitted with a star-shaped nozzle. Allow the icing to set slightly before serving.

Each biscuit (10g) provides:
ENERGY 195kJ/47kcal | FAT 2.6g | SATURATES 1.5g | SUGARS 3.5g | SALT trace

Typical values per 100g: Energy 1945kJ/465kcal
Each biscuit provides:
5.4g carbohydrate | 0.1g fibre | 0.4g protein

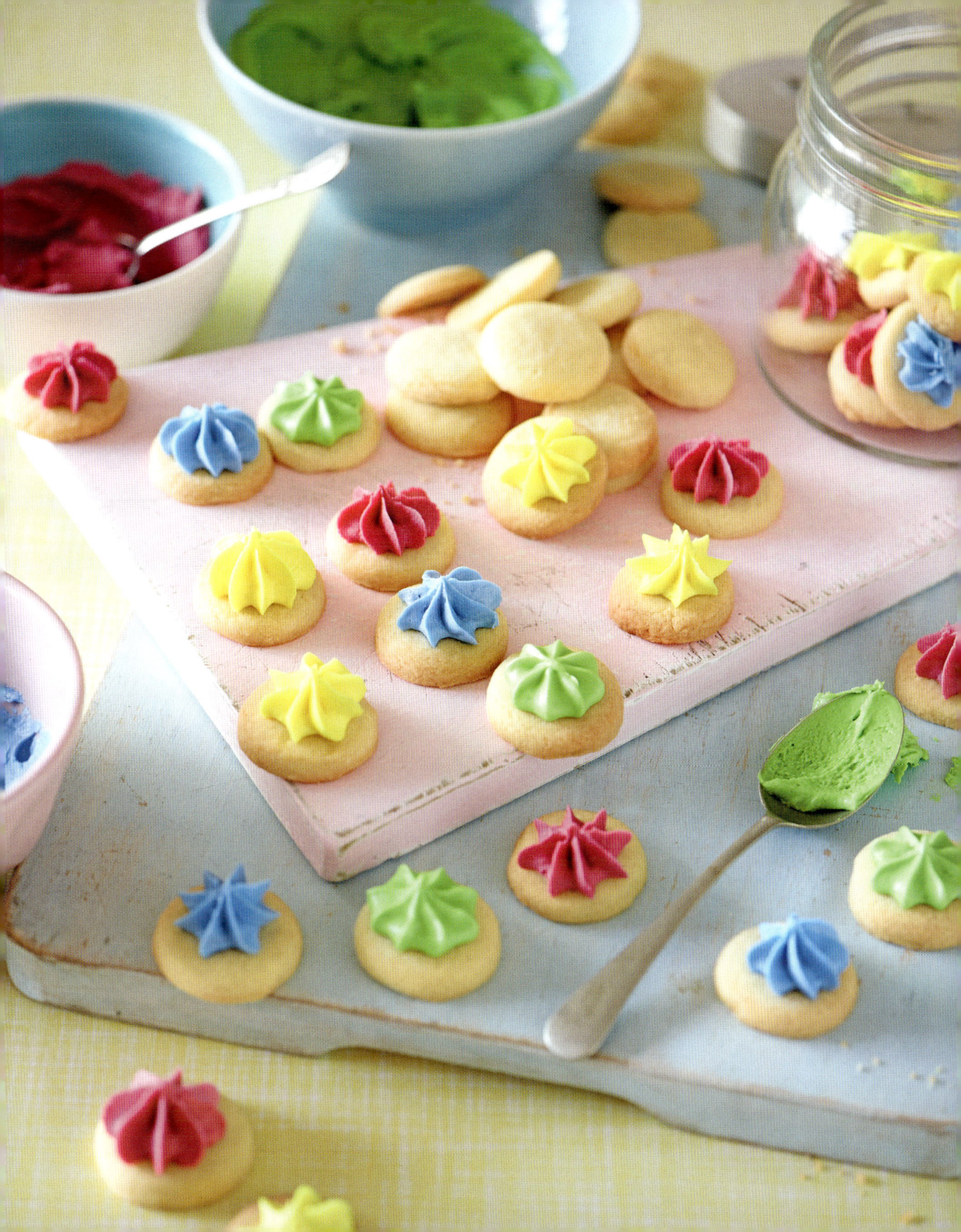

MAKES 8
PREP TIME 20 mins
COOK TIME 20 mins

Pinwheel scones

Delicious served hot or cold, you can use any cheese and herb combo you like to make these tasty scones

1 tsp vegetable oil, for brushing
250g plain flour, plus extra for dusting
1 tbsp baking powder
Pinch of cayenne pepper
30g unsalted butter, cubed
180ml semi-skimmed milk
100g mature British Cheddar by Sainsbury's, plus a little extra for sprinkling
1 tbsp chopped fresh flat-leaf parsley

1. Preheat the oven to 200°C, fan 180°C, gas 6. Brush the base and sides of a 20cm round cake tin with the oil.

2. Sift the flour, baking powder and cayenne pepper into a mixing bowl. Using your fingertips, rub the butter into the flour until the mixture resembles breadcrumbs. Add enough milk so the mixture comes together as a dough, but be careful not to make it too sticky.

3. Tip the dough out onto a floured surface and roll out to a rectangle that's roughly 20cm x 30cm. Sprinkle over the cheese and the parsley. Starting at the long side, roll to a log. Cut the log into 8 rounds.

4. Place one round in the centre of the prepared tin. Arrange the remaining rounds around it to create a 'flower'. Sprinkle the extra cheese over the pinwheel and bake for 20 mins until risen and golden.

5. Remove from the oven and allow to cool slightly before serving. These are best eaten on the same day they're baked.

Each scone (64g) provides:
ENERGY	FAT	SATURATES	SUGARS	SALT
872kJ 208kcal	8.7g	5.1g	1.6g	0.6g

Typical values per 100g: Energy 1363kJ/325kcal
Each scone provides:
24.3g carbohydrate | 1.2g fibre | 7.5g protein

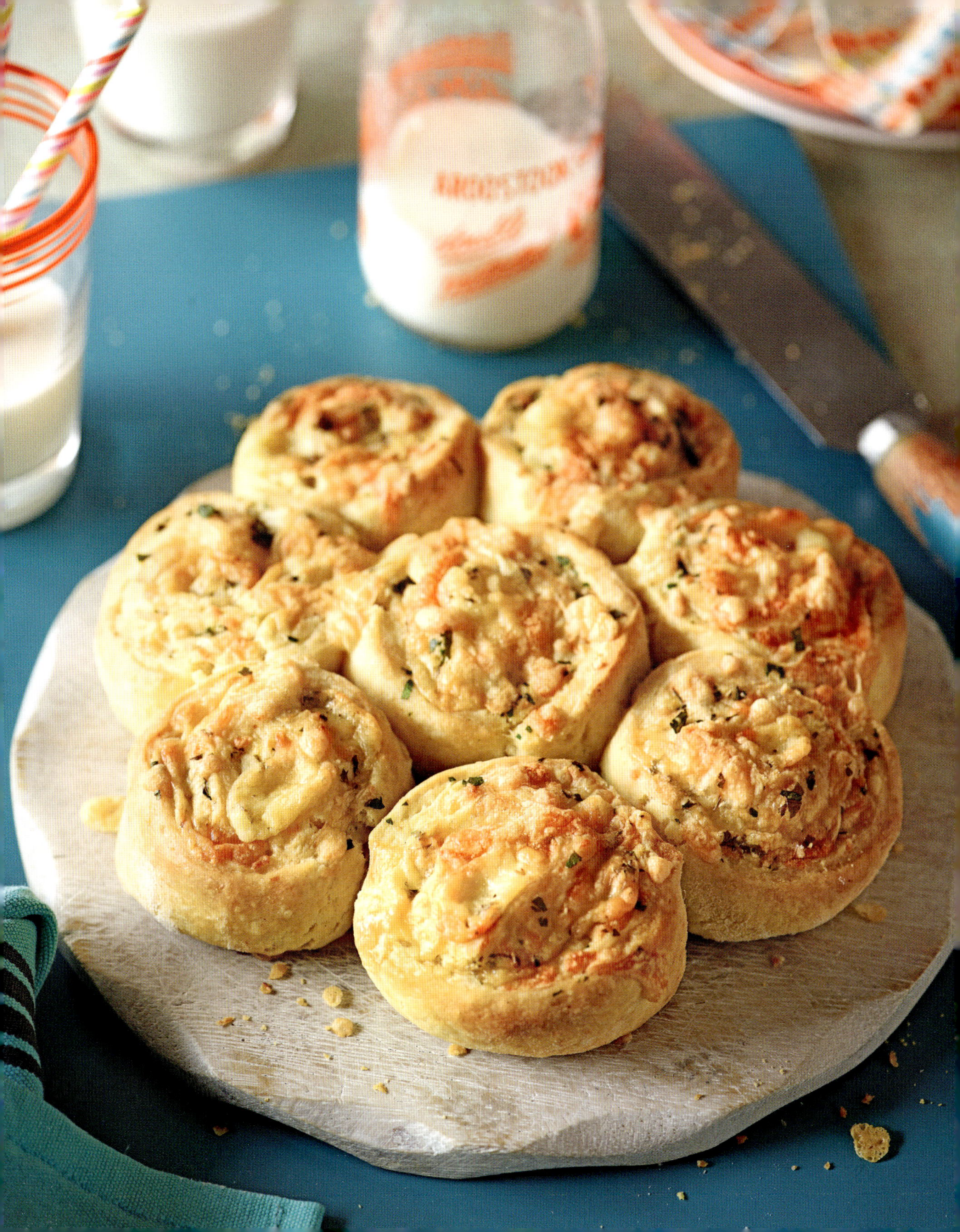

baking with kids

MAKES 8
PREP TIME 25 mins, plus chilling
COOK TIME 20-25 mins

Tomato & mozzarella hand pies

These little pies make perfect finger food - enjoy them warm or cold

175g plain flour, plus extra for dusting
150g unsalted butter, chilled and cubed
90ml be good to yourself soured cream
100g cherry tomatoes, quartered
½ x 125g pack be good to yourself mozzarella, torn
3 tbsp torn fresh basil
1 egg, beaten

1. Put the flour and butter in a large bowl. Rub together with your fingertips until the mixture resembles breadcrumbs. Add the sour cream and stir to form a dough. Shape into a flat disc, wrap in cling film and chill in the fridge for 30 mins.

2. While the dough is chilling, mix together the tomatoes, mozzarella and basil in a bowl. Pour off any excess liquid.

3. Remove the dough from the fridge. Roll out on a floured surface to the thickness of a £1 coin. Use a biscuit cutter to stamp out 8 x 10cm circles (you may need to re-roll the trimmings).

4. Divide the filling between the pastry circles, putting it on one half of each circle and leaving a 2cm border. Dampen the edges of the dough with water, then fold over the pastry to make a semi-circular parcel. Press the edges together, then crimp or seal with a fork. Arrange on a baking sheet lined with baking paper and freeze for 10 mins to firm up before baking.

5. Meanwhile, preheat the oven to 190°C, fan 170°C, gas 5. Brush the pies all over with the beaten egg and bake for 20-25 mins until golden. Cool on a cooling rack before serving.

Cook's tip
Ask kids to decorate the pies by using cookie cutters to cut out shapes from the pastry trimmings. Brush the back of the shapes with egg wash to help them stick, then brush all over with more egg wash before baking.

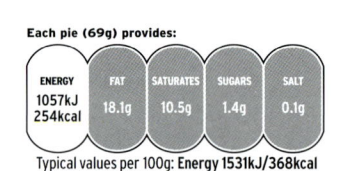

Each pie (69g) provides:

ENERGY	FAT	SATURATES	SUGARS	SALT
1057kJ 254kcal	18.1g	10.5g	1.4g	0.1g

Typical values per 100g: Energy 1531kJ/368kcal
Each pie provides:
17.2g carbohydrate | 0.9g fibre | 5.2g protein

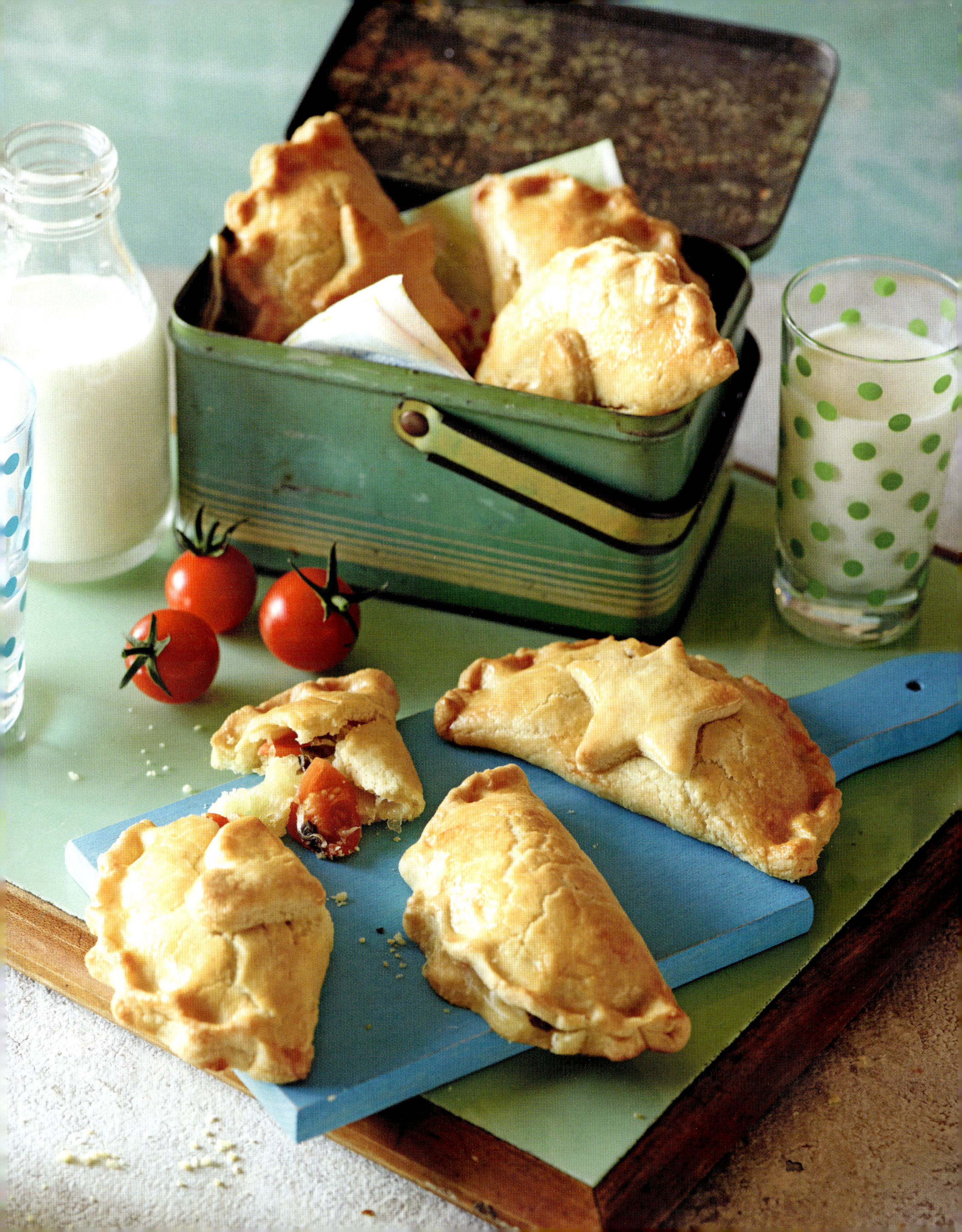

baking with kids

MAKES 12
PREP TIME 10 mins
COOK TIME 20 mins

Ham & pineapple muffins

Delicious breakfast-style muffins that make a nice change from ham and cheese toasties

Butter, for greasing
250g self-raising flour
50g mature British Cheddar by Sainsbury's, grated
50g honey roast ham slices by Sainsbury's, shredded

200g tinned pineapple, finely cubed
1 egg
75ml whole milk
50ml olive oil

1. Preheat the oven to 200°C, fan 180°C, gas 6. Grease a 12-hole muffin tin.

2. Sift the flour into a large bowl, then add the cheese, ham and pineapple. Use a wooden spoon to stir until combined. Make a well in the centre.

3. In a large jug, whisk together the egg, milk and oil. Pour into the well in the dry ingredients and mix to form a soft, wet dough.

4. Divide the mixture between the muffin holes and bake for 20 mins until the muffins are risen and golden. Cool slightly on a cooling rack and serve warm.

Cook's tips
Don't over-mix the muffin fixture – this will help ensure the muffins are nice and light and airy. If you like, you could sprinkle a few pumpkin or poppy seeds on top just before baking.

Each muffin (52g) provides:

ENERGY	FAT	SATURATES	SUGARS	SALT
596kJ 142kcal	6.1g	1.9g	2.3g	0.3g

Typical values per 100g: Energy 1146kJ/276kcal
Each muffin provides:
16.7g carbohydrate | 0.7g fibre | 4.7g protein

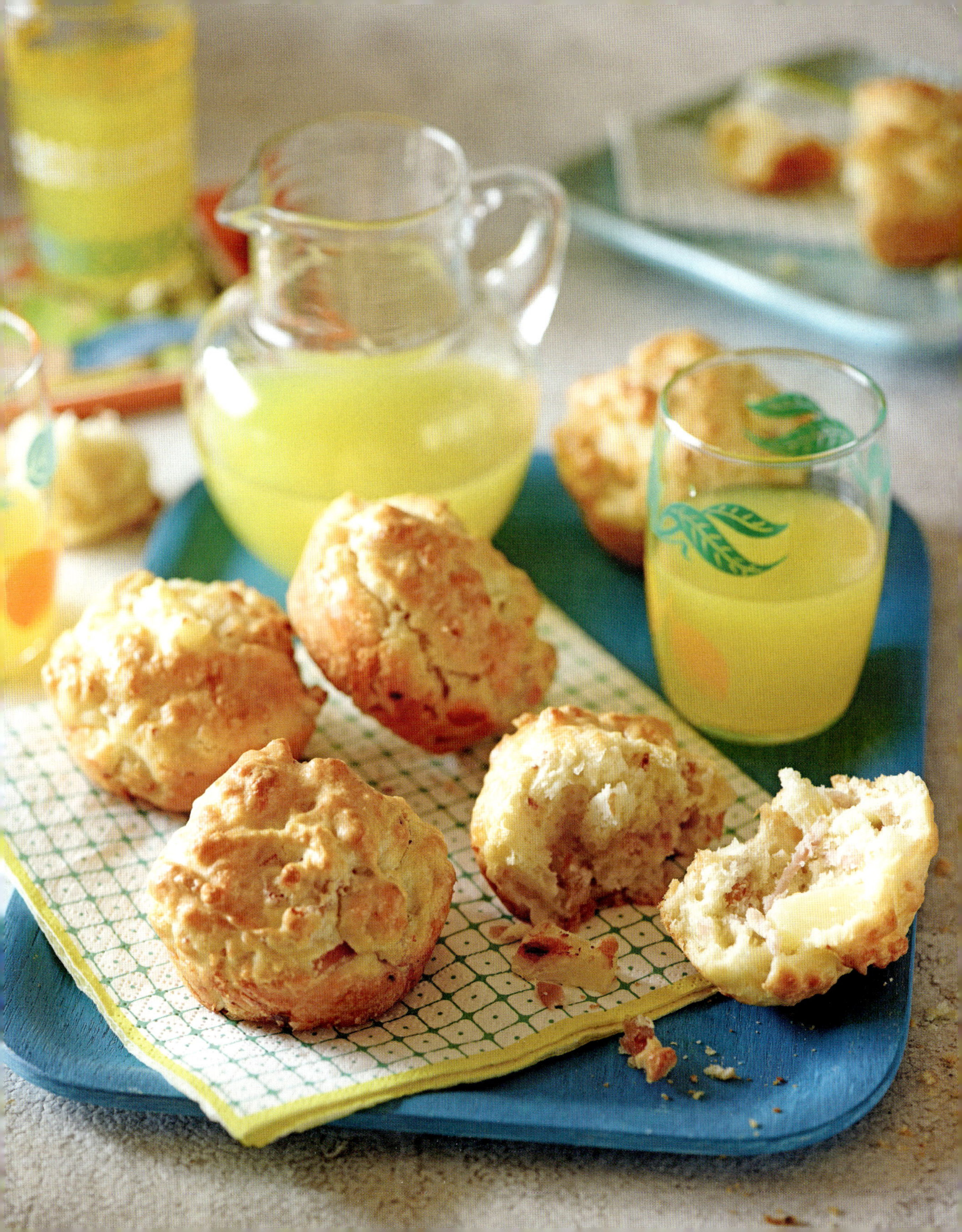

Best bites

Girls' night in, mates coming over to watch the big match or afternoon tea with the parents? These tasty savoury tartlets make the perfect finger food for sharing. Find the recipe on p124.

bakes for sharing with friends

irresistible ideas for grown-up get-togethers

Chocolate olive oil cake	104
Apple & Calvados tart	106
Butternut squash, orange & rosemary loaf cake	108
Salted caramel & peanut brownies	110
Apple & coconut cake	112
Earl Grey tea cake	114
Black pepper shortbread	116
Orange blossom polenta cake	118
Coconut & almond bites	120
Ginger stout cake	122
Spinach & feta tartlets	124
Chorizo-spiced sausage rolls	126
Mushroom, pancetta & Taleggio tart	128
Cheesy oatcakes	130
Stromboli	132
Pizzettas	134

SERVES 12
PREP TIME 15 mins
COOK TIME 30 mins

Chocolate olive oil cake

A deliciously moist cake that will win over any lover of chocolate

---

150ml extra virgin olive oil by Sainsbury's, plus extra for greasing
50g cocoa powder
200g caster sugar
150g ground almonds

1/2 tsp ground mixed spice
Zest of 1 orange
Zest of 1 lemon
3 large free ranges eggs, separated
Icing sugar, for dusting

---

1. Heat the oven to 180°C, fan 160°C, gas 4. Grease a 20cm springform tin and line with baking paper.

2. In a large bowl, mix together the olive oil, cocoa, caster sugar, ground almonds, mixed spice, orange and lemon zests, and egg yolks until well combined.

3. In a spotlessly clean bowl, beat the egg whites with an electric hand-held whisk, until soft peaks form (see p7). Using a large metal spoon, loosen the chocolate almond mix by adding one spoonful of the egg whites and gently folding in. Once combined, gently fold in the remaining egg whites.

4. Pour the mixture into the prepared tin and bake for 30 mins or until a skewer inserted into the centre of the cake comes out clean. Leave to cool completely in the tin - the cake will deflate and crack slightly as it cools and the centre should still be quite moist and squidgy. Remove from the tin, put on a serving plate and dust with the icing sugar (see Cook's tip) to serve.

Cook's tip
This easy icing-sugar decoration is done using a paper lace doily as a stencil (or cut out your own stencil from a circular piece of paper). Place it on top of the cake, put icing sugar in a sieve or tea strainer, then dust it evenly over the stencil and carefully remove it to serve.

Each serving (51g) provides:

ENERGY	FAT	SATURATES	SUGARS	SALT
1165kJ 280kcal	19.7g	3g	18g	0.1g
14%	28%	15%	20%	1%

% of the Reference Intakes
Typical values per 100g: Energy 2285kJ/550kcal
Each serving provides:
18.6g carbohydrate | 2.1g fibre | 5.9g protein

sharing with friends

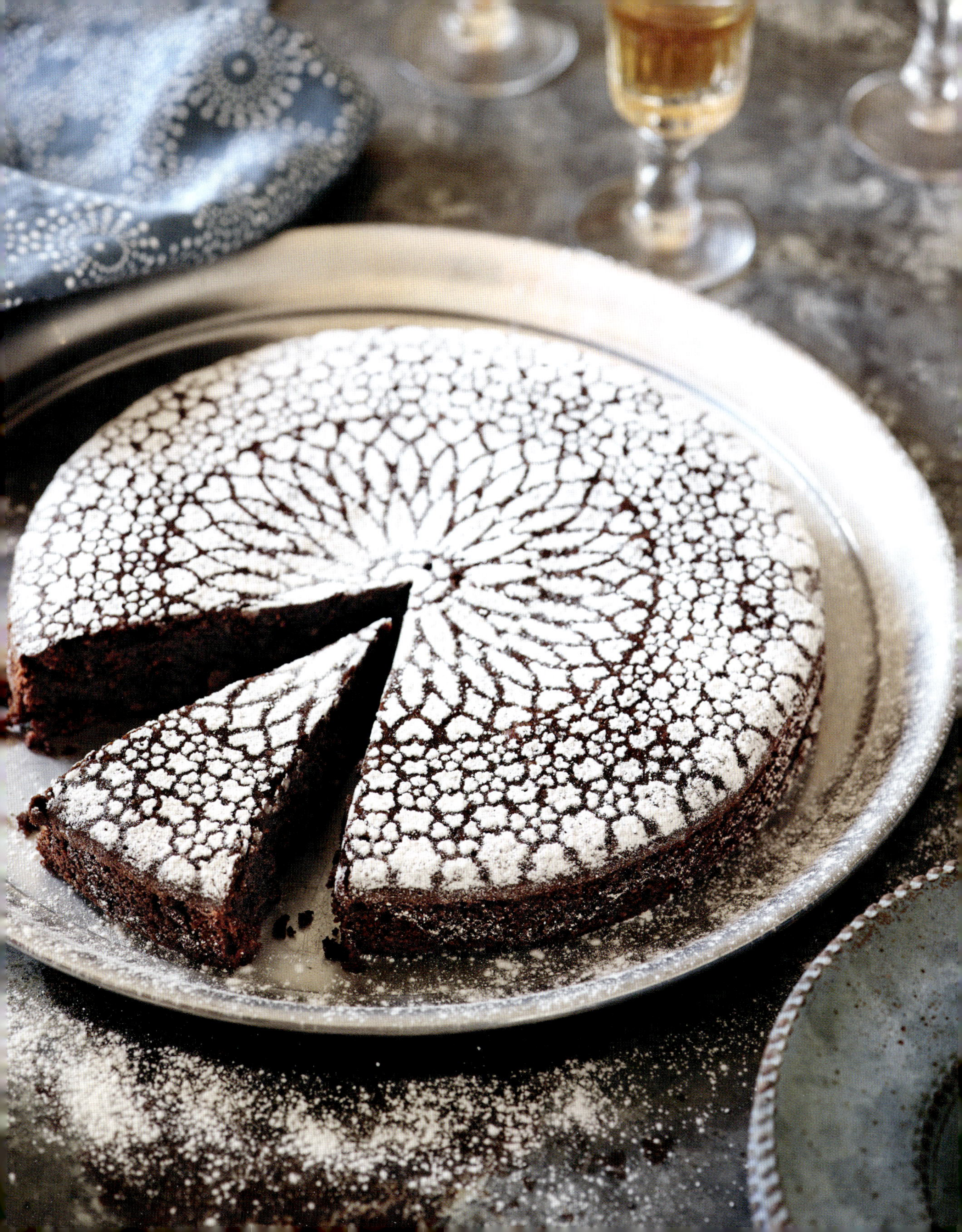

SERVES 12
PREP TIME 30 mins, plus chilling
COOK TIME 1 hour 20 mins

Apple & Calvados tart

This delicious tart is the perfect ending to a special-occasion meal

200g plain flour, plus extra for dusting
100g unsalted butter, chilled and cubed
50g caster sugar
1 egg yolk

FOR THE CUSTARD
150ml fresh double cream
250ml semi-skimmed milk
1 Fairtrade Madagascan vanilla pod by Sainsbury's, split with a knife
80g caster sugar
6 egg yolks
1 tbsp Calvados or brandy

FOR THE CARAMELISED APPLES
70g unsalted butter
3 tbsp caster sugar
3 red apples, cored and cut into thick slices

1. Make the pastry. Put the flour and butter in a food processor or hand blender and pulse until the mixture resembles breadcrumbs. Add the sugar, pulse again, then add one egg yolk and 2 tbsp cold water. Process until the mixture comes together to form a dough. Wrap in cling film and chill in the fridge for 30 min.

2. Preheat the oven to 190°C, fan 170°C, gas 5, along with a large baking sheet. Roll out the pastry on a floured surface so it's big enough to line a deep 23cm loose-bottomed fluted tart tin. Rest the case in the fridge for 30 mins, then trim the edges and prick all over with a fork. Line the pastry base with baking paper and fill with baking beans or rice. Put on the baking sheet and bake for 15 mins, then remove the beans/rice and paper. Cook for a further 5-10 mins until golden.

3. Meanwhile, make the custard. Heat the cream, milk and vanilla pod in a pan over a low heat until just about to boil. Remove from the heat and discard the vanilla pod. Whisk together the sugar and egg yolks in a large heatproof jug, then slowly pour in the cream mixture, whisking until combined. Stir in the Calvados.

4. Reduce the oven temperature to 140°C, fan 120°C, gas 1. While the pastry case is still in the oven, carefully pour in the custard, making sure it doesn't spill over the sides. Bake for 40 mins or until set. Allow the tart to cool completely in the tin, then transfer it to a serving plate.

5. Make the caramelised apples. Melt the butter and sugar in a large pan over a low heat. When it bubbles, add the apples and cook for around 5 mins until caramelised. Remove from the heat and cool slightly. Decorate the tart with the apples.

*See p191 for a list of recipes to use leftover egg yolks.

Each serving (97g) provides:

ENERGY	FAT	SATURATES	SUGARS	SALT
1397kJ 335kcal	21.5g	11.8g	17.6g	trace
17%	31%	59%	20%	<1%

% of the Reference Intakes
Typical values per 100g: Energy 1441kJ/346kcal
Each serving provides:
29.6g carbohydrate | 1.4g fibre | 4.5g protein

sharing with friends

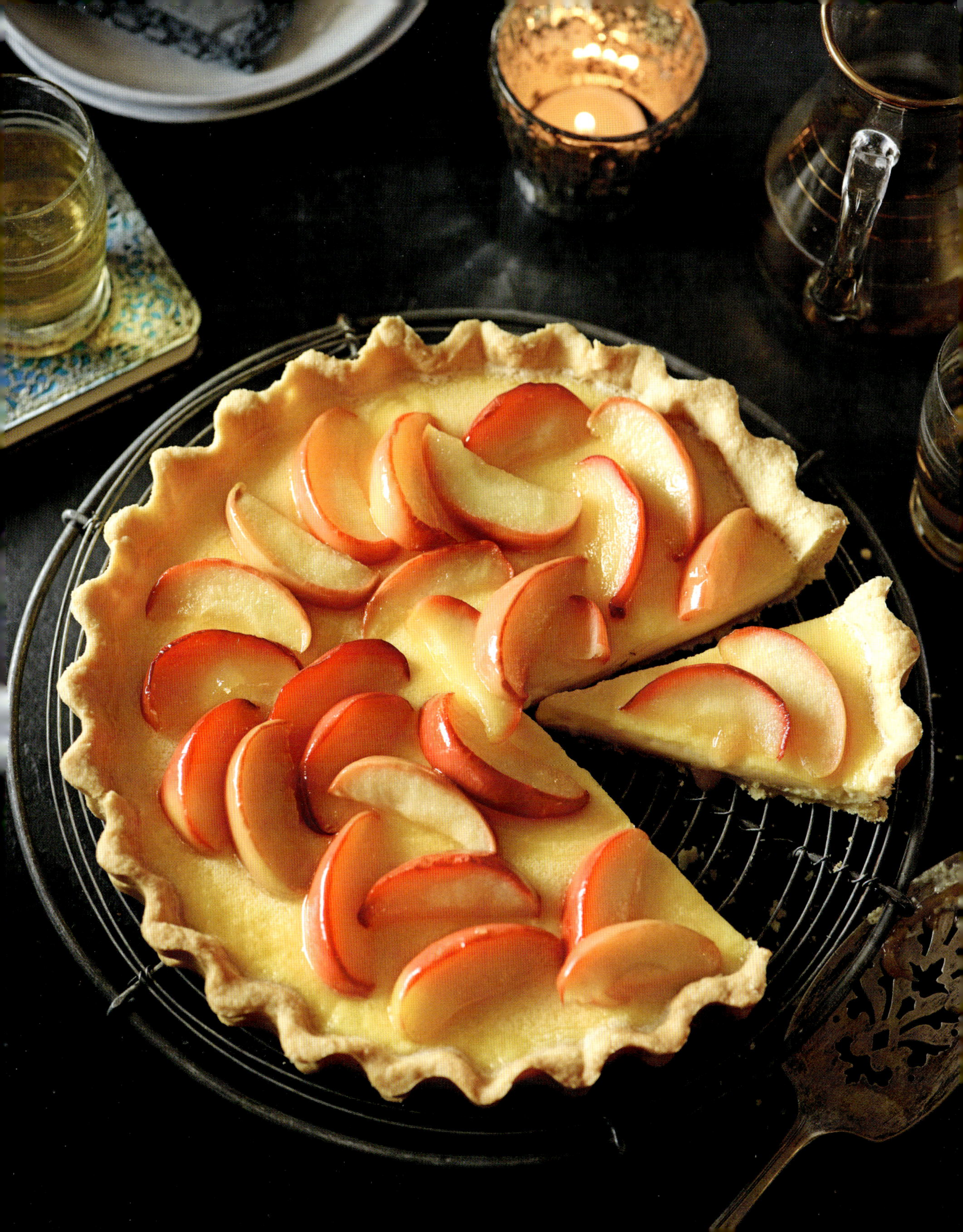

SERVES 12
PREP TIME 20 mins
COOK TIME 2 hours

Butternut squash, orange & rosemary loaf cake

This loaf cake with a difference uses roasted butternut squash for a dense, moist texture and interesting flavour

150g unsalted butter, softened, plus extra for greasing
1 small butternut squash, halved and deseeded (about 400g raw weight)
1 tbsp olive oil
1 sprig fresh rosemary, leaves picked and finely chopped, plus extra to decorate
150g light brown soft sugar by Sainsbury's
3 large eggs
225g self-raising flour
Grated zest and juice of 1 orange
100g icing sugar

1   Preheat the oven to 200°C, fan 180°C, gas 6. Grease and line a 2lb loaf tin with baking paper or a Sainsbury's loaf tin liner.

2   Put the butternut squash in a roasting tin, rub all over with the olive oil, then sprinkle over the chopped rosemary. Roast for 1 hour, or until tender. Cool slightly, then scoop out the roasted flesh and purée it, using either a hand blender or a potato masher. You'll need 300g to go in the cake.

3   In a large bowl, beat together the butter and sugar until light and fluffy. Beat in the eggs, one at a time, adding a spoonful of flour between each one. Sift in the remaining flour, then add the orange zest and 300g butternut purée. Fold in until the mixture is combined.

4   Spoon the mixture into the prepared tin and bake for 1 hour, or until a skewer inserted into the centre of the loaf comes out clean. Leave to cool in the tin for a few minutes, then transfer to a cooling rack to cool completely.

5   To decorate, mix the icing sugar with 2 tbsp of the orange juice. Beat until smooth, then drizzle over the top of the cake. Decorate with the extra rosemary and cut into thick slices to serve.

Each serving (85g) provides:

ENERGY	FAT	SATURATES	SUGARS	SALT
1128kJ 269kcal	13g	6.8g	20.6g	0.2g
13%	19%	34%	23%	3%

% of the Reference Intakes
Typical values per 100g: Energy 1328kJ/317kcal
Each serving provides:
33.9g carbohydrate | 0.7g fibre | 3.9g protein

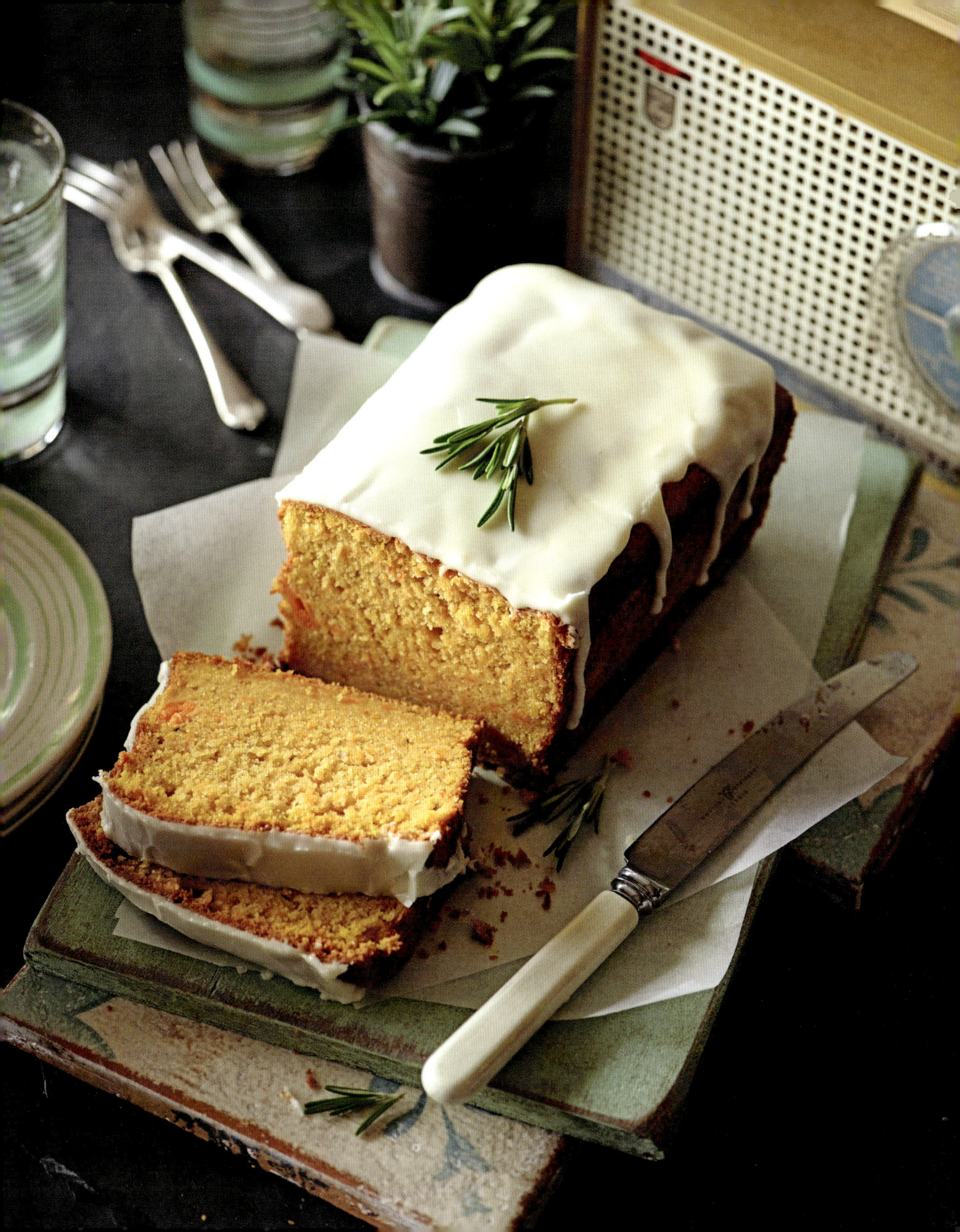

Salted caramel & peanut brownies

A little bit naughty, and a lot nice! Dense, gooey brownies made even more decadent with a salted caramel and peanut topping

MAKES 16
PREP TIME 15 mins
COOK TIME 45 mins

115g unsalted butter, plus extra for greasing
50g cocoa
2 large eggs
225g caster sugar
½ tsp Taste the Difference Madagascan vanilla extract
75g self-raising flour, sifted
150g Taste the Difference salted caramel sauce
35g salted peanuts, finely chopped

1 Preheat the oven to 180°C, fan 160°C, gas 4. Grease and line a 23cm square cake tin with baking paper.

2 Melt the butter in a small pan over a medium heat. Remove from the heat and stir in the cocoa until smooth.

3 Whisk the eggs, sugar and vanilla together in a large bowl until pale and foamy. Stir in the cocoa mixture followed by the flour. Spoon the mixture into the prepared tin and level the top. Bake for 40 mins, until the top has risen slightly and the cake looks slightly softer in the middle than around the edges.

4 Cool in the tin for 10 mins, then turn out onto a cooling rack. Drizzle over the salted caramel sauce and scatter over the peanuts. Let cool completely before cutting into 16 even pieces.

Cook's tip
With brownies, timing is everything to get that all-important squidgy centre. To check they're ready, insert a skewer into the centre of the cake. If it comes out with wet cake mixture, it's underdone. If it has a slightly gooey mixture stuck to it, it's ready.

Each brownie (41g) provides:

ENERGY	FAT	SATURATES	SUGARS	SALT
818kJ 196kcal	10.8g	5.9g	17.8g	0.2g
10%	15%	30%	20%	3%

% of the Reference Intakes
Typical values per 100g: Energy 1994kJ/447kcal
Each brownie provides:
21.3g carbohydrate | 1.2g fibre | 2.8g protein

sharing with friends

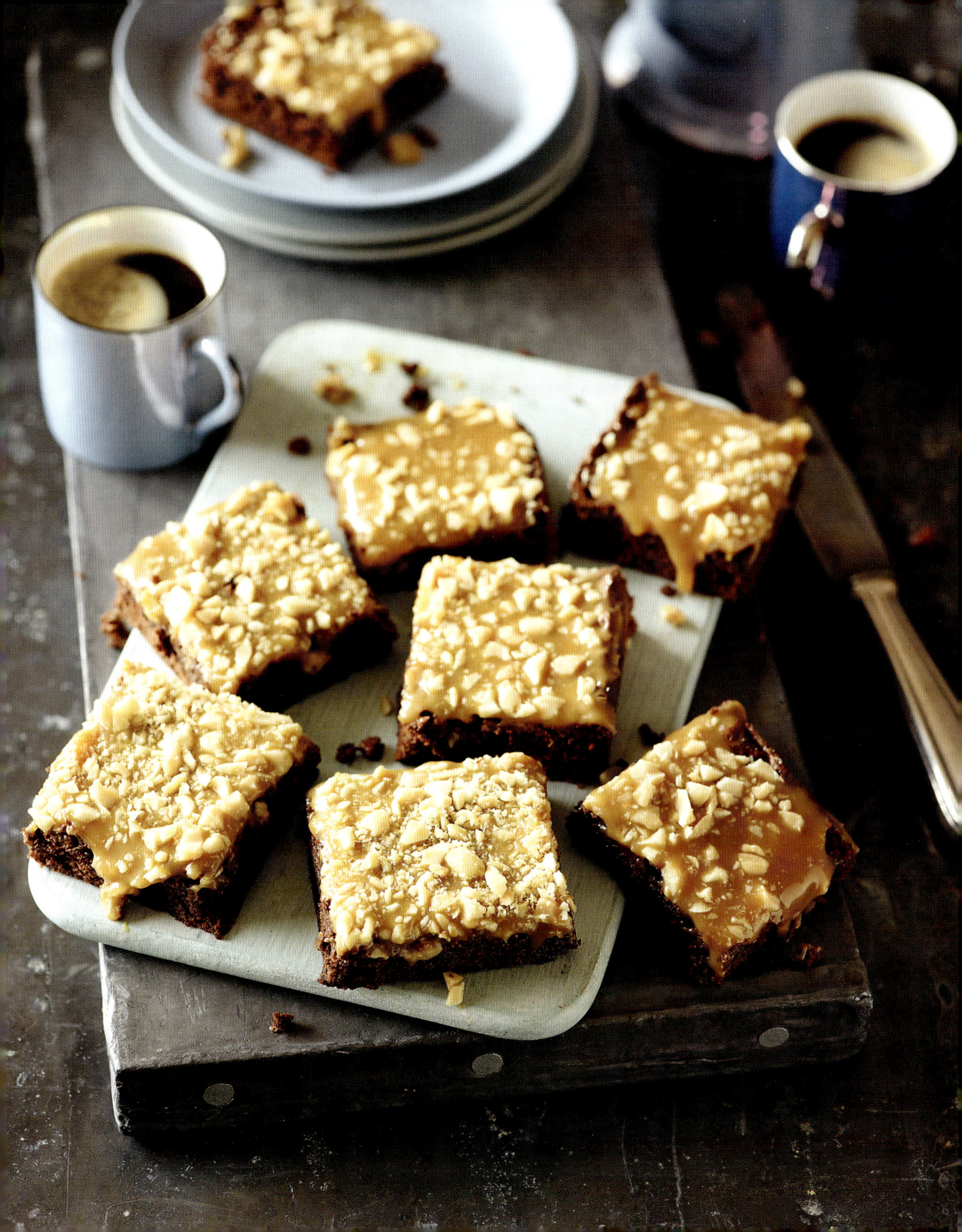

SERVES 12
PREP TIME 15 mins
COOK TIME 40 mins

Apple & coconut cake

This is an easy but delicious cake that uses everyday ingredients, so it's great to make at short notice for last-minute guests

125g butter at room temperature, plus extra for greasing
175g caster sugar
200g self-raising flour
2 eggs
1 tbsp semi-skimmed milk
50g desiccated coconut

½ tsp Taste the Difference Madagascan vanilla extract
1 eating apple, cored, peeled and sliced
Juice of ½ a lemon
¼ tsp ground cinnamon
½ tbsp demerara sugar
Icing sugar, for dusting

1. Preheat the oven to 180°C, fan 160°C, gas 4. Grease a 20cm round springform tin and line with baking paper.

2. Put the butter, caster sugar, flour, eggs, milk, coconut and vanilla extract into a bowl and beat with a hand-held electric whisk for 1-2 mins until all of the ingredients are well combined. Spoon the cake mixture into the prepared tin.

3. In a separate bowl, toss together the apple slices, lemon juice, cinnamon and demerara sugar. Carefully arrange the apple slices on the top of the cake mix and bake for 40 mins or until the apple is starting to brown and a skewer inserted into the centre of the cake comes out clean. Carefully remove from the tin and cool on a cooling rack. Dust with icing sugar to serve.

Cook's tip
For those with a gluten allergy or intolerance, this cake also works well using gluten-free self raising flour, instead of wheat flour.

Each serving (57g) provides:

ENERGY	FAT	SATURATES	SUGARS	SALT
985kJ 235kcal	12.3g	7.7g	16.4g	0.2g
12%	18%	39%	18%	3%

% of the Reference Intakes
Typical values per 100g: Energy 1727kJ/413kcal
Each serving provides:
27.5g carbohydrate | 1.3g fibre | 3g protein

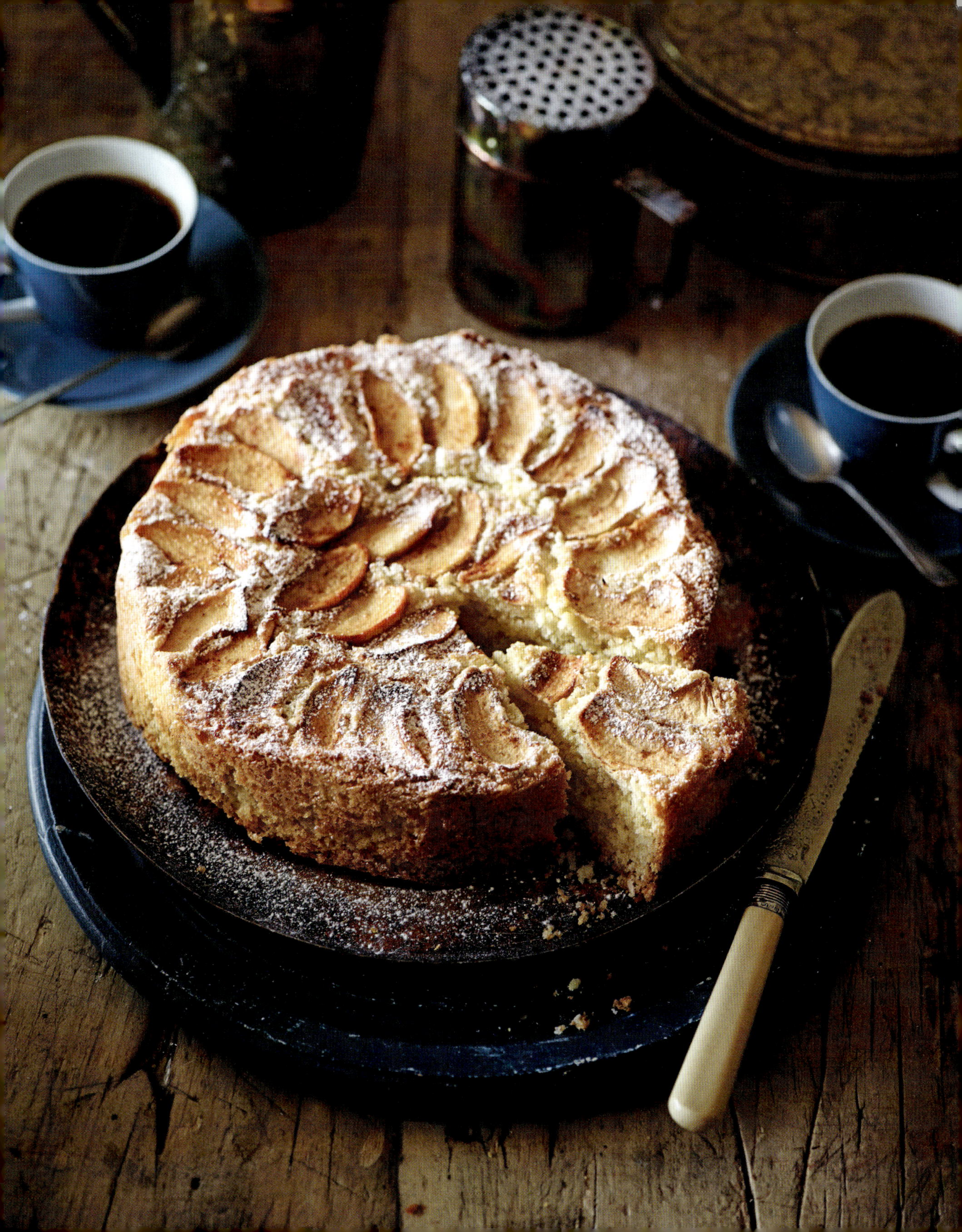

SERVES 10
PREP TIME 15 mins, plus soaking
COOK TIME 1 hour 15 mins

Earl Grey tea cake

Dotted with plump fruit, infused with Earl Grey tea, and topped with a whisky glaze, this loaf is packed with delicious flavours

375g mixed fruit with cranberries and apricots by Sainsbury's
2 tsp ground mixed spice
Zest and juice of 1 lemon
Zest and juice of 1 orange
1 tbsp clear honey
225ml Earl Grey tea, made with 1 Taste the Difference Earl Grey tea bag
50g unsalted butter, melted, plus extra for greasing

350g self-raising flour
200g light brown soft sugar
2 large eggs, lightly beaten

FOR THE GLAZE
3 tbsp Taste the Difference breakfast marmalade
1 tbsp whisky (optional), or water

1 Combine the dried fruit, mixed spice, the lemon and orange zest and juice, honey and tea in a large mixing bowl. Cover with cling film and leave to soak for 4-5 hours, or overnight.

2 Preheat the oven to 170°C, fan 150°C, gas 3 1/2. Grease a 2lb loaf tin and line with baking paper, or a Sainsbury's loaf tin liner.

3 Add the flour, sugar, melted butter and beaten eggs to the fruit mixture. Beat with a wooden spoon until the mixture is well combined and you have a stiff mixture. Spoon into the prepared tin and bake for 1 hour 15 mins until the top of the loaf is golden and a skewer inserted into the centre comes out clean. Carefully remove from the tin and cool slightly on a cooling rack.

4 While the loaf is cooling, make the glaze. In a small pan over a medium heat, gently melt the marmalade, then stir in the whisky, if using, or water. Brush all over the loaf and serve.

sharing with friends

Each serving (142g) provides:

ENERGY	FAT	SATURATES	SUGARS	SALT
1548kJ 366kcal	6.3g	3.1g	45.3g	0.4g
18%	9%	16%	50%	6%

% of the Reference Intakes
Typical values per 100g: Energy 1090kJ/258kcal
Each serving provides:
69.8g carbohydrate | 2.6g fibre | 5.6g protein

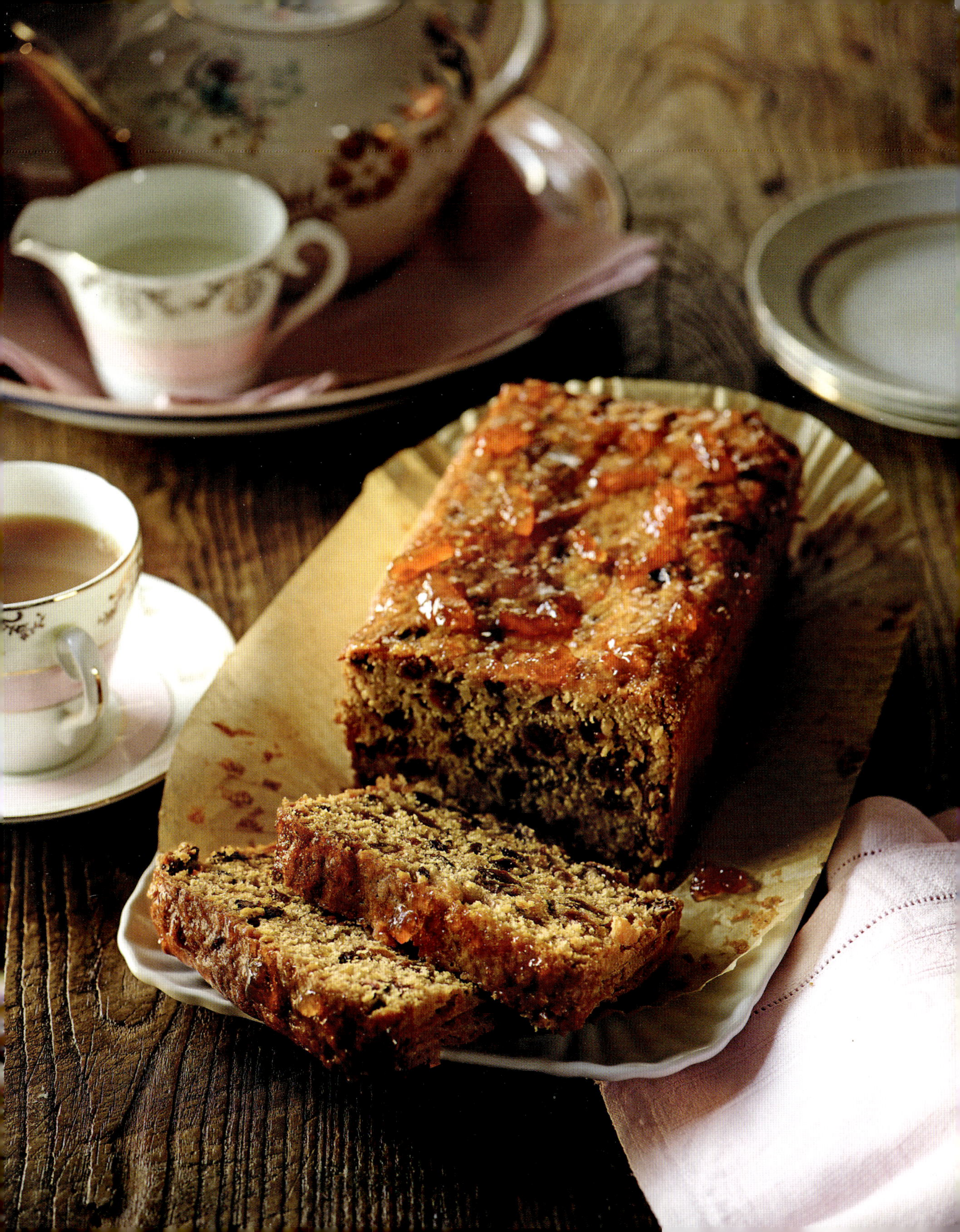

sharing with friends

MAKES 12
PREP TIME 25 mins
COOK TIME 30 mins

Black pepper shortbread

These buttery shortbread biscuits are simple to make - you only need 5 ingredients. The pepper gives them a hint of spicy warmth

115g unsalted butter, at room temperature, plus extra for greasing
55g caster sugar, plus extra for dusting
½ tsp freshly ground black pepper
Finely grated zest of 1 lemon
175g plain flour, plus extra for dusting

1. Preheat the oven to 160°C, fan 140°C, gas 3. Grease a shallow 20cm square cake tin and line with baking paper.

2. In a large bowl, beat together the butter, sugar, pepper and lemon zest with a wooden spoon.

3. Sift in the flour and mix with a fork until a dough starts to form. Gather into a ball and knead briefly on a lightly floured work surface with your hands until smooth. Gently push the dough into the prepared tin and lightly prick all over with a fork.

4. Bake for 30 mins until pale golden, being careful not to let it brown. Remove from the oven and use a sharp knife to mark into fingers while warm, then leave to cool on a cooling rack. Dust with the extra sugar, cut into fingers and serve.

Cook's tip
Make these even more special by adding 60g chopped nuts – pistachios work well – or by dipping the ends of the biscuits in melted dark chocolate.

Each biscuit (26g) provides:

ENERGY	FAT	SATURATES	SUGARS	SALT
592kJ 142kcal	8.1g	4.7g	5.4g	trace
7%	12%	24%	6%	<1%

% of the Reference Intakes
Typical values per 100g: Energy 2277kJ/545kcal
Each biscuit provides:
15.5g carbohydrate | 0.5g fibre | 1.5g protein

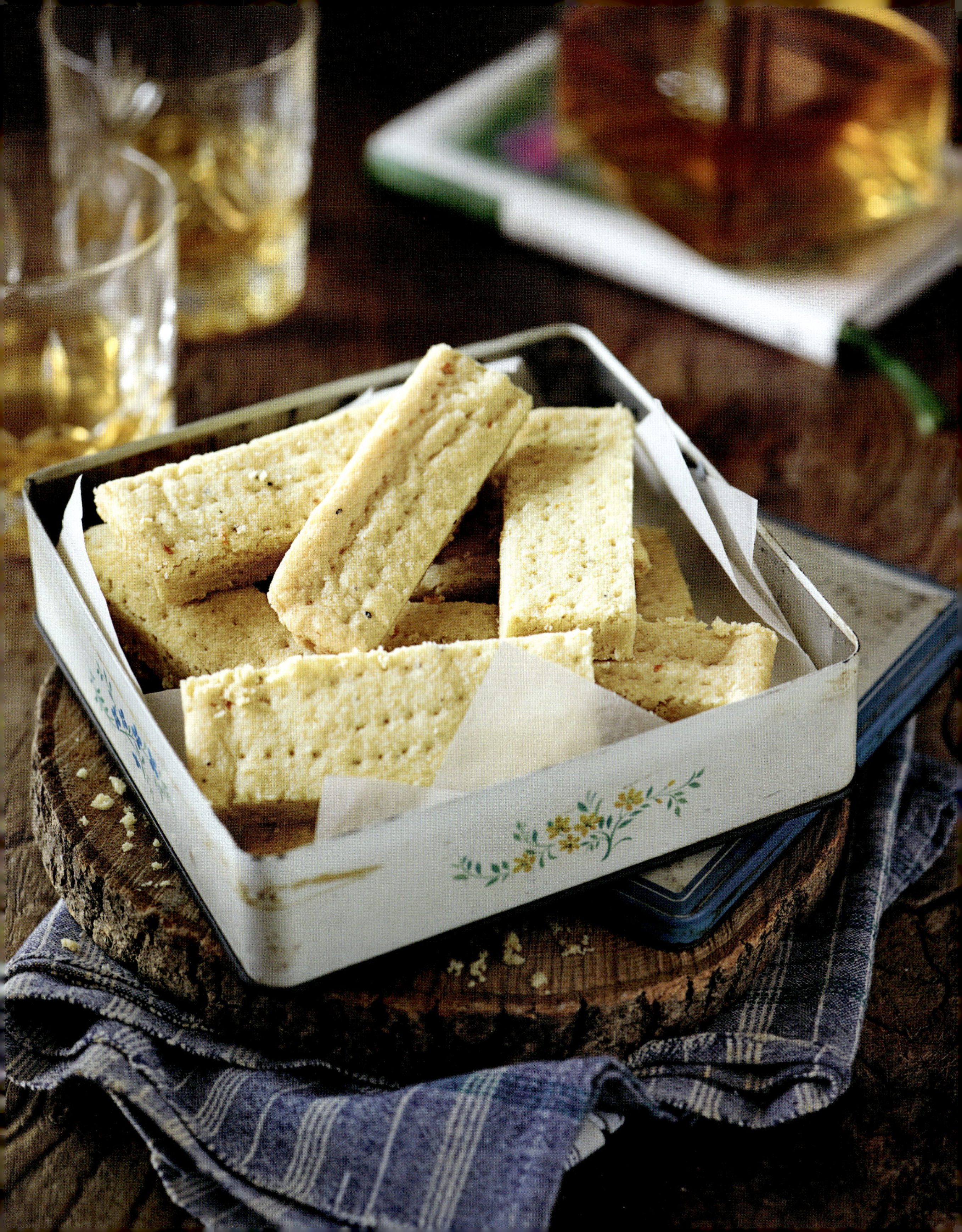

SERVES 12
PREP TIME 20 mins
COOK TIME 45 mins

Orange blossom polenta cake

Middle Eastern flavours of orange, pistachios and cardamom combine in this deliciously fragrant cake

---

200g unsalted butter, at room temperature, plus extra for greasing
100g polenta by Sainsbury's
200g unsalted roasted pistachio nuts, finely ground in a food processor or hand blender, plus a few extra roughly chopped pistachios to decorate
200g caster sugar
3 large eggs
Finely grated zest of 2 oranges

2 tsp orange blossom water, or 1/2 tsp Taste the Difference Valencian orange extract
3 cardamon pods, outer shell removed and seeds ground
1 tsp baking powder

FOR THE SYRUP
100g caster sugar
Zest and juice of 1 orange
Juice of 1 lemon

---

1. Preheat the oven to 180°C, fan 160°C, gas 4. Grease a 20cm round springform tin and line with baking paper.

2. Put the butter, polenta, ground pistachios, caster sugar, eggs, orange zest, orange blossom water or extract, cardamon and baking powder into a large mixing bowl, and beat with a hand-held electric whisk until all of the ingredients are combined.

3. Pour the cake mixture into the prepared tin and bake for 45 mins until golden and a skewer inserted into the centre of the cake comes out clean. Turn out of the tin onto a cooling rack and leave to cool.

4. Meanwhile, make the syrup. In a small pan over a medium heat, gently dissolve the sugar in the orange and lemon juice, then boil for a couple of minutes until it reduces slightly. Take off the heat, add the orange zest and leave to cool slightly.

5. Poke a few holes in the top of the cake with a cocktail stick or skewer, then slowly drizzle over the syrup and zest, and sprinkle over the extra pistachios to serve.

Each serving (78g) provides:

ENERGY	FAT	SATURATES	SUGARS	SALT
1541kJ 370kcal	23.6g	9.7g	25.2g	0.2g
18%	34%	49%	28%	3%

% of the Reference Intakes
Typical values per 100g: Energy 1950kJ/468kcal
Each serving provides:
32g carbohydrate | 1.5g fibre | 6.7g protein

sharing with friends

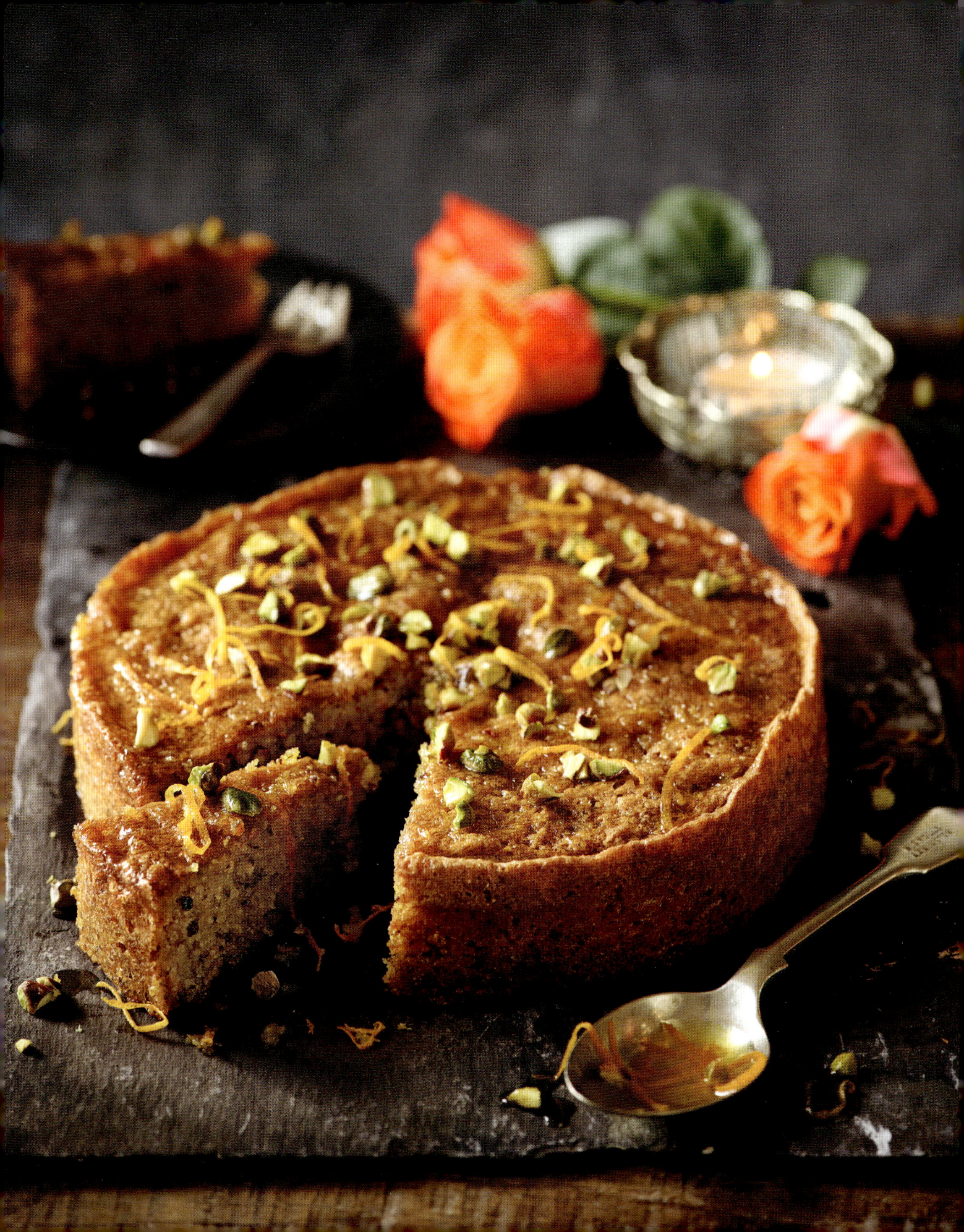

MAKES 14
PREP TIME 15 mins, plus chilling
COOK TIME 2 mins

Coconut & almond bites

These tasty bites are super simple to make - toasting the coconut to roll them in gives them lots of nutty flavour

215g desiccated coconut by Sainsbury's
50g raw coconut oil, melted
80g agave nectar
½ tsp Taste the Difference French almond extract

1. Line a baking tray with baking paper. Toast 40g of the dessicated coconut in a large frying pan over a low heat for 2 mins, or until it just starts to turn golden. Transfer to a large plate to cool down.

2. Put the remaining desiccated coconut in a food processor or hand blender and add the coconut oil, agave syrup and almond extract. Process until the mixture just starts to come together.

3. Shape the coconut mixture into 14 equal balls. Roll in the toasted coconut and put on the prepared baking tray. Chill in the refrigerator for 1 hour or until solid.

Cook's tips
Agave syrup is an organic sweetener. You could use clear honey in this recipe instead, but it won't be suitable for vegans.

Each bite (24g) provides:

ENERGY	FAT	SATURATES	SUGARS	SALT
583kJ 141kcal	12.7g	11.2g	4.3g	trace
7%	18%	56%	5%	<1%

% of the Reference Intakes
Typical values per 100g: Energy 2430kJ/580kcal
Each bite provides:
4.9g carbohydrate | 2g fibre | 0.8g protein

sharing with friends

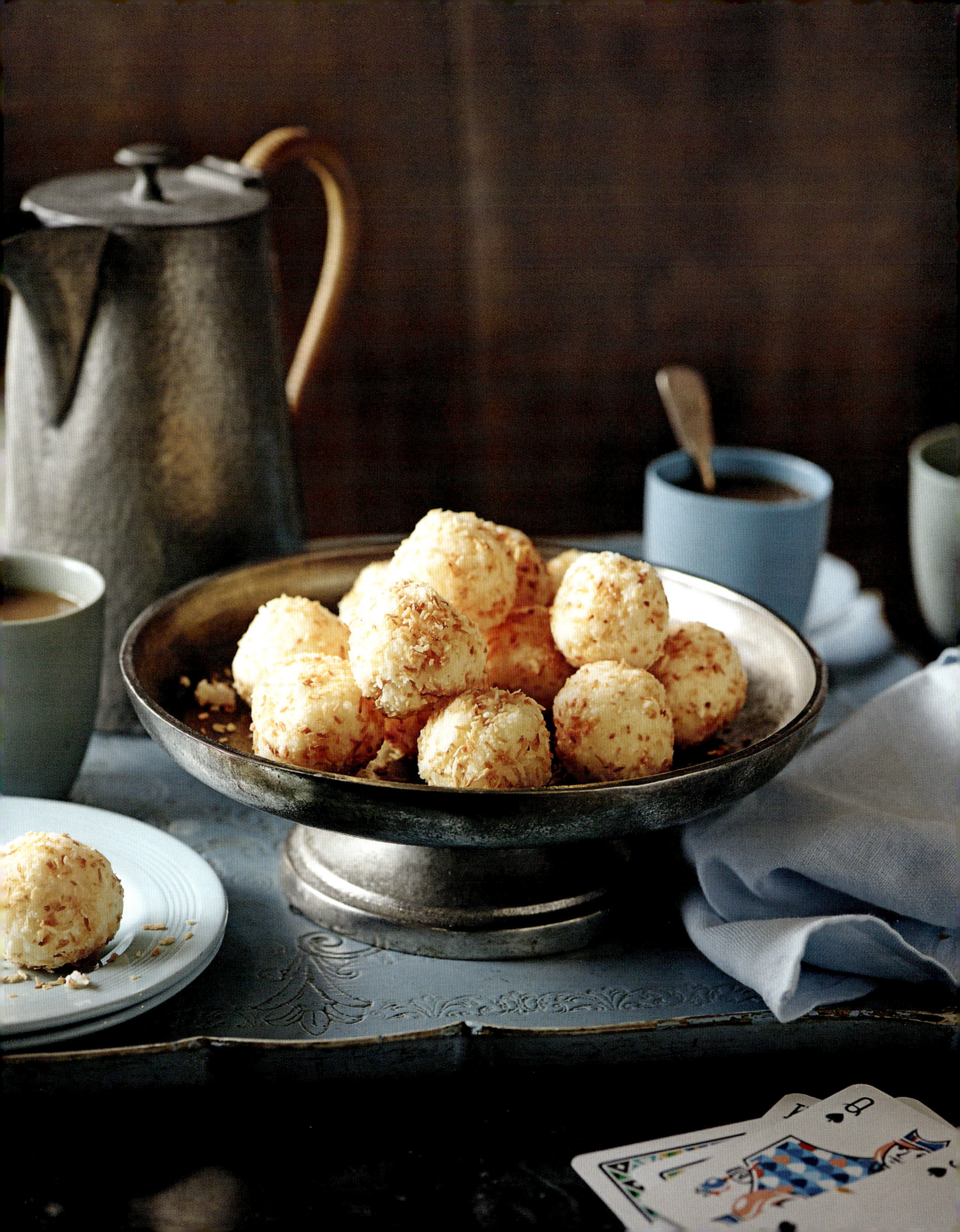

SERVES 16
PREP TIME 15 mins
COOK TIME 40-45 mins

Ginger stout cake

A dense, sticky cake with a hint of warming spice. The stout adds an earthy richness and keeps the cake deliciously moist

200g unsalted butter, plus extra for greasing
200ml stout
200g caster sugar
50g dark brown soft sugar
3 tbsp black treacle
2 tsp ground ginger
1/2 tsp mixed spice

2 large eggs
100ml buttermilk
300g self-raising flour
1/2 tsp bicarbonate of soda
4 tbsp diced stem ginger in sugar syrup by Sainsbury's

1. Preheat the oven to 180°C, fan 160°C, gas 4. Grease a 20cm square cake tin and line with baking paper. Put the stout, butter, both sugars, treacle, ginger and mixed spice in a medium pan. Stir over a medium heat for 3-4 mins until the butter has melted – don't allow the mixture to boil. Remove from the heat and let cool slightly.

2. In a large bowl, whisk together the eggs and buttermilk, then pour over the stout mixture. Sift in the flour and bicarbonate of soda, and beat with a hand-held electric whisk until combined.

3. Pour the cake mixture into the prepared tin and bake for 35-40 mins or until a skewer inserted in the centre of the cake comes out clean.

4. Carefully remove from the tin and cool on a cooling rack. Spoon over the diced stem ginger in syrup while the cake is still warm.

sharing with friends

Each serving (72g) provides:

ENERGY	FAT	SATURATES	SUGARS	SALT
1062kJ 253kcal	11.4g	6.5g	20.9g	0.3g
13%	16%	33%	23%	6%

% of the Reference Intakes
Typical values per 100g: Energy 1475kJ/352kcal
Each serving provides:
33.5g carbohydrate | 0.7g fibre | 3.2g protein

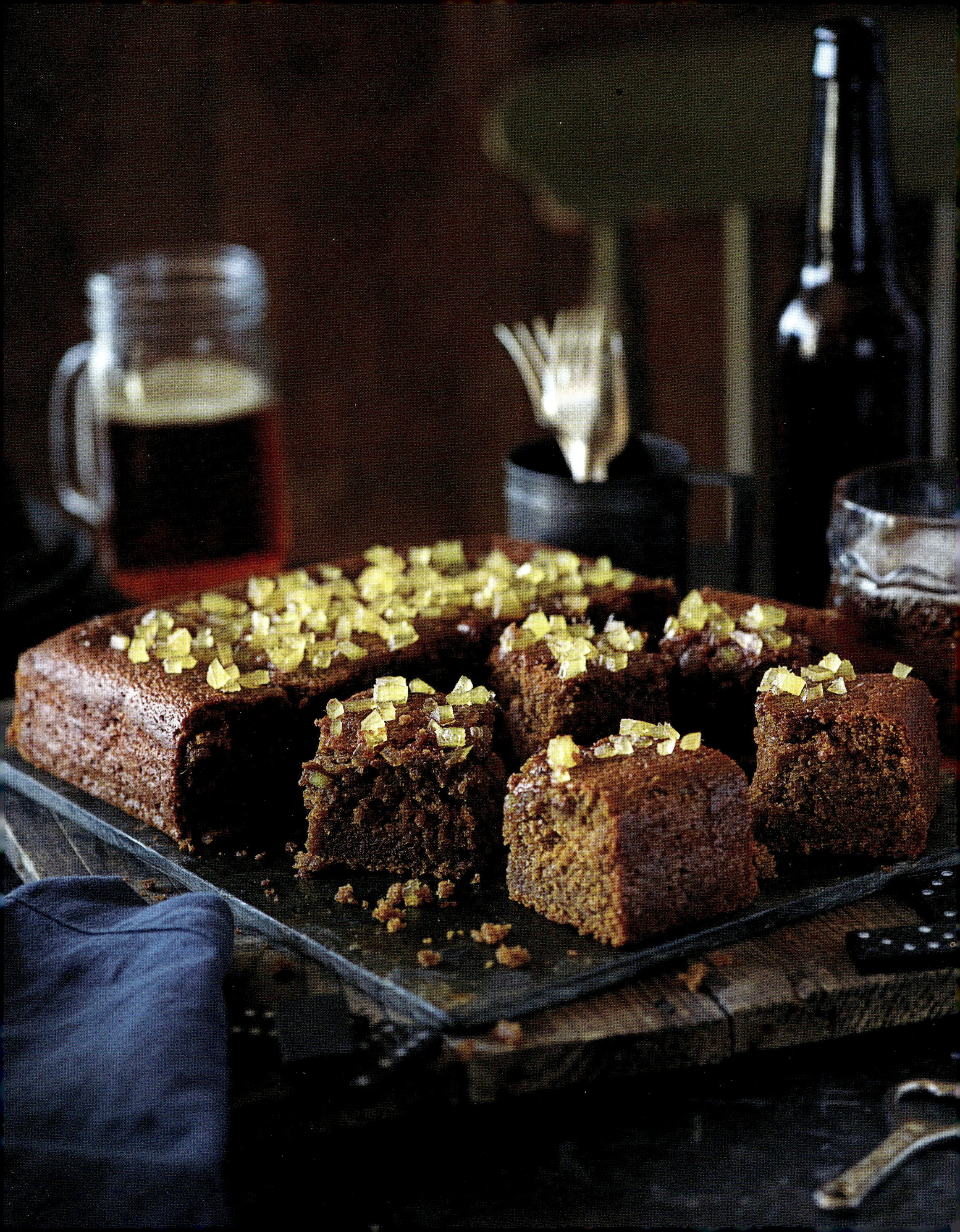

MAKES 12
PREP TIME 25 mins, plus chilling
COOK TIME 20 mins

Spinach & feta tartlets

The tasty morsels are filled with a classic combination – feta cheese and spinach – with plenty of extra Mediterranean flavours

---

150g plain flour, plus extra for dusting
30g walnut halves by Sainsburys, finely ground in a food processor or hand blender
75g unsalted butter, cubed
1 large egg, beaten
100g feta cheese, crumbled
25g parmesan cheese, grated

100g baby leaf spinach, cooked and roughly chopped, any moisture squeezed out
5 Kalamata olives, pitted and roughly chopped
1 small red onion, finely chopped
50ml fresh single cream

---

1. Make the pastry. Put the flour, ground walnuts and butter in a large mixing bowl and rub together with your fingertips until the mixture resembles breadcrumbs. Add 25ml cold water a little at a time (you may not need all of it), mixing as you go until everything comes together to form the pastry. Knead briefly on a lightly floured work surface until smooth. Shape into a disk, wrap in cling film and chill in the fridge for 30 mins.

2. Preheat the oven to 200°C, fan 180°C, gas 6. Roll out the pastry on a lightly floured work surface until it's about 4mm thick. Cut out 12 rounds with a 7cm biscuit cutter (you may need to reroll the trimmings) and use them to line a 12-hole shallow bun tin.

3. In a medium bowl, combine the egg, feta cheese, parmesan cheese, spinach, olives, onion and cream. Carefully divide the mixture between the pastry cases, being careful not to overfill them.

4. Bake for 20 mins until the pastry is golden and the filling has just set. Serve warm or cold.

Cook's tip
Save time by cooking the spinach for this recipe in a microwave. Put it in a covered, microwave-safe bowl (you don't need to add any water) and cook on high for 2 mins, then allow to cool.

Each tartlet (49g) provides:

ENERGY	FAT	SATURATES	SUGARS	SALT
677kJ 163kcal	11.1g	5.6g	0.8g	0.3g
8%	16%	28%	<1%	5%

% of the Reference Intakes
Typical values per 100g: Energy 1382kJ/332kcal
Each tartlet provides:
10.5g carbohydrate | 0.9g fibre | 4.9g protein

sharing with friends

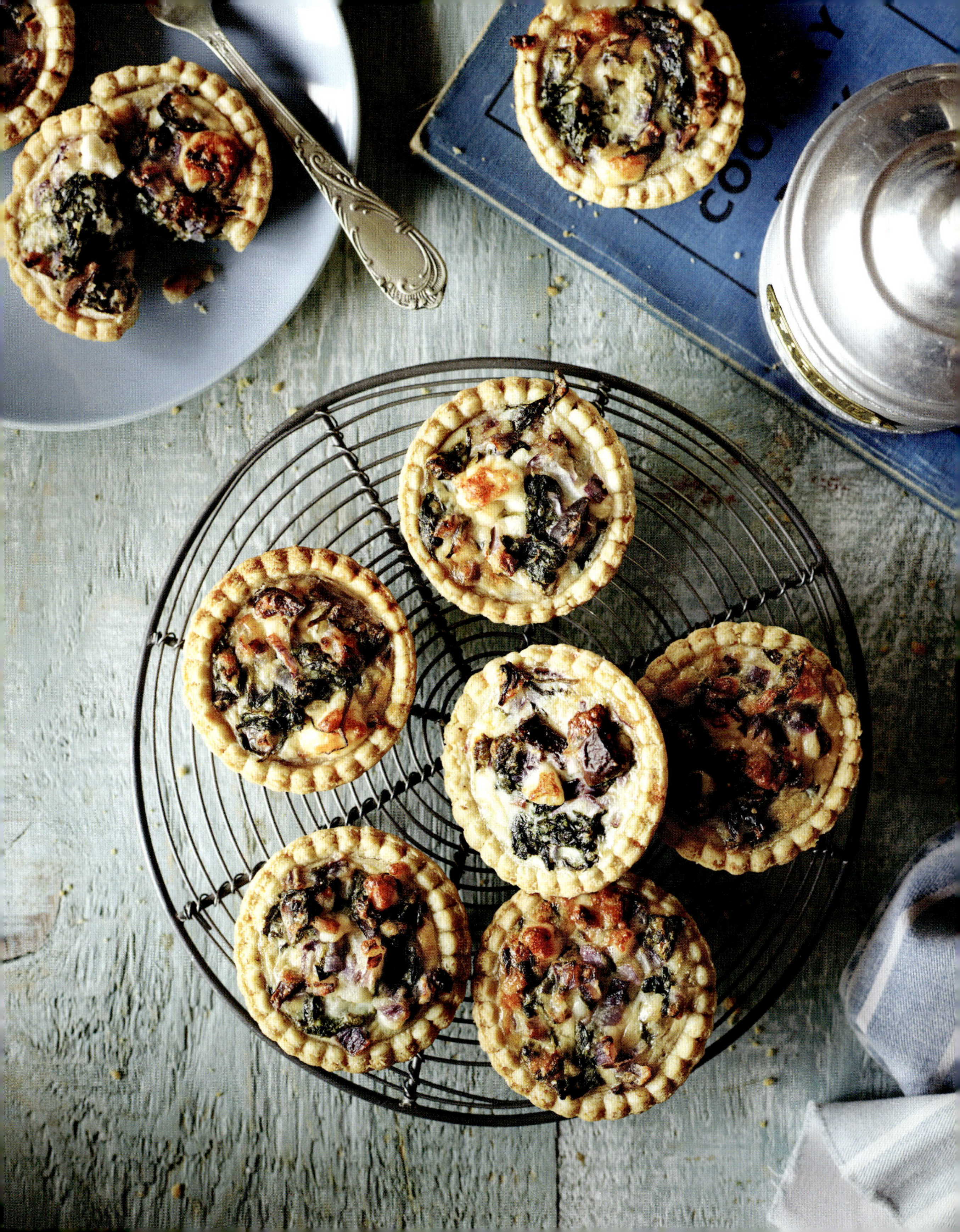

MAKES 20
PREP TIME 15 mins
COOK TIME 15-20 mins

Chorizo-spiced sausage rolls

The humble sausage roll gets a grown-up makeover with some chorizo-style spiciness and a hint of fennel

---

375g pack ready rolled lighter puff pastry by Sainsbury's
1 tsp fennel seeds
400g pack Taste the Difference outdoor bred pork ultimate sausages
1 clove garlic, crushed

1 tsp smoked paprika, plus extra to sprinkle
¼ tsp cayenne pepper
1 tbsp chopped fresh flat-leaf parsley
1 large egg, lightly beaten with a splash of semi-skimmed milk

---

1. Preheat the oven to 220°C, fan 200°C, gas 7.

2. In a small frying pan, lightly toast the fennel seeds over a medium heat, then remove from the heat and crush using a pestle and mortar.

3. Squeeze the sausages from their skins and put the meat into a large bowl. Add the crushed fennel seeds, garlic, smoked paprika, cayenne pepper and parsley. Mix until everything is well combined.

4. Unroll the pastry and cut in half lengthways. Form the sausage meat into two thick sausage shapes down the centre of the two pieces of pastry. Brush the pastry edges with the egg mixture, then roll and seal by pressing the edges tightly together.

5. Cut each roll into 10 mini rolls and transfer to a large baking sheet with the seam underneath. Brush the pastry tops with more egg wash and sprinkle with the extra paprika. Bake for 10-15 mins until the pastry is crisp and golden, and the meat is cooked through with no pink remaining.

Each mini roll (36g) provides:

ENERGY	FAT	SATURATES	SUGARS	SALT
514kJ 123kcal	7.7g	3.1g	0.5g	0.4g
6%	11%	16%	<1%	6%

% of the Reference Intakes
Typical values per 100g: Energy 1428kJ/342kcal
Each mini roll provides:
7g carbohydrate | 0.5g fibre | 6.2g protein

sharing with friends

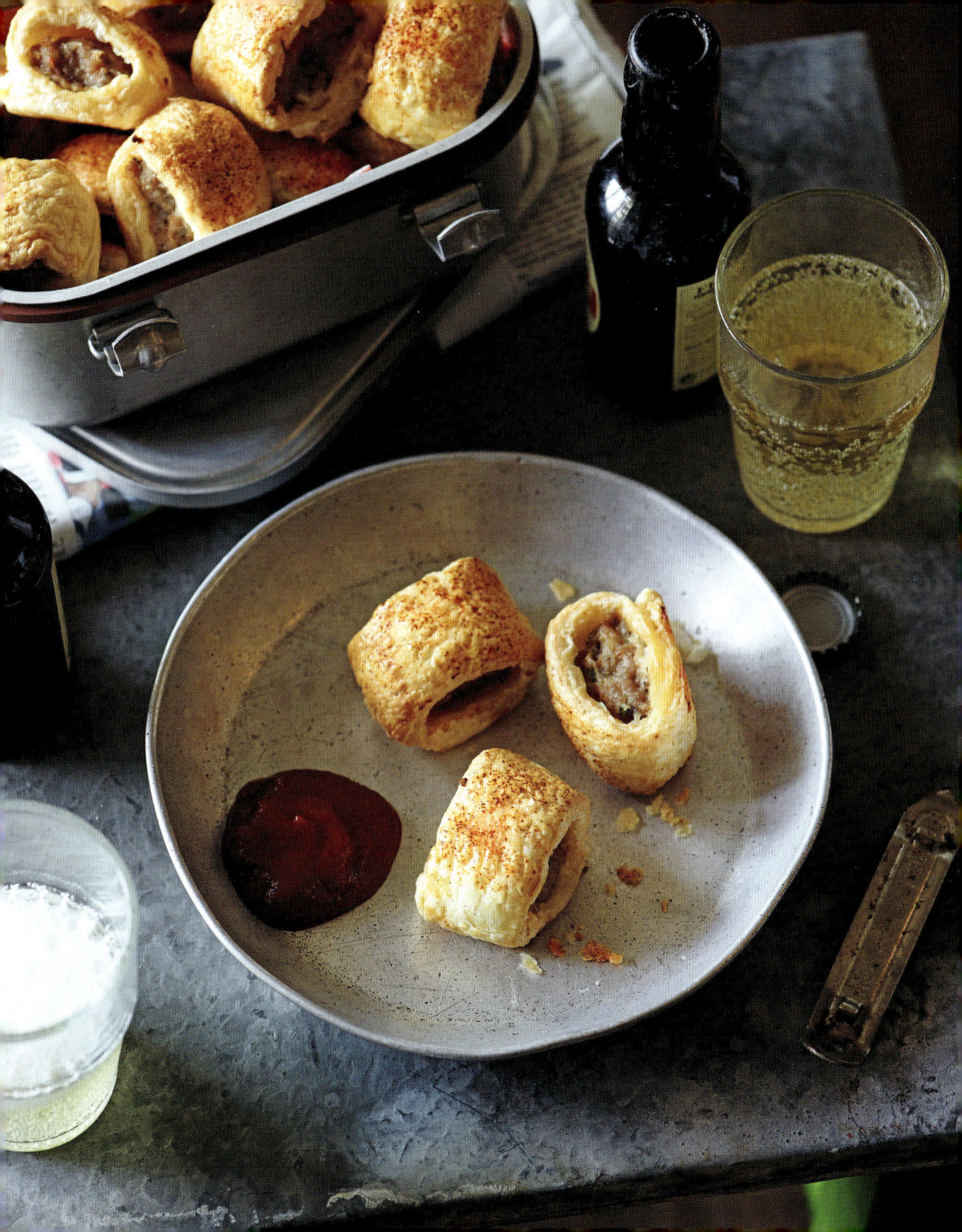

SERVES 8
PREP TIME 10 mins
COOK TIME 30 mins

Mushroom, pancetta & Taleggio tart

This easy tart is packed with savoury flavours and is great served in slices with drinks, or as a quick weekend lunch with a green salad

---

375g pack ready rolled lighter puff pastry by Sainsbury's
1 tbsp olive oil
160g pack cooking smoked cubetti di pancetta by Sainsbury's
1 clove garlic, crushed

500g wild mushrooms (or a selection of your favourite mushrooms), roughly chopped
1 tsp chopped fresh thyme leaves
200g Taste the Difference Italian Taleggio cheese, cubed

---

1. Preheat the oven to 220°C, fan 200°C, gas 7. Line a large baking sheet with baking paper. Unroll the puff pasty and transfer to the baking sheet.

2. Score a border around the pastry 2cm in from the edge, being careful not to cut right through the pastry. Prick inside the border all over with a fork and set aside.

3. Heat the olive oil in a large frying pan over a medium heat. Fry the pancetta for 2-3 mins until it starts to become golden, then add the garlic and mushrooms, and fry for a further 4-5 mins until the mushrooms soften. Stir in the thyme.

4. Spoon the mushroom and pancetta mixture onto the pastry, keeping within the border, then scatter the cheese on top. Bake for 20 mins or until the pastry is golden and the cheese melted. Allow to cool slightly before serving.

sharing with friends

Each serving (120g) provides:

ENERGY	FAT	SATURATES	SUGARS	SALT
1341kJ 322kcal	21.3g	9.9g	1.4g	1.7g
16%	30%	50%	2%	29%

% of the Reference Intakes

Typical values per 100g: Energy 1118kJ/268kcal
Each serving provides:
17.6g carbohydrate | 1.5g fibre | 14.2g protein

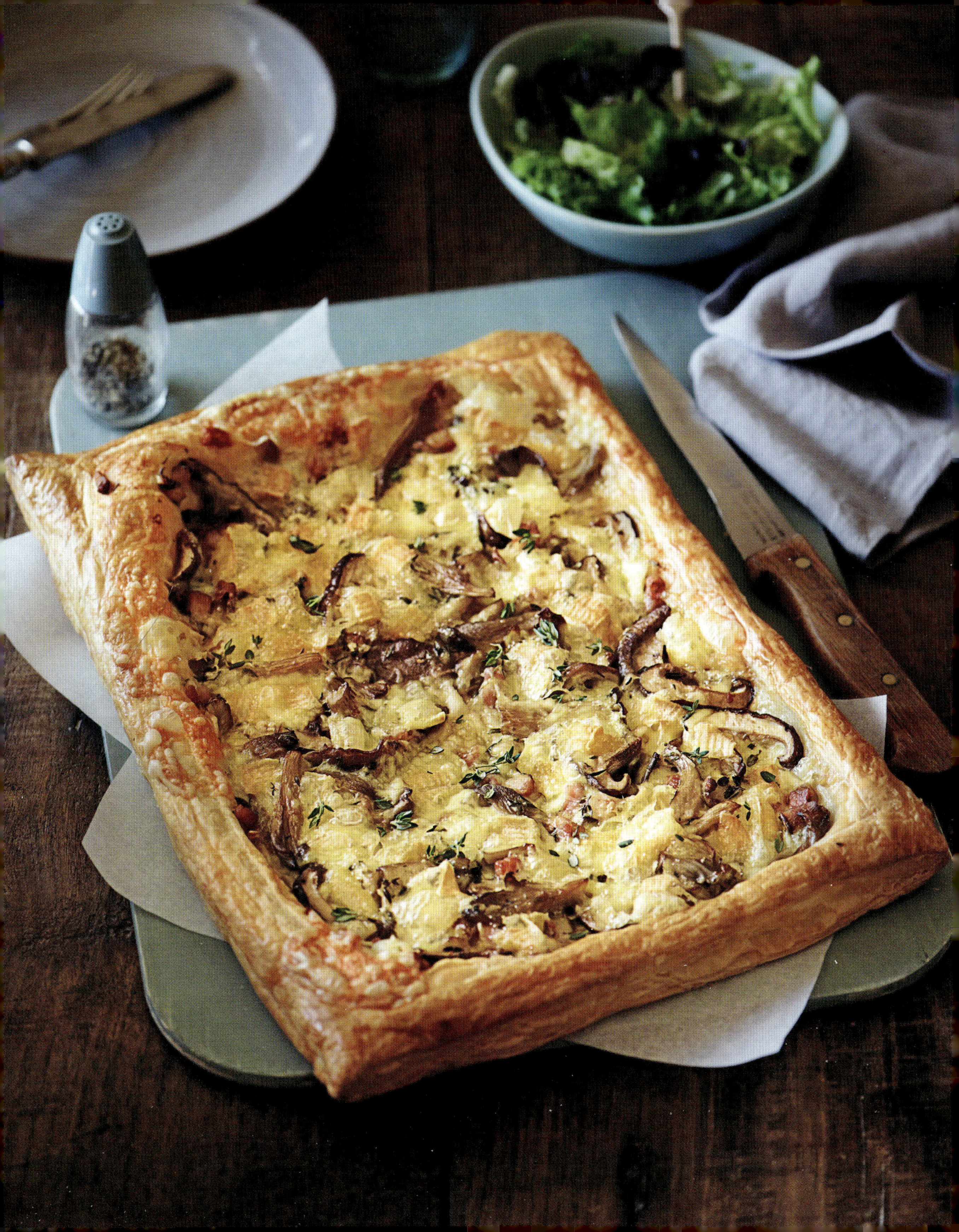

MAKES 20
PREP TIME 20 mins
COOK TIME 20 mins

Cheesy oatcakes

Impress friends by making your own biscuits for cheese – these crumbly, oaty ones taste great topped with a creamy Stilton

---

225g Scottish porridge oats by Sainsbury's, plus extra for dusting
60g wholemeal bread flour by Sainsbury's
¼ tsp table salt
½ tsp bicarbonate of soda
80g Taste the Difference extra mature West Country farmhouse Cheddar, grated
60g unsalted butter

---

1. Preheat the oven to 180°C, fan 160°C, gas 4. In a large bowl, mix together the oats, flour, salt, bicarbonate of soda and grated cheese. Add the butter and rub with your fingertips until the mixture resembles large breadcrumbs.

2. Add 80ml water, a little at a time, until you have a thick dough you can form into a ball – you may not need to use all of the water.

3. Roll out the dough on a lightly floured surface to a thickness of about ½ cm and stamp out as many 6cm rounds as possible, using a biscuit cutter. Gather up the dough scraps, knead lightly and roll and stamp out more rounds – you should get 20 biscuits.

4. Transfer the oatcakes to a large baking tray and bake for 20 mins or until they are crisp and golden. Cool on a cooking rack, then store for up to 7 days in an airtight container.

Cook's tip
If you find the dough a little too crumbly, try rolling it out between two pieces of cling film.

Each biscuit (26g) provides:

ENERGY	FAT	SATURATES	SUGARS	SALT
369kJ 88kcal	4.7g	2.5g	0.2g	0.3g
4%	7%	13%	<1%	5%

% of the Reference Intakes
Typical values per 100g: Energy 1420kJ/340kcal
Each biscuit provides:
8g carbohydrate | 1.3g fibre | 2.8g protein

sharing with friends

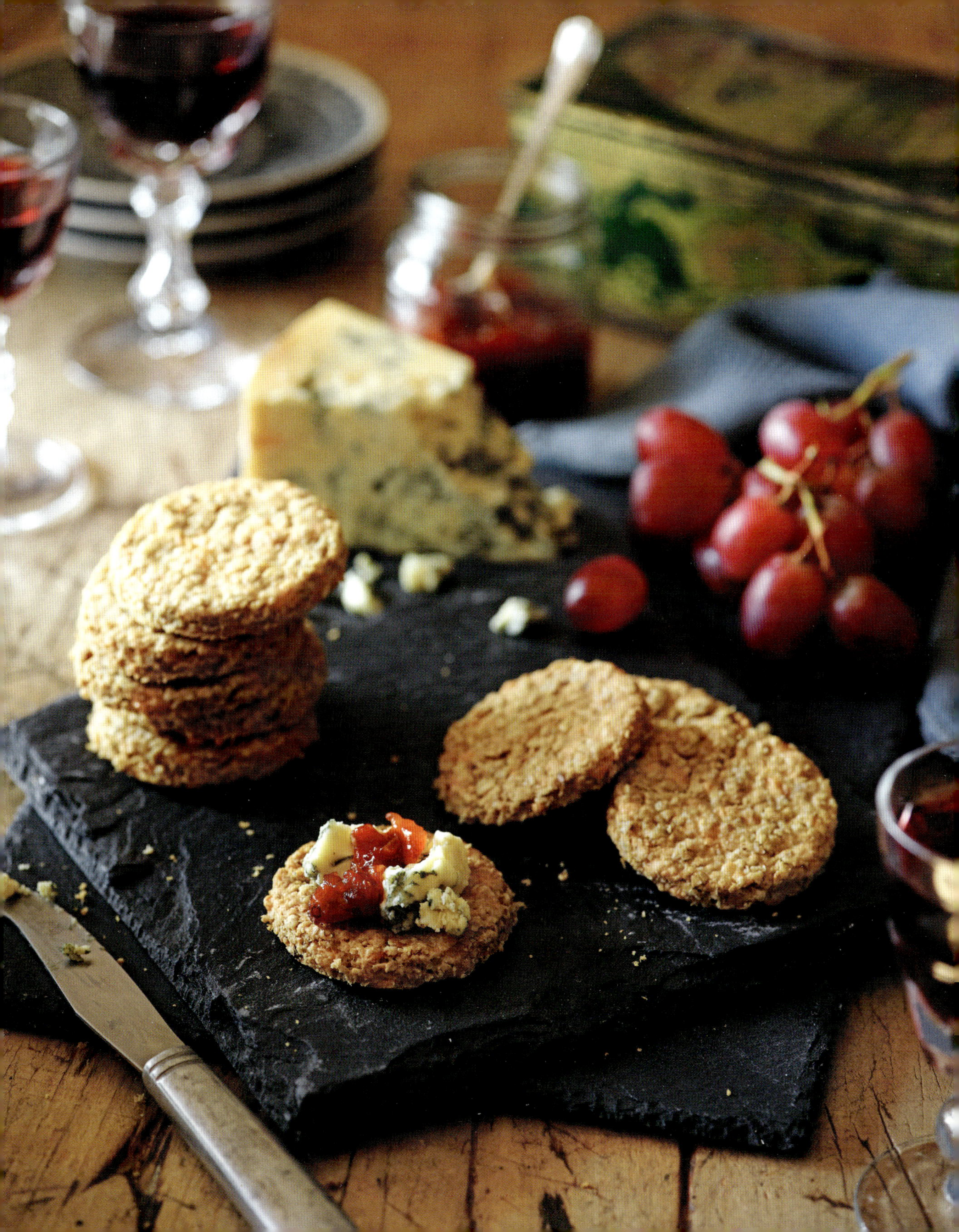

SERVES 10
PREP TIME 20 mins, plus rising
COOK TIME 20 mins

Stromboli

This filled and rolled bread is a great for feeding a crowd - you can mix and match the filling to suit your guests, and serve it either warm or cold

500g pack crusty white bread mix by Sainsbury's
1 tbsp olive oil, plus extra for brushing
Plain flour, for dusting
150g tub fresh Italian green pesto by Sainsbury's
120g pack Taste the Difference prosciutto cotto di vignola
100g grated mozzarella by Sainsbury's
8 sun-dried tomatoes, roughly chopped
10 Kalamata olives, pitted and roughly chopped

1 Put the bread mix into a large bowl, slowly add the olive oil and 310ml lukewarm water and mix to make a soft dough.

2 Knead the dough on a lightly floured surface for 10 mins until smooth and elastic.

3 Return to the bowl, cover with lightly oiled cling film and leave in a warm place until doubled in size. This should take about 1 hour.

4 Tip the dough onto a lightly floured surface and knead for a couple of minutes, then roll out to a rectangle measuring approximately 25cm x 35cm.

5 Spread the pesto over the dough, leaving a small border all around. Top with the prosciutto, then scatter over the cheese, tomatoes and olives. Fold the short sides in by about 2cm and roll the long side up tightly, as you would a large Swiss roll. Put seam-side down on a lightly floured baking sheet and brush all over with the extra olive oil. Set aside to rise again for 30 mins.

6 Meanwhile, preheat the oven to 220°C, fan 200°C, gas 7. Bake for 20 mins until well risen and golden. Leave to cool slightly, then slice and serve.

Each serving (119g) provides:

ENERGY	FAT	SATURATES	SUGARS	SALT
1151kJ 275kcal	13.8g	3.9g	2.3g	1.6g
14%	20%	20%	3%	27%

% of the Reference Intakes

Typical values per 100g: Energy 967kJ/231kcal
Each serving provides:
24.7g carbohydrate | 2.4g fibre | 12g protein

sharing with friends

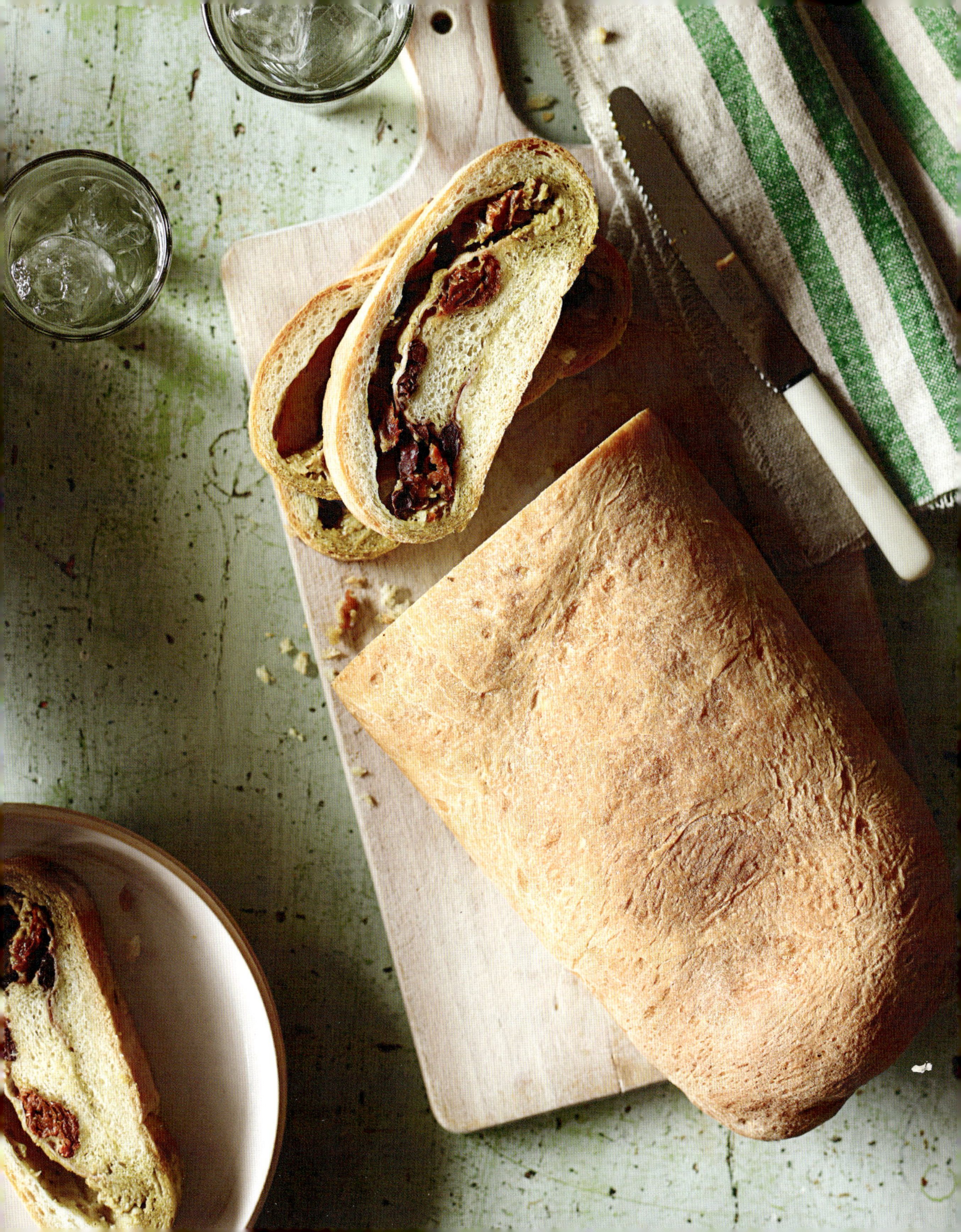

SERVES 8
PREP TIME 20 mins mins, plus proving
COOK TIME 12-15 mins

Pizzettas

Making your own mini pizzas is far easier than you might think – get creative with the toppings and experiment with different flavours

500g Taste the Difference very strong Canadian white bread flour, plus extra for dusting
1/2 tbsp table salt
7g sachet fast action dried yeast by Sainsbury's
1/2 tbsp caster sugar
3 tbsp olive oil, plus extra for greasing

FOR THE TOPPING
190g jar sun-dried tomato paste by Sainsbury's
280g jar artichoke antipasto by Sainsbury's, drained and cut into chunks if large
250g ricotta
8 Parma ham slices
70g rocket leaves

1 To make the dough, put the flour and salt in a large mixing bowl and make a well in the centre. Put 300ml tepid water into a jug and stir in the yeast, sugar and oil. Pour into the well a bit a time, mixing with a wooden spoon as you go, until you have a rough dough. Tip onto a lightly floured surface and knead for 5 mins, dusting with more flour if needed. Once the dough is smooth and elastic, shape into a rough ball and put in a lightly greased mixing bowl. Cover with cling film and leave in a warm place to rise until doubled in size – this will take about 1 hour.

2 Preheat the oven to 240°C, fan 220°C, gas 9 with 3 large baking sheets inside. Once the dough has risen, tip it onto a floured surface and knead for 1-2 mins. Divide into 8 equal balls. Roll them out, one at a time, until they are about 18cm in diameter. Spread each base with the sun-dried tomato paste, then scatter over the artichokes and dot with small spoonfuls of ricotta. Top with the Parma ham and season with black pepper.

3 Scatter some flour over the hot baking sheets and carefully slide the pizzettas onto them. Bake for 12-15 mins until the pizzetta bases are crisp.

4 Remove from the oven and serve scattered with the rocket leaves.

Each pizzetta (181g) provides:

ENERGY	FAT	SATURATES	SUGARS	SALT
1973kJ 472kcal	23.8g	5g	4.1g	2.3g
24%	34%	25%	5%	38%

% of the Reference Intakes
Typical values per 100g: Energy 1090kJ/261kcal
Each pizzetta provides:
45g carbohydrate | 4.1g fibre | 17.2g protein

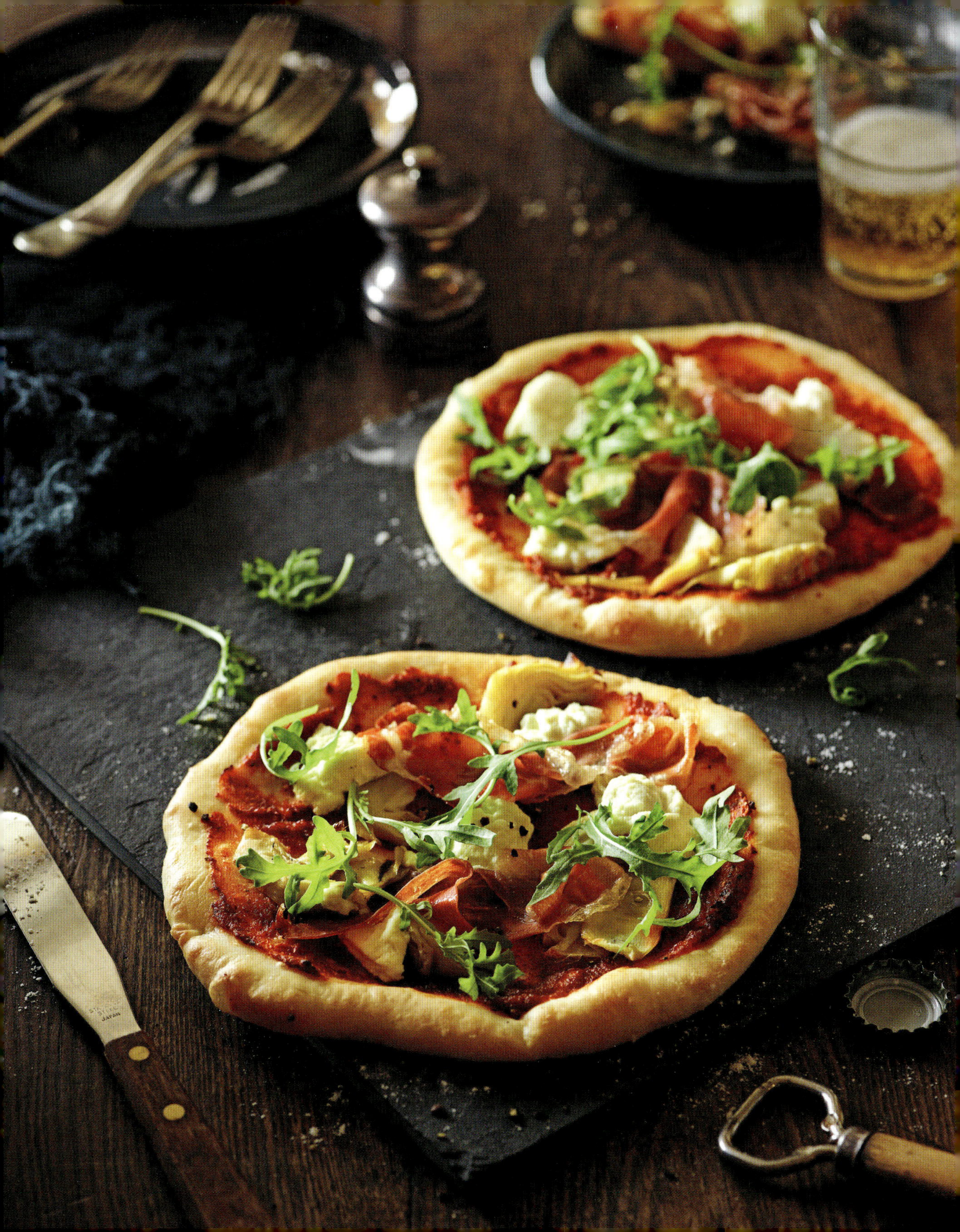

Posh pud

Need a dessert for a special occasion? This pavlova is simple to make but guaranteed to impress. Brown sugar gives it a tempting, golden colour. Find the recipe on p142.

bakes for entertaining

perfect puds and sweet treats to finish off a special meal

Mango & coconut tarte tatin	138
Molten butterscotch puddings	140
Peach Melba pavlova	142
Greek milk pie (Galaktoboureko)	144
Passionfruit meringue pie	146
Chocolate & cherry meringue roulade	148
New York cheesecake	150
Plum, vanilla & star anise galette	152
Chocolate & hazelnut millefeuille	154
Mini baked Alaskas	156
Chocolate spiced cheesecake	158
Churros with cinnamon sugar	160
Tosca cake	162
Pistachio & sour cherry biscotti	164

SERVES 8
PREP TIME 10 mins
COOK TIME 35-40 mins

Mango & coconut tarte tatin

A simple, tropical take on the classic tarte tatin recipe – with a warming kick of dark rum

150g caster sugar
20g unsalted butter, cubed
2 tbsp rum
2 mangos, peeled, destoned and cut into slices
Plain flour, for dusting

375g pack ready rolled lighter puff pastry by Sainsbury's
20g desiccated coconut by Sainsbury's
20g coconut flakes by Sainsbury's, toasted
100g lighter crème fraîche, to serve

1. Preheat the oven to 200°C, fan 180°, gas 6. Put the sugar in a large, heavy-based ovenproof 20cm frying pan. Heat very gently until the sugar dissolves and turns brown. Add the butter and rum, then quickly whisk until you have a smooth, glossy caramel. Take the pan off the heat and arrange the mango slices in the caramel.

2. Unroll the pastry on a floured surface and scatter over the desiccated coconut. Using a rolling pin, further roll out to a rough circle that's 5mm thick, pushing the coconut in as you go. Lightly prick all over with a fork, then drape over the mango, coconut-side down. Tuck the sides of the pastry down the sides of the pan and around the mango and bake in the oven for 25-30 mins, until the pastry is puffed up and golden.

3. Meanwhile, toast the coconut flakes in a dry frying pan over a medium heat until golden. Carefully invert the tarte tatin onto a plate and decorate with the toasted coconut. Serve warm with the crème fraîche.

Each serving (123g) provides:
ENERGY	FAT	SATURATES	SUGARS	SALT
1343kJ 321kcal	14.8g	8.8g	24.3g	0.3g
16%	21%	44%	27%	5%

% of the Reference Intakes
Typical values per 100g: Energy 1093kJ/261kcal
Each serving provides:
41.4g carbohydrate | 1.4g fibre | 4.8g protein

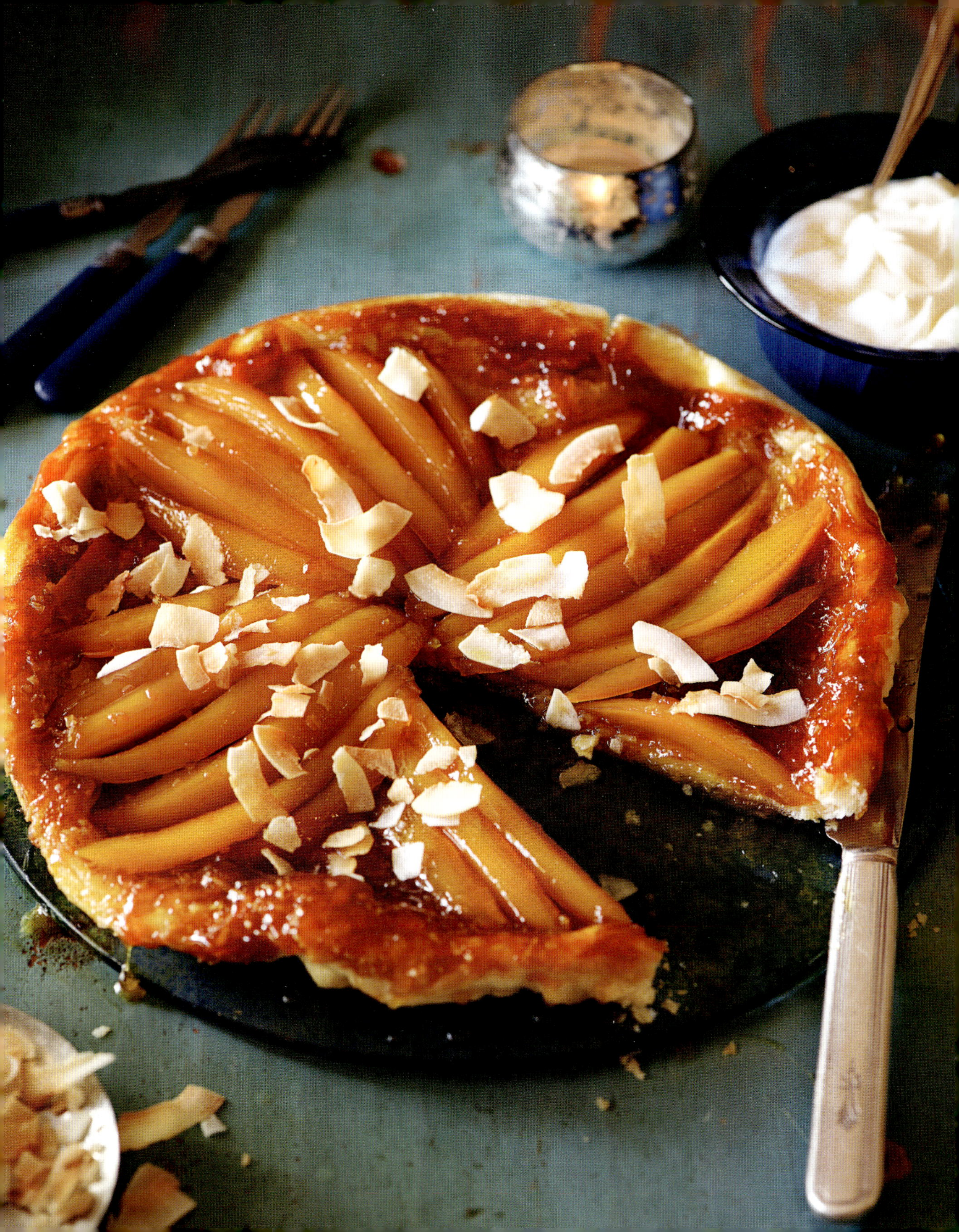

Molten butterscotch puddings

An indulgent but easy pudding with a sweet caramel surprise inside

MAKES 4
PREP TIME 20 mins, plus chilling
COOK TIME 40 mins

125g butterlicious by Sainsbury's, plus extra for greasing
125g light brown soft sugar
2 eggs
½ tsp Taste the Difference Madagascan vanilla extract
125g plain flour, sifted

4 tbsp half-fat créme fraîche, to serve

FOR THE BUTTERSCOTCH
100g light brown soft sugar
80ml double fresh cream
10g unsalted butter, diced
1 tbsp golden syrup

1. Make the butterscotch. Heat the sugar and 60ml cold water in a medium pan over a low heat, stirring often, for 5 mins or until the sugar has dissolved. Increase the heat to high and bring to the boil. Bubble for 8 mins without stirring, remove from the heat and carefully stir in the cream. Stir in the butter and golden syrup until melted and combined – you should have a thick, glossy sauce. Pour half into a heatproof bowl, let cool slightly for 5 mins, then cover and chill in the freezer for 30 mins to set. Cover the remaining sauce and set aside.

2. Remove the butterscotch from the freezer, divide into 4 equal pieces and shape into balls. Return to the freezer until needed.

3. Preheat the oven to 200°C, fan 180°C, gas 6. Grease 4 x 150ml pudding moulds or ramekins. In a medium bowl, beat together the butterlicious and sugar using a hand-held electric whisk, until pale and fluffy. Add the eggs and vanilla, then beat until combined. Fold in the flour until smooth, then divide the mixture between the prepared moulds, reserving 4 tbsp of the mixture.

4. Press a butterscotch ball into the centre of each pudding and cover with the remaining mixture – the butterscotch should be completely covered. Transfer to a baking tray and bake for 22 mins until the puddings are golden and risen, and spring back when lightly pressed.

5. Remove from the oven and cool for 2 mins, then run a knife around the edges and turn out onto plates. Gently reheat the extra butterscotch sauce. Serve the puddings with the extra sauce and the créme fraîche.

Each pudding (165g) provides:

ENERGY	FAT	SATURATES	SUGARS	SALT
2624kJ 627kcal	31.6g	13.2g	55.6g	0.5g
31%	45%	66%	62%	9%

% of the Reference Intakes

Typical values per 100g: Energy 1590kJ/380kcal
Each pudding provides:
77.4g carbohydrate | 1.7g fibre | 7.5g protein

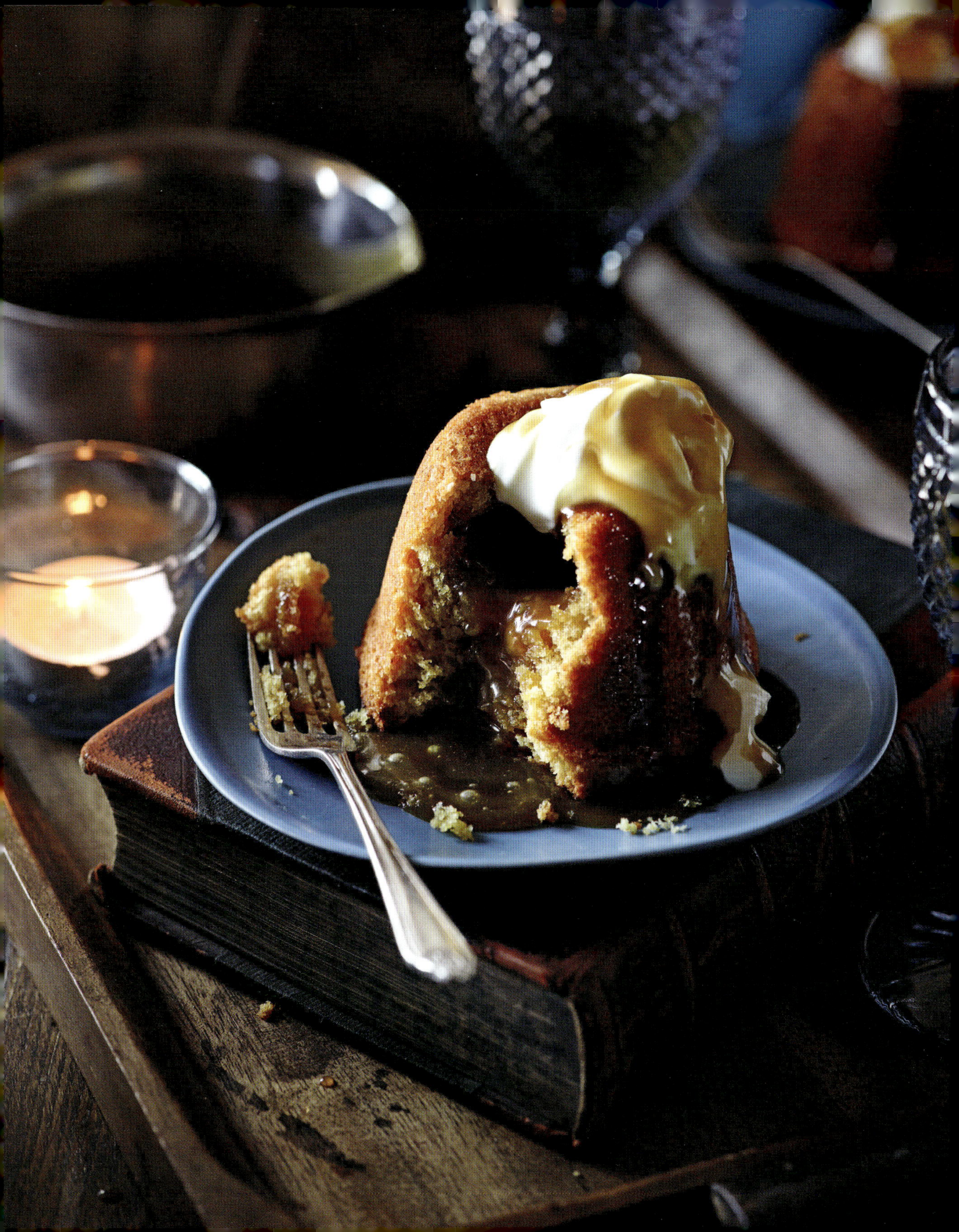

SERVES 10
PREP TIME
30 mins,
plus cooling
COOK TIME
1 hour 30 mins

Peach Melba pavlova

Crisp on the outside, mallowy on the inside – this is topped with the classic combination of peaches and raspberries

---

5 egg whites
150g caster sugar
100g light brown soft sugar
1 tbsp cornflour
1 tsp white wine vinegar
225g fresh raspberries
300ml tub fresh double cream by Sainsbury's

1 tbsp icing sugar
1 tsp rose water
4 tbsp Greek-style natural yogurt by Sainsbury's
3 peaches, halved, stones removed and thinly sliced

---

1 Preheat the oven to 140°C, fan 120°C, gas 1. Line a large baking sheet with baking paper and trace a 22cm diameter circle on it.

2 In a large, spotlessly clean bowl, whisk the eggs whites* until soft peaks form, using a hand-held electric whisk (see p7). Mix together the sugars and add to the egg whites, 1 tbsp at a time, whisking constantly. Continue to whisk until the egg whites are glossy and form stiff peaks. Fold in the cornflour and vinegar with a metal spoon.

3 Scrape the mixture onto the baking paper. Use a spatula to spread it to the edge of the circle, shaping it so that the edge comes up higher than the centre. Bake for 1 hour 30 mins until the meringue is crisp and firm. Turn off the heat and let the meringue cool in the oven.

4 Push 150g of the raspberries through a sieve to make a purée (discarding the pulp in the sieve). Stir in 1/2 tbsp of the icing sugar and set aside. Pour the cream into a large bowl, add the rest of the icing sugar and the rose water, and whip together until soft peaks form. Gently fold in the yogurt. Spoon the cream mixture into the dip of the pavlova, then arrange the peach slices and remaining raspberries on top. Drizzle over the raspberry coulis just before serving.

*See p191 for a list of recipes to use leftover egg yolks.

Each serving (122g) provides:

ENERGY	FAT	SATURATES	SUGARS	SALT
1104kJ 264kcal	14.9g	9.2g	28.8g	0.1g
13%	21%	46%	32%	2%

% of the Reference Intakes
Typical values per 100g: Energy 905kJ/216kcal
Each serving provides:
29.2g carbohydrate | 0.2g fibre | 3.3g protein

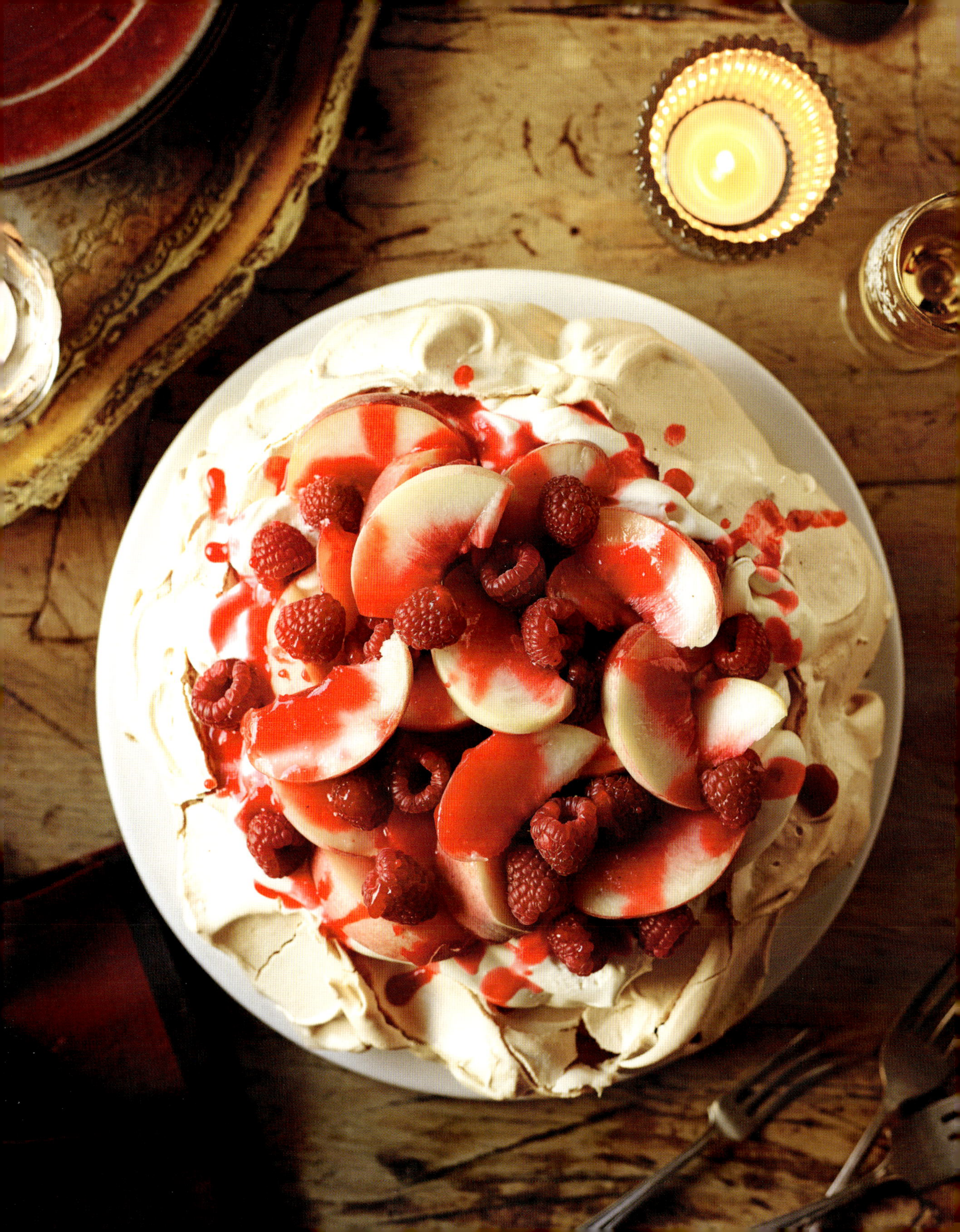

SERVES 10
PREP TIME 20 mins
plus cooling
COOK TIME
50-55 mins

Greek milk pie

Also known as *galaktoboureko*, this easy filo pastry pie is filled with custard and sweetened with a lemon syrup that's poured over after baking

150g semolina by Sainsbury's
200g caster sugar
400ml semi-skimmed milk
400ml fresh single cream
2 tbsp freshly squeezed lemon juice
4 eggs, lightly beaten
50g unsalted butter, melted

220g pack ready rolled filo pastry by Sainsbury's
25g pistachio kernels, roughly chopped, to decorate

FOR THE SYRUP
75g caster sugar
4 tbsp freshly squeezed lemon juice

1. Put the semolina, 100g of the sugar, the milk and cream into a large pan set over a medium heat. Cook for 4-5 mins, whisking continuously to prevent lumps forming, until the mixture has thickened. Remove from the heat and allow to cool for a few minutes. Whisk in the lemon juice, remaining sugar and eggs until well combined. Preheat the oven to 200°C, fan 180°C, gas 6.

2. Brush a deep 20cm x 25cm baking dish with a little of the melted butter. Line with one sheet of the filo, then brush all over with melted butter. Repeat with 6 layers of filo. Pour the custard over the pastry, then top with a sheet of filo pastry. Brush all over with butter then repeat until you have used up all the pastry and butter. Bake for 40-45 mins until the pastry is crisp and golden brown. Remove from the oven and let cool for 20 mins.

3. Make the syrup. Put the sugar and lemon juice in a small pan with 50ml of water. Heat gently over a low heat until the sugar has dissolved, then bring to the boil, reduce the heat and simmer for 4-5 min until you have a syrup. Pour over the top of the pie, then sprinkle with the pistachios.

4. Let cool for at least an hour before serving.

Each serving (150g) provides:

ENERGY	FAT	SATURATES	SUGARS	SALT
1703kJ 406kcal	16g	8.1g	29.4g	0.2g
20%	23%	41%	33%	4%

% of the Reference Intakes
Typical values per 100g: Energy 1135kJ/270kcal
Each serving provides:
53.6g carbohydrate | 1.8g fibre | 10.9g protein

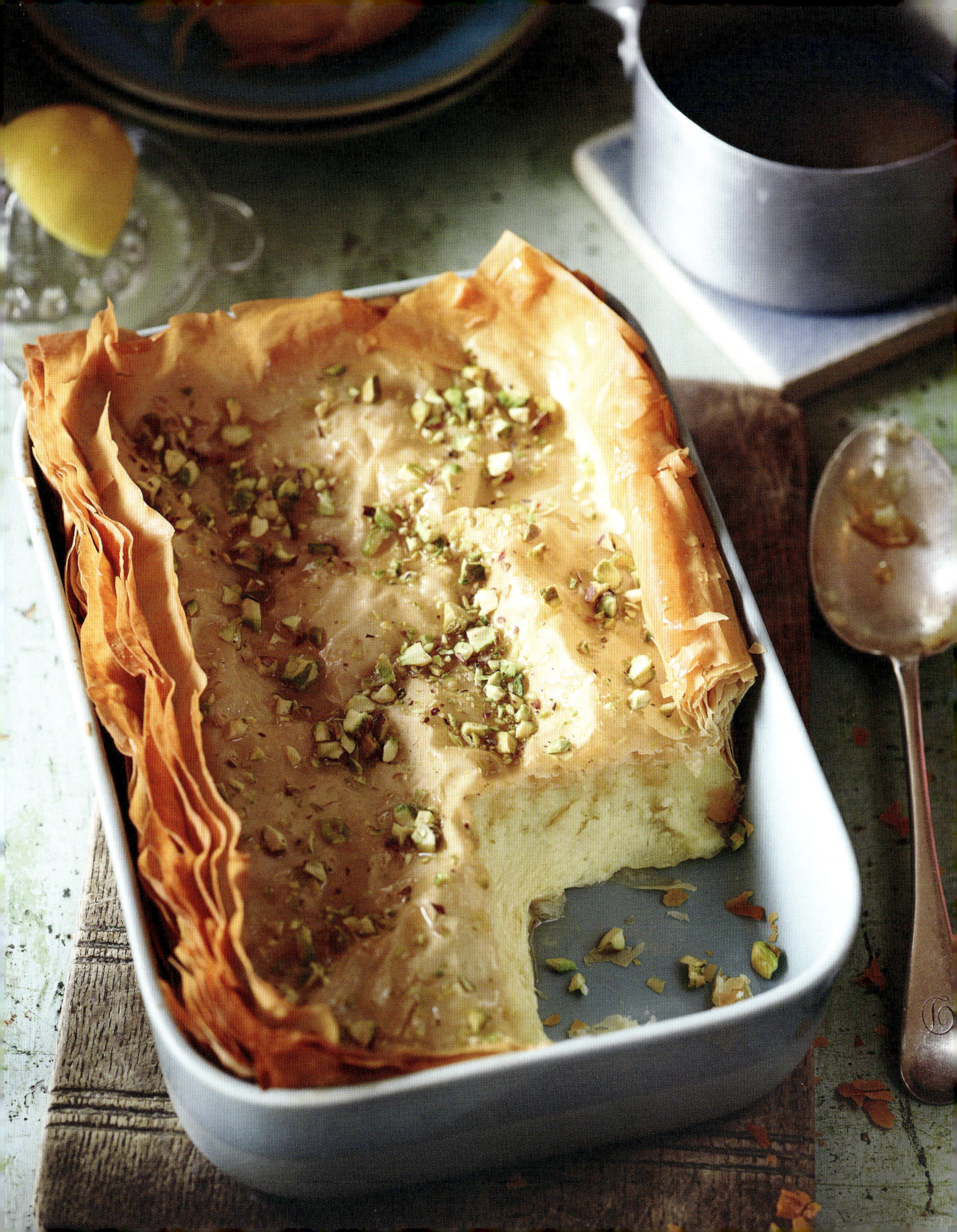

SERVES 12
PREP TIME 25 mins, plus chilling
COOK TIME 45 mins

Passionfruit meringue pie

A tropical version of a classic lemon meringue pie, made from a tempting combination of crisp pastry, passionfruit curd and fluffy meringue

Plain flour, for dusting
300g dessert pastry, from a 500g block by Sainsbury's
12 passionfruit, halved and pulp scooped out
4 tbsp cornflour
300g caster sugar
4 eggs, separated
2 tbsp icing sugar, for dusting

1. Dust a work surface with flour and roll out the pastry to a 26cm round that's about the thickness of a £1 coin. Use it to line a 23cm loose-bottomed tart tin. Trim the edges and prick all over with a fork. Chill in the freezer for 20 mins.

2. Preheat the oven to 200°C, fan 180°C, gas 6, along with a large baking sheet. Line the pastry case with baking paper and fill with baking beans or rice. Put on the pre-heated baking sheet and blind-bake for 20 mins, then remove the beans/rice and paper and bake again for 5 mins until golden and dry on top. Remove from the oven and set aside to cool. Reduce the oven temperature to 180°C, fan 160°C, gas 4.

3. Meanwhile, make the filling. Press the passionfruit pulp through a sieve into a bowl and discard the seeds. Put the cornflour and 100g of the sugar in a medium non-stick pan and pour over the passionfruit juice and 200ml cold water. Cook over a medium-low heat, stirring constantly, until the mixture just comes to a boil and thickens. Remove from the heat and whisk in the egg yolks. Let cool slightly then spread over the base of the pastry case.

4. Using a hand-held electric whisk, whisk the egg whites until stiff peaks form (see p7), then gradually add the remaining caster sugar, a spoonful at a time, and continue to whisk until the mixture is thick and glossy. Spoon the meringue over the filling, using the back of a spoon to create swirls and peaks.

5. Bake for 20 mins until the meringue is lightly golden. Dust with the icing sugar before serving.

Each serving (81g) provides:

ENERGY	FAT	SATURATES	SUGARS	SALT
1126kJ 268kcal	8.9g	3.2g	30.5g	0.2g
13%	13%	16%	34%	3%

% of the Reference Intakes
Typical values per 100g: Energy 1391kJ/330kcal
Each serving provides:
43g carbohydrate | 0.3g fibre | 3.8g protein

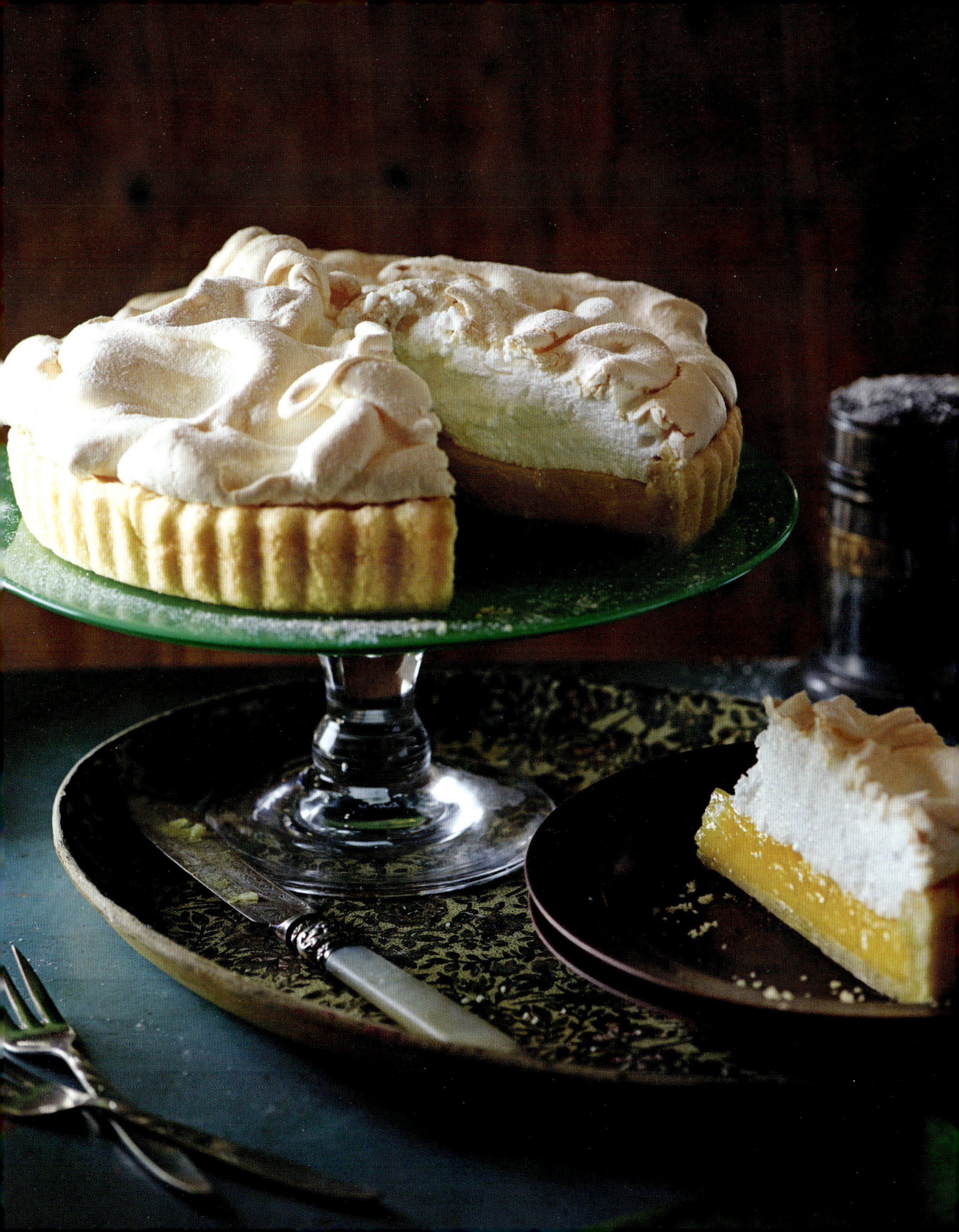

SERVES 10
PREP TIME 30 mins, plus cooling
COOK TIME 15-20 mins

Chocolate & cherry meringue roulade

Juicy dark cherries and dark chocolate is a match made in heaven – try them in this Black Forest gateau-inspired dessert

4 large egg whites
250g caster sugar, plus a little extra for sprinkling
3 tbsp cocoa powder
1 tsp white wine vinegar
1 tsp cornflour
300ml double fresh cream
200g Taste the Difference morello cherry compote
50g dark chocolate, melted (see p7)

1. Preheat the oven to 200°C, fan 180°C, gas 6. Line a 20cm x 30cm Swiss roll tin or roasting tin with baking paper.

2. In a large bowl, whisk the egg whites* using a hand-held electric whisk until stiff peaks form (see p7). Gradually add the sugar, a tablespoon at a time, whisking for 2-3 mins until the mixture is stiff and glossy. Whisk in the cocoa powder, then fold in the vinegar and cornflour.

3. Spoon the mixture into the prepared tin, gently levelling it with the back of a spoon. Bake for 10 mins. Reduce the oven temperature to 160°C, fan 140°C, gas 3 and cook for a further 5-10 mins until the top springs back when lightly pressed. Carefully lift out of the tin, still in the paper lining, and invert onto a large sheet of baking paper sprinkled with the extra sugar. Leave to cool for 2 hours.

4. Whip the cream until soft peaks form. Carefully peel the paper from the base of the cooled meringue, then spread first with the cherry compote, then the whipped cream, leaving a 1cm border all around. Carefully roll up the meringue from the shorter side, then put it, seam-side down, on a platter to serve. Drizzle over the melted chocolate, then serve.

*See p191 for a list of recipes to use leftover egg yolks.

Each serving (83g) provides:

ENERGY	FAT	SATURATES	SUGARS	SALT
1220kJ 292kcal	16.1g	10g	32.2g	0.1g
15%	23%	50%	36%	2%

% of the Reference Intakes

Typical values per 100g: Energy 1469kJ/352kcal
Each serving provides:
33.3g carbohydrate | 1.2g fibre | 2.9g protein

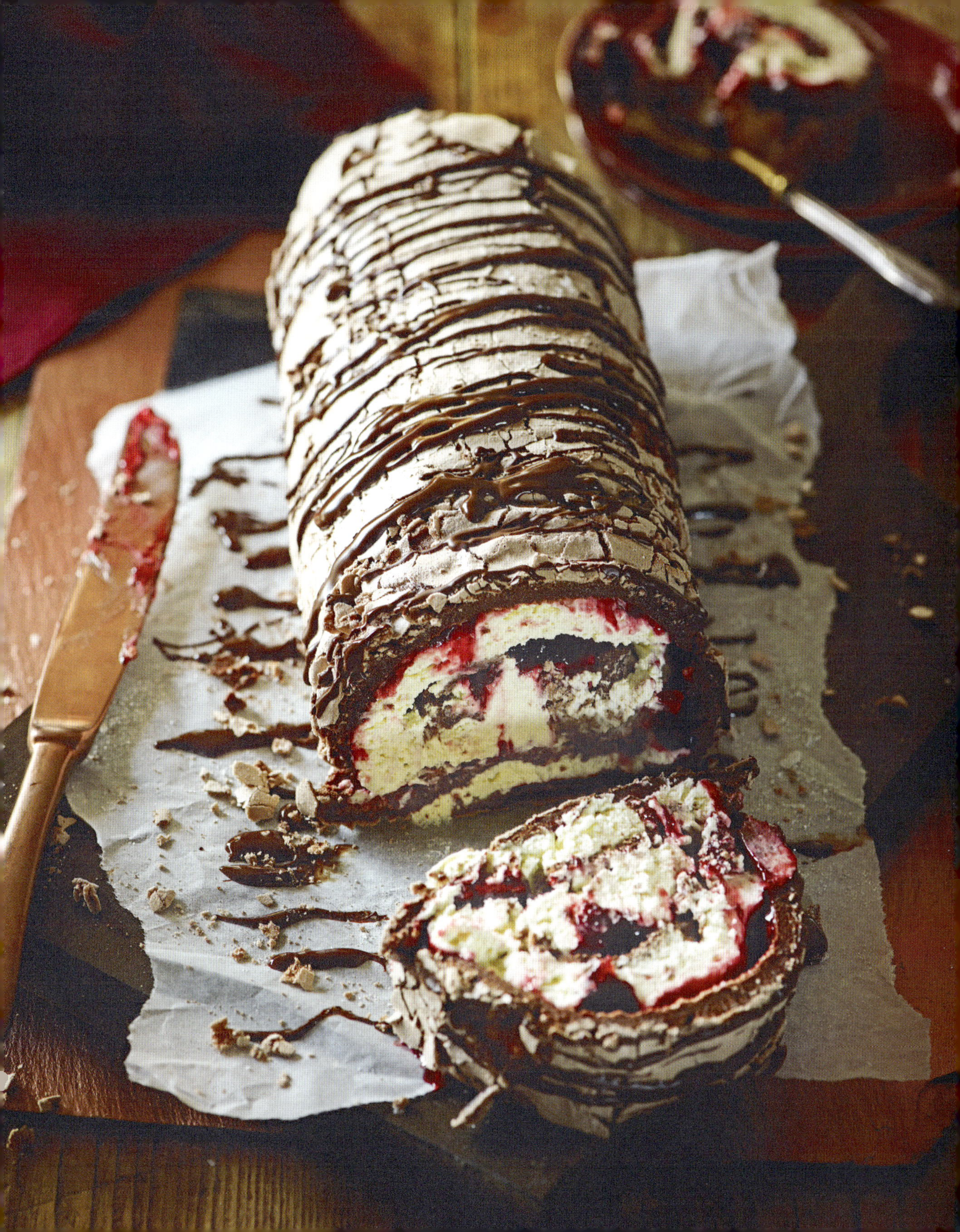

SERVES 14
PREP TIME
30 mins, plus overnight chilling
COOK TIME
1 hour

New York cheesecake

This delicious baked cheesecake makes a great special-occasion dessert

80g unsalted butter, melted, plus extra for greasing
200g sweatmeal digestives by Sainsbury's
3 x 300g tubs full-fat soft cheese by Sainsbury's
200g caster sugar, plus an extra 1 tbsp
3 tbsp plain flour
1½ tsp Taste the Difference Madagascan vanilla extract
Grated zest and juice of 2 small lemons
3 large eggs
300ml soured cream by Sainsbury's

1. Preheat the oven to 180°C, fan 160°C, gas 4. Grease and line the base of a 20cm loose-bottomed tin with baking paper. Put the biscuits in a food processor and process until you have fine crumbs, or put them in a sealed plastic food bag and crush with a rolling pin. Tip into a bowl and mix with the melted butter. Press the mixture evenly into the prepared tin. Bake for 10 mins, then set aside to cool.

2. Meanwhile, make the filling. Using a wooden spoon, mix the soft cheese and sugar together in a medium bowl until smooth. Stir in the flour, vanilla, zest and half the juice. Using a hand-held electric whisk, beat in the eggs, one at a time, followed by 150ml of the soured cream until you have a smooth mixture. Be careful to not overwhisk.

3. Increase the oven temperature to 200°C, fan 180°C, gas 6. Lightly grease the sides of the springform tin and spoon the filling over the biscuit base. Put the tin on a baking sheet and bake for 10 mins. Reduce the oven temperature to 110°C, fan 90°C, gas ¼ and bake for a further 35 mins until the top is golden and set at the edges, but still a bit wobbly in the middle. Turn off the oven, open the door and leave the cheesecake to cool for 2 hours in the oven.

4. Make the topping. Mix the remaining soured cream, 1 tbsp caster sugar and the remaining lemon juice together and spread over the cheesecake in a thin, even layer. Cover loosely with foil and chill in the fridge for at least 6 hours or overnight, before serving.

Each serving (132g) provides:

ENERGY	FAT	SATURATES	SUGARS	SALT
1645kJ 396kcal	28.6g	17.2g	19.4g	0.6g
20%	41%	86%	22%	10%

% of the Reference Intakes

Typical values per 100g: Energy 1246kJ/300kcal
Each serving provides:
27g carbohydrate | 1.1g fibre | 6.9g protein

entertaining

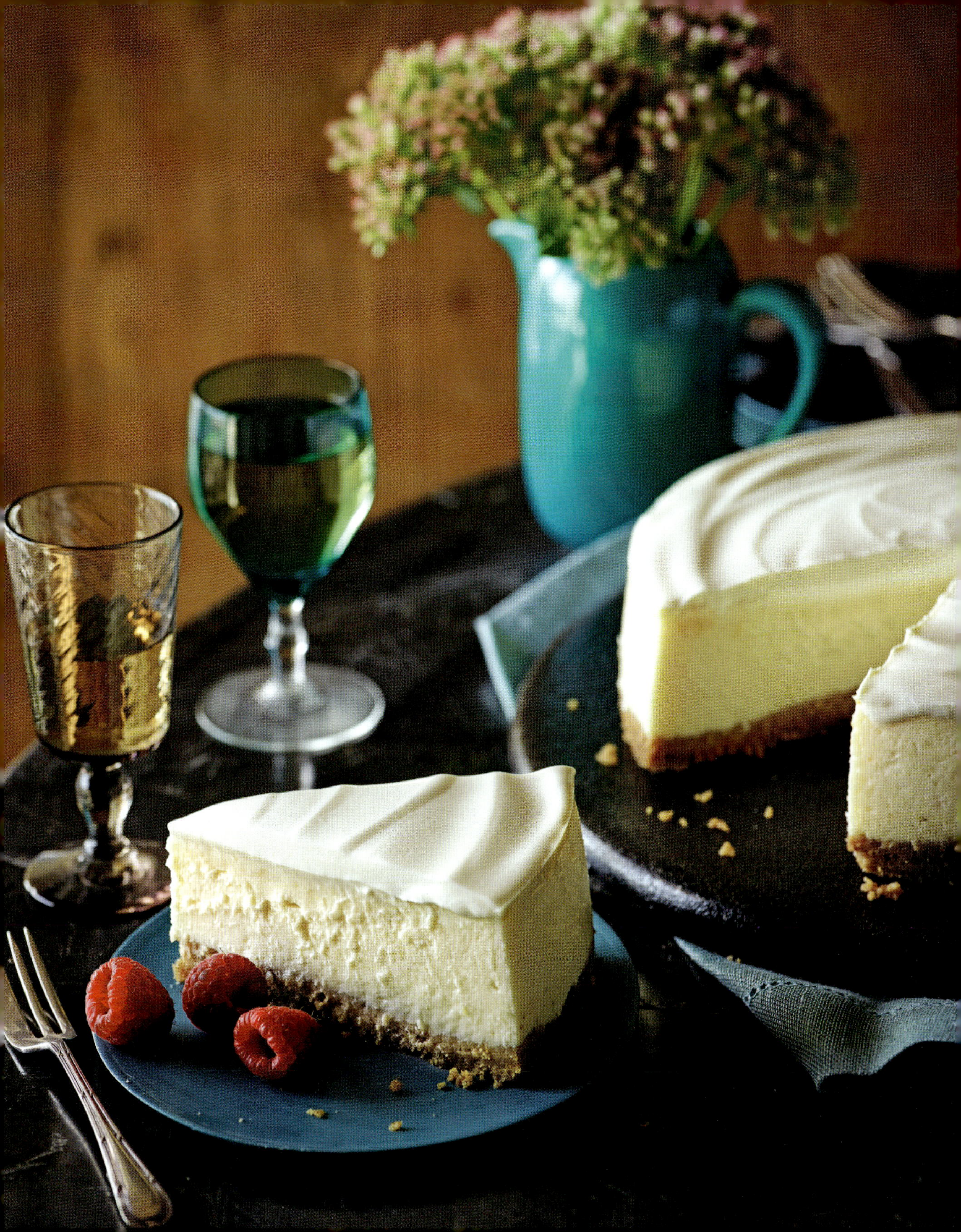

SERVES 8
PREP TIME 25 mins, plus chilling
COOK TIME 50 mins-1 hour

Plum, vanilla & star anise galette

This fruity open pie with warming vanilla and spicy star anise is the perfect way to end a special meal

75g whole almonds
2 tbsp caster sugar
4 tbsp plain flour
1 Fairtrade Madagascan vanilla pod, halved lengthways and seeds scraped out
Few drops almond extract

500g pack shortcrust pastry block by Sainsbury's
6 ripe plums, halved, stones removed and flesh cut into thin slices
3 whole star anise
2 tbsp single cream

1. Put the almonds, sugar, half the flour, the vanilla seeds and almond extract into a food processor or hand blender and pulse to coarse crumbs.

2. Dust a clean surface with the remaining flour and roll out the pastry to a 35cm large circle that's approximately 5mm thick. Transfer to a baking sheet lined with baking paper.

3. Spread the almond mixture over the pastry with the back of a spoon, leaving a 5cm border around the edge, then arrange the plum slices on top, overlapping them slightly. Bring the sides of the pastry up to cover some of the filling. Top with the vanilla pod and the star anise, and chill in the fridge for 20 mins.

4. Preheat the oven to 180°C, fan 160°C, gas 4. Brush the pastry crust with the cream, then bake the galette for 50 mins-1 hour until the pastry is golden and the plums are soft. Discard the vanilla pod and star anise before serving.

entertaining

Each serving (120g) provides:

ENERGY	FAT	SATURATES	SUGARS	SALT
1692kJ / 406kcal	26.9g	9.8g	7g	0.3g
14%	38%	49%	8%	5%

% of the Reference Intakes
Typical values per 100g: Energy 1410kJ/339kcal
Each serving provides:
26.9g carbohydrate | 2.5g fibre | 6g protein

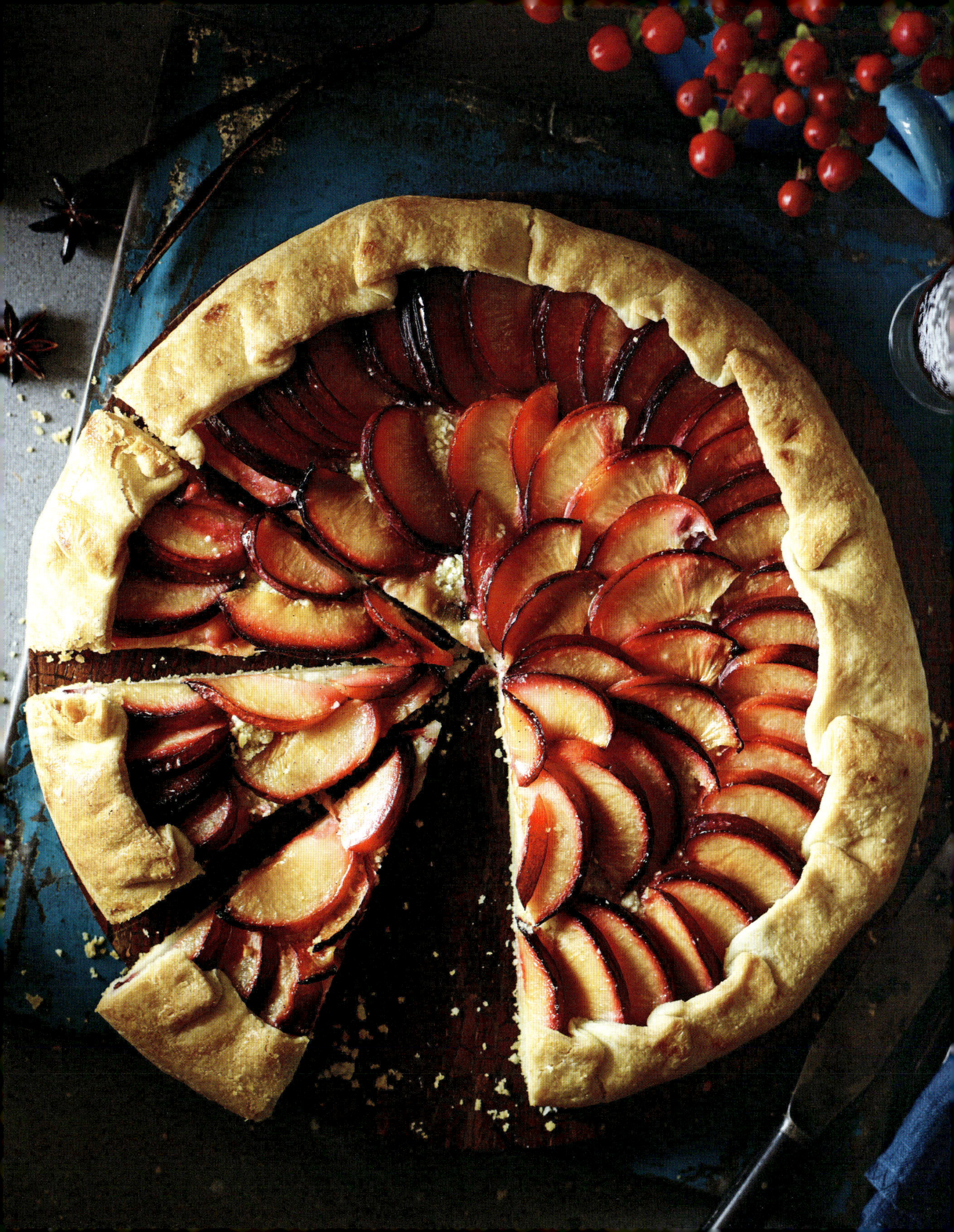

MAKES 6
PREP TIME 30 mins
COOK TIME 35 mins

Chocolate & hazelnut millefeuille

An easy but impressive dessert with a filling made from hazelnut milk

Icing sugar, for dusting
375g pack ready rolled lighter puff pastry by Sainsbury's
100g caster sugar
4 egg yolks
25g plain flour
15g cornflour

300ml hazelnut milk
35g cook's Belgian dark chocolate by Sainsbury's, broken into pieces
35g cook's Belgian milk chocolate by Sainsbury's, broken into pieces
100ml fresh double cream

1 Preheat the oven to 200°C, fan 180°C, gas 6. Line 2 baking trays with baking paper.

2 Lightly dust a work surface with icing sugar and unroll the pastry. Trim the edges to neaten, then cut the pastry into 18 even-sized rectangles. Transfer to the trays and cover with another sheet of baking paper. Lay another heavy baking tray on top and bake for 20 mins until crisp and golden, then set aside to cool.

3 Meanwhile, in a large heatproof bowl, whisk together the sugar, egg yolks*, flour and cornflour until combined. Bring the hazelnut milk to boiling point over a medium heat. Gradually whisk the hot milk over the egg mixture until smooth and combined. Return to the pan and continue to cook over a medium heat until you have a thick custard. Transfer to a bowl, cover with cling film and leave to cool.

4 Put the chocolate into a heatproof bowl. Bring the cream to boiling point over a medium heat, then pour it over the chocolate. Leave for 30 seconds then stir until the chocolate is melted. Set aside to cool.

5 To assemble the millefeuille, spread 12 of the pastry rectangles with the chocolate ganache. Put the hazelnut custard in a piping bag fitted with a round nozzle and pipe blobs of custard over the chocolate. Sandwich two of these layers together so you have 6 double layered stacks and 6 pastry tops. Top each stack with a pastry top and dust with icing sugar to serve.

*See p191 for a list of recipes to use leftover egg whites.

Each millefeuille (152g) provides:

ENERGY	FAT	SATURATES	SUGARS	SALT
2073kJ 496kcal	27g	13.5g	28.6g	0.5g
25%	39%	68%	32%	8%

% of the Reference Intakes
Typical values per 100g: Energy 1523kJ/365kcal
Each millefeuille provides:
55g carbohydrate | 3.1g fibre | 8.6g protein

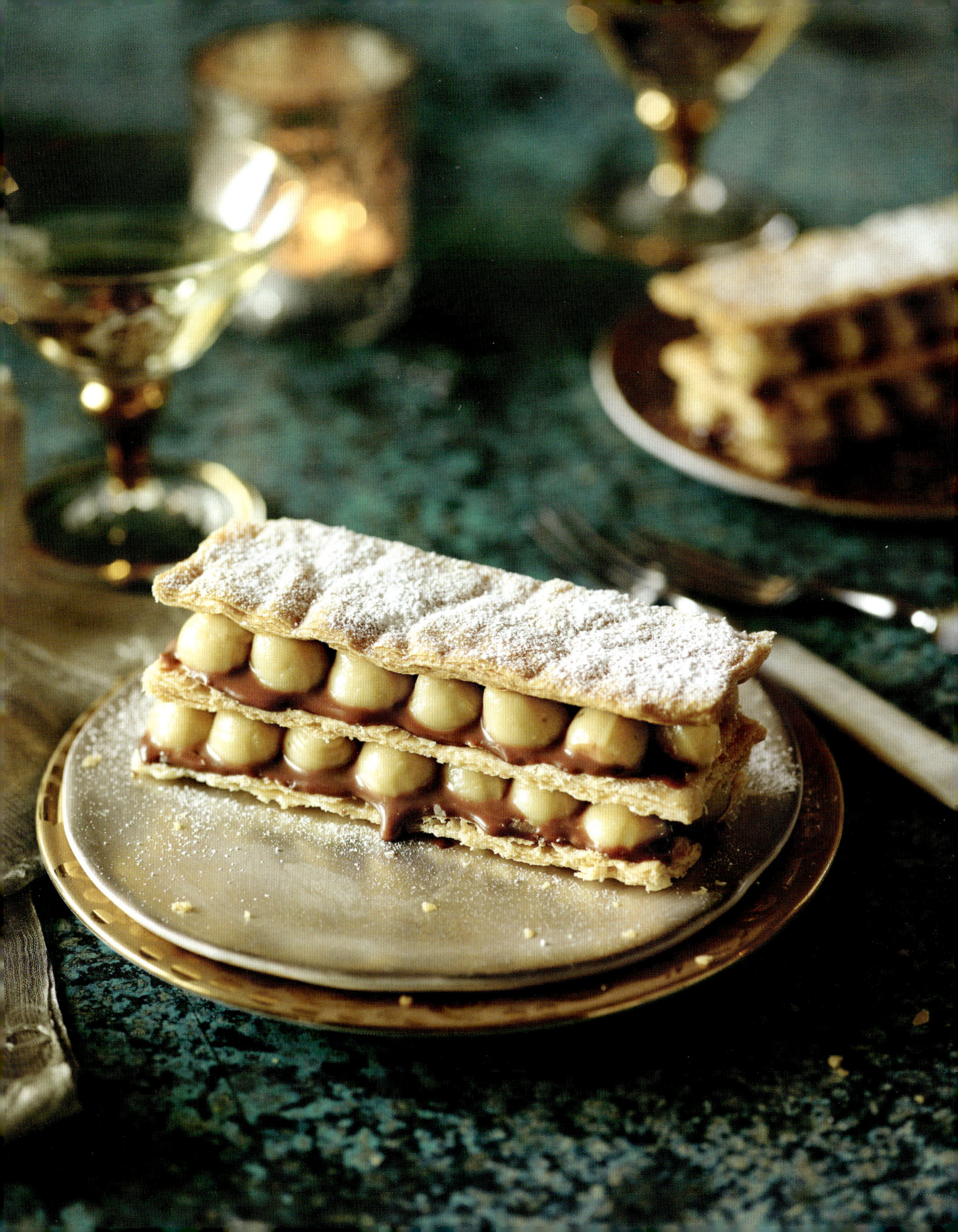

MAKES 4
PREP TIME 20 mins, plus freezing
COOK TIME 4 mins

Mini baked Alaskas

These gorgeous desserts are an irresistible mix of sponge, fresh berries, ice cream and baked meringue

---

1 tsp sunflower oil, for greasing
500ml Taste the Difference Madagascan vanilla dairy ice cream
4 thick slices (120g total) raspberry sponge roll by Sainsbury's
100g caster sugar
2 large egg whites
16 fresh raspberries

---

1. Grease 4 small dariole moulds or ramekins with the sunflower oil, then line with cling film. Divide the ice cream between the moulds and freeze for 2 hours until hardened. Preheat the oven to 220°C, fan 200°C, gas 7.

2. Put the sponge roll slices onto a baking sheet lined with baking paper, leaving a large gap between each. Top each slice with 4 raspberries and gently press with the back of a spoon to crush. Set aside.

3. In a large bowl, whisk the egg whites* with a hand-held electric whisk until stiff peaks form (see p7). Gradually whisk in the sugar, whisking well between each addition. Continue to whisk until the mixture is glossy and very stiff peaks form.

4. Assemble the Alaskas. Lift the ice cream from the moulds and remove the cling film. Put each ice cream mound on top of the crushed raspberries. Working quickly, spoon the meringue all over the ice cream, ensuring there are no gaps. Use the back of the spoon to make swirls in the meringue.

5. Bake for 4 mins at 220°C, fan 200°C, gas 7 until golden all over. Transfer to plates and serve immediately.

*See p191 for a list of recipes to use leftover egg yolks.

Cook's tip
The baked Alaskas can be made a few hours ahead of time up to the end of step 4, then put in the freezer until just before you need to bake and serve them.

Each baked Alaska (178g) provides:

ENERGY	FAT	SATURATES	SUGARS	SALT
1890kJ 451kcal	20.1g	13g	52.2g	0.4g
23%	29%	65%	58%	7%

% of the Reference Intakes
Typical values per 100g: Energy 1062kJ/253kcal
Each baked Alaska provides:
59g carbohydrate | 1.5g fibre | 7.7g protein

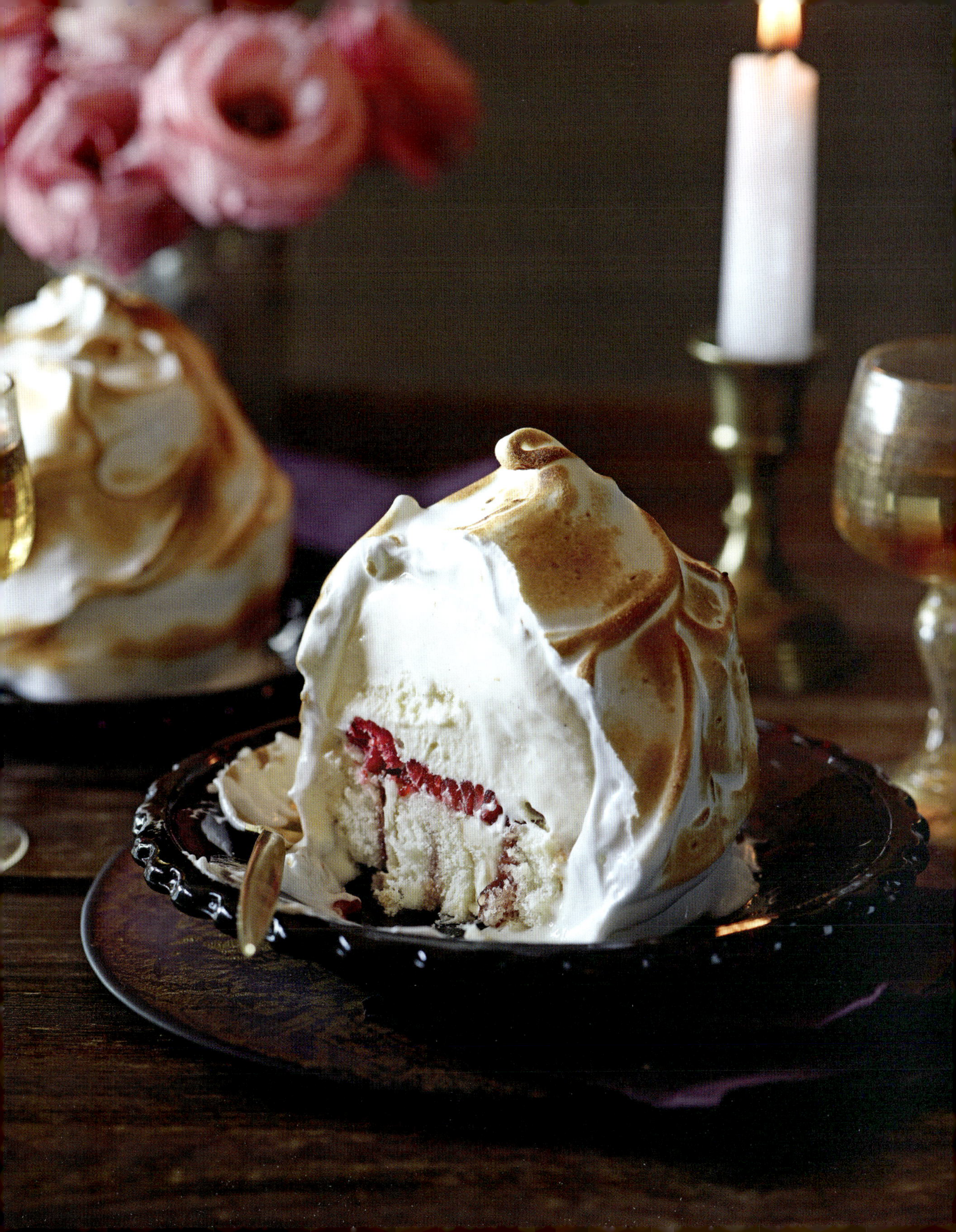

SERVES 12
PREP TIME
30 mins, plus chilling time
COOK TIME
8 mins

Chocolate spiced cheesecake

This unusual cheesecake combines chocolate and vanilla with mixed spices for a Asian-inspired dessert

---

75g unsalted butter, melted, plus extra for greasing
175g ginger snap biscuits, by Sainsburys, roughly broken
500g lighter soft cheese by Sainsbury's
100g icing sugar
300ml fresh double cream

175g dark chocolate, melted (see p7)
1 tbsp Taste the Difference Madagascan vanilla extract
½ tsp mixed spice
1 tsp ground cinnamon, plus extra, for dusting
1 tsp ground ginger
2 tbsp demerara sugar

---

1. Grease a 20cm loose-bottomed tin and line with baking paper. Put the ginger snaps in a food processor and process until you have fine crumbs, or put them in a sealed plastic food bag and crush with a rolling pin. Tip into a medium bowl and mix with the melted butter. Transfer to the lined tin and press down firmly to create an even base. Chill in the fridge for 30 mins to set firmly.

2. Put the soft cheese and icing sugar in a bowl, then beat with a hand-held electric whisk until smooth. Pour over the double cream and continue beating until the mixture is smooth, thick and combined.

3. Divide the mixture between two bowls. Stir the melted chocolate through the cheese mixture in one of the bowls, and the vanilla and spices through the other. Put a spoonful of the chocolate mixture into the tin, followed by a spoonful of the vanilla mixture, and repeat until all the mixtures are in the tin. Drag a skewer or knife through them to create a marble effect. Using the back of a spoon, level the top, then press the spoon lightly into the mixture to create a swirl. Transfer to the fridge to set for at least 3 hours or overnight.

4. To serve, take out of the tin, remove the baking paper and transfer to a serving plate, then sprinkle over the demerara sugar and cinnamon.

Each serving (114g) provides:

ENERGY	FAT	SATURATES	SUGARS	SALT
1664kJ 400kcal	28.7g	17.5g	22g	0.4g
20%	41%	88%	24%	6%

% of the Reference Intakes
Typical values per 100g: Energy 1460kJ/351kcal
Each serving provides:
27.8g carbohydrate | 2g fibre | 6.6g protein

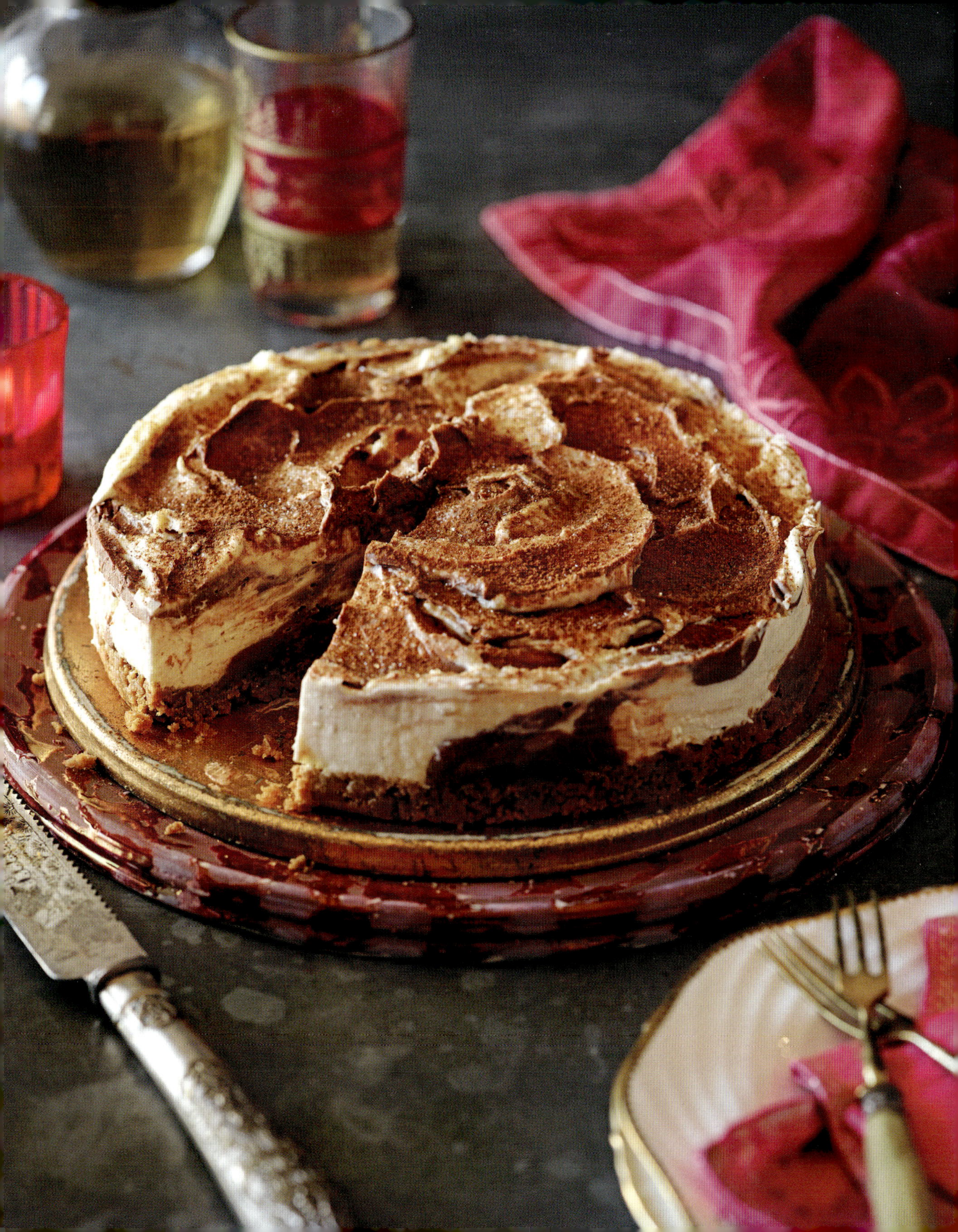

> **SERVES** 8
> **PREP TIME** 10 mins, plus chilling
> **COOK TIME** 40 mins

Churros with cinnamon sugar

These doughnut-style treats are popular in Spain and are great for parties. Serve them on a big platter for everyone to help themselves

25g unsalted butter
½ tsp Taste the Difference Madagascan vanilla extract
125g self-raising flour, sifted
3 tbsp caster sugar
Pinch of salt

2 eggs
500ml sunflower oil, for frying
1 tsp cinnamon
260g jar Taste the Difference Belgian chocolate sauce

1. Put the butter and vanilla extract in a medium pan along with 175ml water. Bring to the boil over a high heat and cook for 3 mins on a rapid boil. Remove from the heat and beat in the flour, 1 tbsp of the sugar and a good pinch of salt until the mixture forms a smooth ball. Cover and leave to cool for 20 mins.

2. Line a large baking tray with kitchen paper. Once the dough has cooled slightly, add the eggs, one at a time, beating thoroughly after each addition until they are fully incorporated and you have a soft, slightly sticky, dough. Spoon into a piping bag fitted with a large star nozzle.

3. In a large, deep, heavy-bottomed pan, heat the oil for deep-frying the churros to 180°C or until a piece of bread takes 45 seconds to colour. Holding the nozzle just above the hot oil, gently squeeze the piping bag and carefully snip off 3-4 x 8cm lengths of the mixture with kitchen scissors. Fry for 4 mins, turning occasionally, until crisp and golden. Lift out with a slotted spoon onto the lined baking tray. Repeat with the remaining dough.

4. Mix the remaining sugar with the cinnamon and sprinkle it over the churros. Serve with the chocolate sauce.

Cook's tip
These are really good eaten warm. You can make the dough ahead of time and keep it in the fridge, covered with cling film, then cook them just before serving.

Each serving (94g) provides:

ENERGY	FAT	SATURATES	SUGARS	SALT
1577kJ 380kcal	28.5g	10.4g	13.4g	0.3g
19%	41%	52%	15%	5%

% of the Reference Intakes
Typical values per 100g: Energy 1678kJ/404kcal
Each serving provides:
25.4g carbohydrate | 2g fibre | 4.4g protein

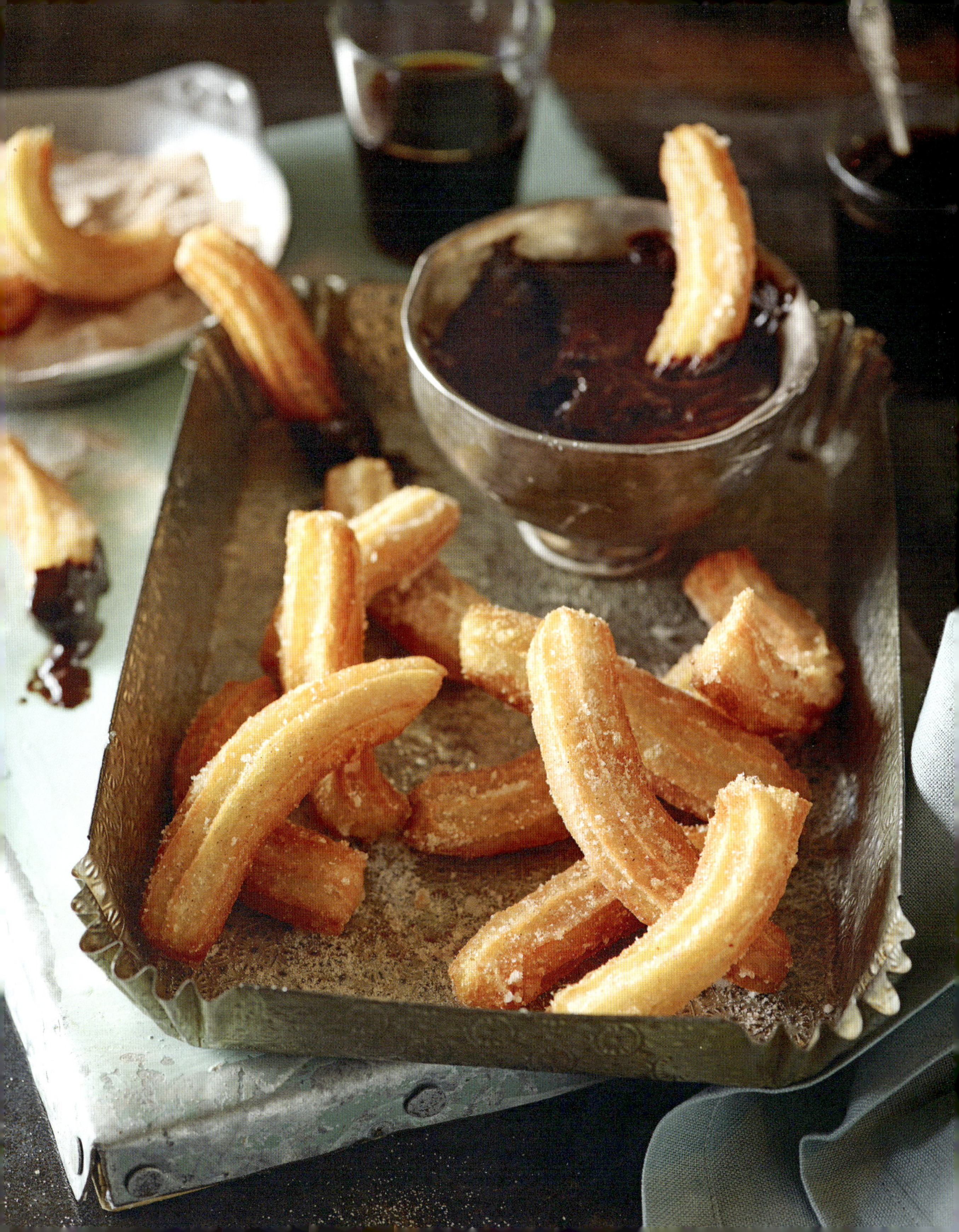

SERVES 12
PREP TIME 20 mins, plus 30 mins soaking and chilling
COOK TIME 45-55 mins

Tosca cake

Known as *toscakaka* in Sweden, this delicious sponge is topped with a layer of caramelised almonds – try serving it with a spoonful of yogurt

225g unsalted butter, softened, plus extra for greasing
225g caster sugar
4 eggs
50g plain flour
200g ground almonds
1 tsp baking powder

FOR THE TOPPING
100g unsalted butter, cubed
100g light brown soft sugar
2 tbsp semi-skimmed milk
100g toasted flaked almonds

1 Preheat the oven to 200°C, fan 180°C, gas 6. Grease a 21cm loose-bottomed cake tin and line the base and sides with baking paper.

2 In a large bowl, beat together the butter and sugar until pale and creamy. Beat in the eggs, one at a time, adding a spoonful of flour between each one. Sift in the remaining flour, then add the ground almonds and baking powder, and fold in gently to combine.

3 Spoon the cake mixture into the prepared tin and gently level the surface. Bake for 40-45 mins, until the top of the cake springs back when lightly pressed.

4 Meanwhile, make the topping. Put all the ingredients in a pan set over a medium heat. Stir well to combine all the ingredients, and leave to gently bubble for 2-3 mins, until thickened slightly.

5 Carefully spoon the topping over the cake and return to the oven for another 5-8 mins, until it's crunchy and golden. Cool the cake in the tin for 10 minutes, then carefully remove from the tin and transfer to a cooling rack to cool completely, or serve still warm.

Each serving (90g) provides

ENERGY	FAT	SATURATES	SUGARS	SALT
2091kJ 503kcal	37.9g	15g	26.7g	0.2g
25%	54%	75%	30%	3%

% of the Reference Intakes
Typical values per 100g: Energy 2323kJ/559kcal
Each serving provides:
30.5g carbohydrate | 2.3g fibre | 8.9g protein

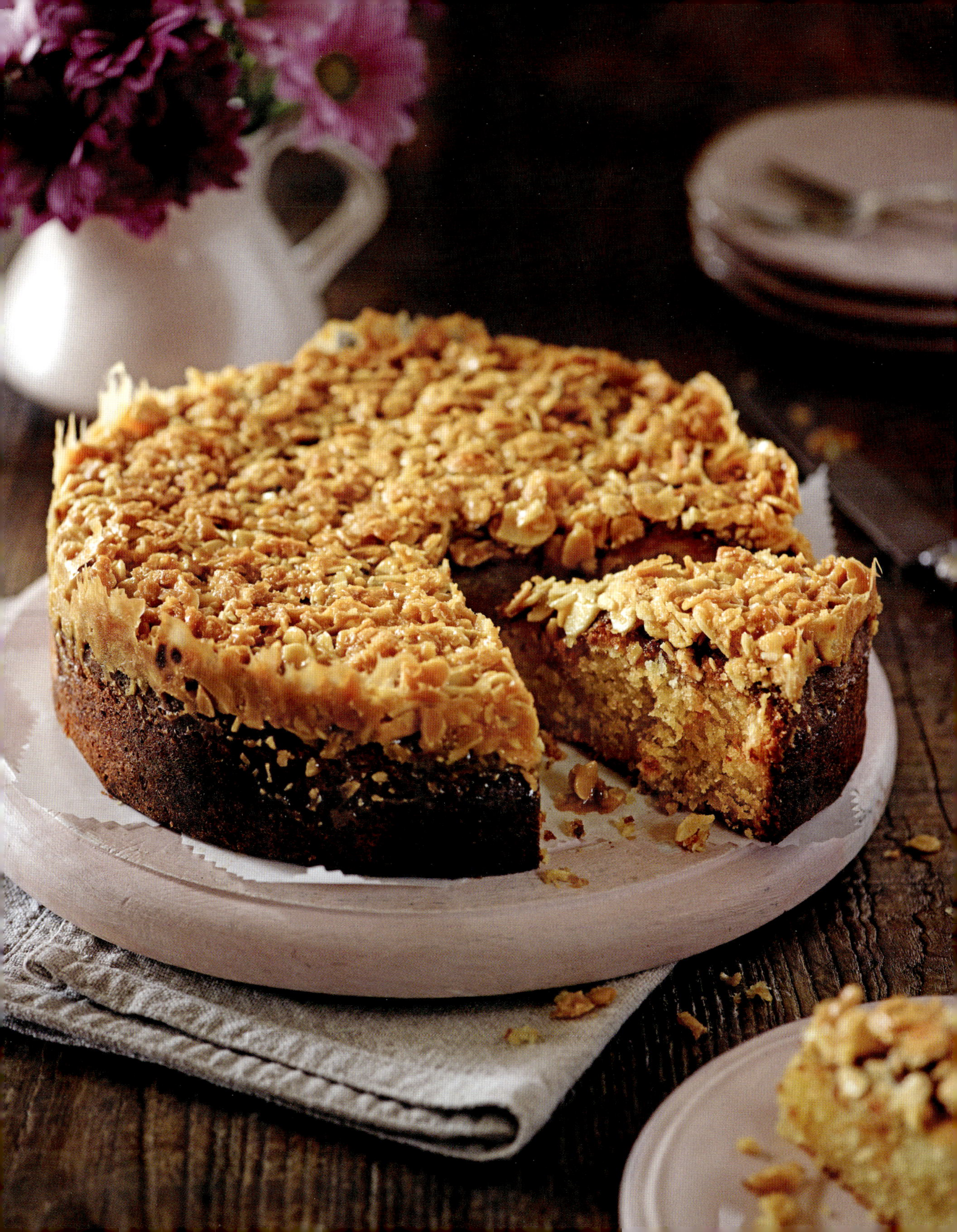

entertaining

MAKES 30
PREP TIME 25 mins
COOK TIME 45 mins

Pistachio & sour cherry biscotti

These Italian fruit and nut biscuits are baked twice for extra crunch and look so appealing. Serve them with coffee as an alternative to dessert

200g caster sugar
2 eggs
Zest of 2 oranges
300g plain flour, plus extra for dusting
1 tsp baking powder
150g pistachio kernels by Sainsbury's, roughly chopped
75g dried cherries by Sainsbury's

1 Preheat the oven to 180°C, fan 160°C, gas 4. Line two large baking sheets with baking paper.

2 Put the sugar, eggs and orange zest in a bowl and whisk together using a hand-held electric whisk. Fold through the flour, baking powder, pistachio kernels and cherries until you have a sticky dough. Turn out onto a lightly floured surface and knead lightly to a smooth dough. Shape into 2 x 30cm sausages. Transfer to the prepared baking sheets and bake for 30 mins until golden.

3 Remove from the oven and set aside for 10 mins to cool a little. Reduce the oven temperature to 150°C, fan 130°C, gas 2. Using a serrated knife, cut the biscotti into 30 x 2cm-thick slices. Arrange side by side, cut-side down, on the baking sheets. Bake for 10 mins until crisp and just beginning to turn golden, then turn the biscotti over and bake for another 5 mins. Cool on a cooling rack.

Cook's tip
Once they've cooled completely, store the biscotti in an airtight container on baking paper. They'll keep for up to 1 month.

Each biscuit (23g) provides:

ENERGY	FAT	SATURATES	SUGARS	SALT
425kJ 101kcal	2.8g	0.4g	8.5g	0.1g
5%	4%	2%	9%	1%

% of the Reference Intakes
Typical values per 100g: Energy 1850kJ/439kcal
Each biscuit provides:
15.8g carbohydrate | 0.8g fibre | 2.7g protein

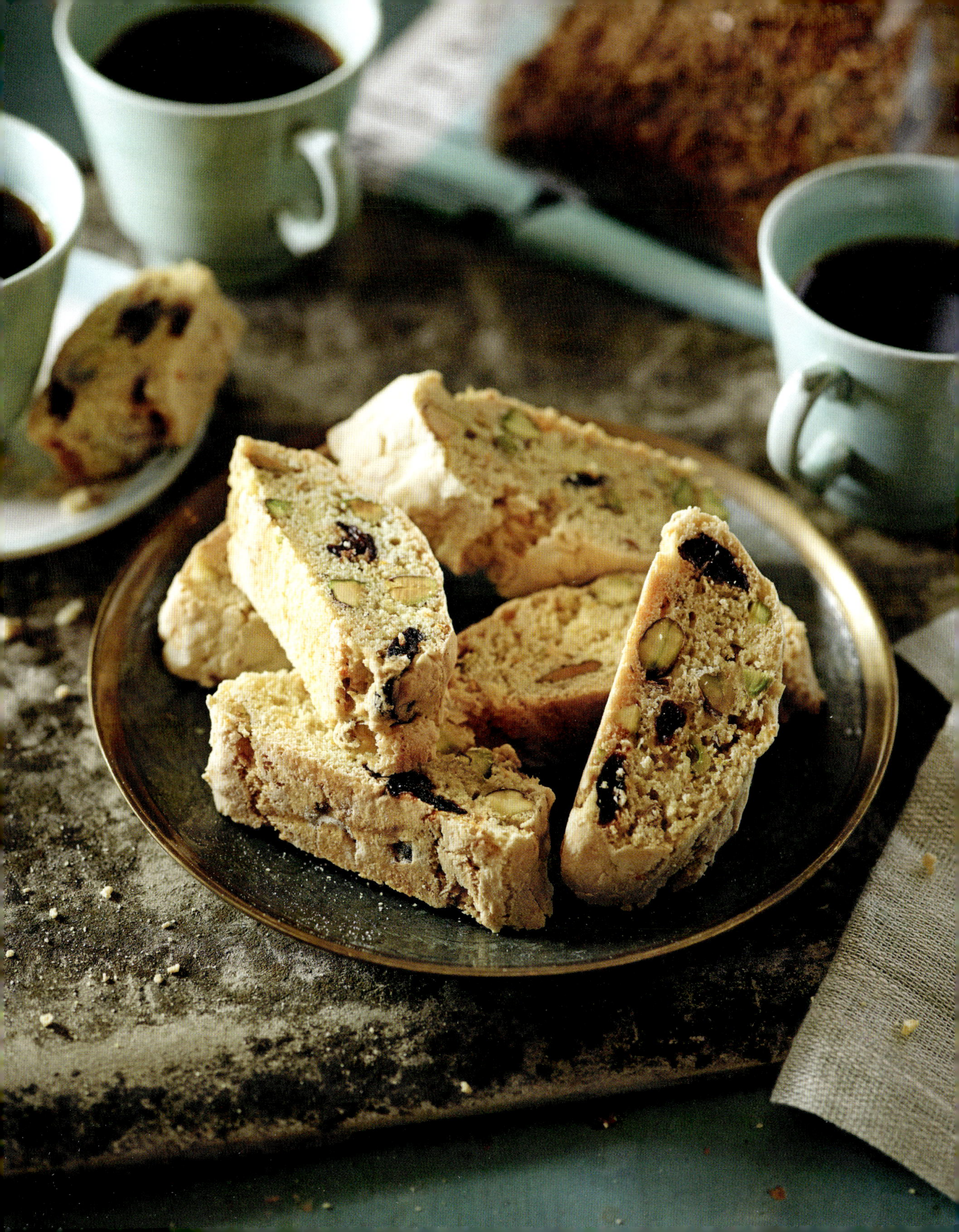

Slice of heaven

White, milk or dark – chocolate is a favourite flavour with bakers. Indulge your passion with a simple chocolate mousse cake on p170, or spectacular honeycomb cake on p174.

bakes for celebrations

show-stopping bakes, just right for special occasions

Berry angel food cake	168
Chocolate mousse cake	170
Hazelnut coffee gateau	172
Honeycomb cake	174
Chocolate crêpe cake	176
Mango meringue layer cake	178
Dulce de leche ice cream cake	180
Tiramisu cake	182
Pink ombre cake	184
White chocolate & cranberry panettone	186
Naked cake	188

celebrations

SERVES 12
PREP TIME 20 mins
COOK TIME 30-35 mins

Berry angel food cake

This light-as-air sponge topped with cream and colourful fresh fruit is a great choice for an outdoor summer party

10 egg whites
1 tsp cream of tartar
275g icing sugar, sifted, plus extra for dusting
1 tsp Taste the Difference Madagascan vanilla extract
90g plain flour
20g cornflour

FOR THE TOPPING
150ml double cream
1 tbsp icing sugar
Seasonal fresh fruit (blackberries, grapes, raspberries, redcurrants, blackcurrants and blueberries)

1 Preheat the oven to 170°C, 150 fan, gas 4. Put the egg whites* in the bowl of a freestanding mixer and add the cream of tartar and a pinch of salt. Whisk until soft peaks form (see p7), then add the sugar, a couple of tablespoons at a time, whisking well between each addition.

2 Add the vanilla extract and half of the flour, gently folding it in until the ingredients are well incorporated. Fold in the rest of the flour and cornflour.

3 Pour the mixture into an ungreased 25cm angel food cake tin. Level the surface with a palette knife to get rid of any air bubbles, then bake for 30-35 mins, or until a skewer inserted into the centre of the cake comes out clean. Remove from the oven, turn the tin upside down and leave on a wire rack to cool completely for around 45 mins to an hour. Run a palette knife around the edges of the cake to release it from the pan.

4 To serve, put the double cream and icing sugar in a bowl and whisk to soft peaks using a hand-held electric whisk. Neaten the top of the cake with a knife if necessary, to make a flat surface, then spread a thick layer of the cream over the top and decorate with the fresh fruit. Finish with a dusting of icing sugar.

*See p191 for a list of recipes to use leftover egg yolks.

Each serving (85g) provides:

ENERGY	FAT	SATURATES	SUGARS	SALT
828kJ 197kcal	6g	3.7g	25.5g	0.2g
10%	9%	19%	28%	4%

% of the Reference Intakes
Typical values per 100g: Energy 975kJ/231kcal
Each serving provides:
31.4g carbohydrate | 0.3g fibre | 4g protein

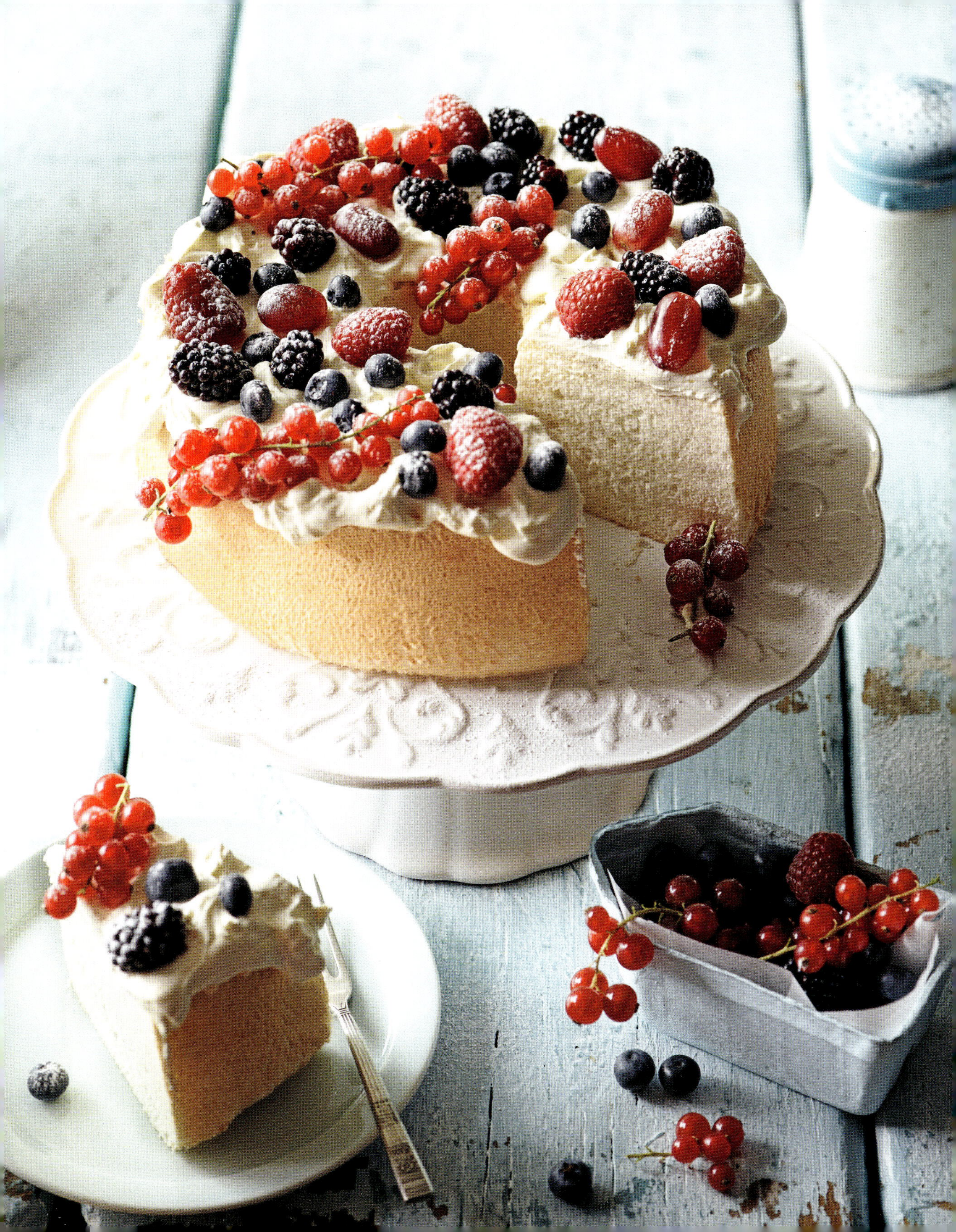

SERVES 16
PREP TIME 25 mins, plus chilling
COOK TIME 35 mins

Chocolate mousse cake

An impressive mousse-topped cake that's perfect for lovers of chocolate

40g cocoa powder
150g self-raising flour
½ tsp baking powder
200g caster sugar
2 large eggs
1 tsp Taste the Difference Madagascan vanilla extract
150g butterlicious by Sainsbury's, melted, plus extra for greasing
2 tbsp brandy (optional)
375g cook's Belgian dark chocolate by Sainsbury's, roughly chopped
400ml fresh whipping cream

1. Preheat the oven to 180°C, fan 160°C, gas 4. Grease a 20cm round spring form cake tin and line with baking paper. In a heatproof bowl, whisk the cocoa and 150ml boiling water until smooth and combined.

2. Sift the flour and baking powder into a large bowl, and stir in the sugar. Add the eggs, vanilla extract, melted butterlicious and cocoa mixture, and beat together using a hand-held electric whisk until smooth and combined.

3. Spoon into the prepared tin and bake for 30 mins or until a skewer inserted into the centre of the cake comes out clean. While the cake is still hot, brush all over with the brandy, if using, then leave to cool in the tin.

4. Melt the chocolate (see p7) and set aside to cool slightly. Whip the cream to soft peaks, then fold through 300g of the melted chocolate until everything is combined. Spoon the chocolate mousse over the cooled cake and level with the back of a spoon. Cover the tin loosely with cling film, then chill in the fridge for at least 4 hours or overnight until the mousse is set.

5. Line a baking sheet with baking paper. Put the remaining melted chocolate (you may need to re-melt it if it is too thick) in a plastic sandwich bag, then snip off one corner of the bag. Pipe heart shapes onto the baking paper (don't worry if they're not perfect), then leave in a cool place to set.

6. Release the cake from the tin and remove the baking paper. Carefully peel the chocolate hearts off the baking paper and use them to decorate the sides and top of the cake.

Each serving (91g) provides:

ENERGY	FAT	SATURATES	SUGARS	SALT
1494kJ 359kcal	24.1g	13.2g	22.3g	0.3g
18%	34%	66%	25%	5%

% of the Reference Intakes
Typical values per 100g: Energy 1642kJ/395kcal
Each serving provides:
29.3g carbohydrate | 2.9g fibre | 3.9g protein

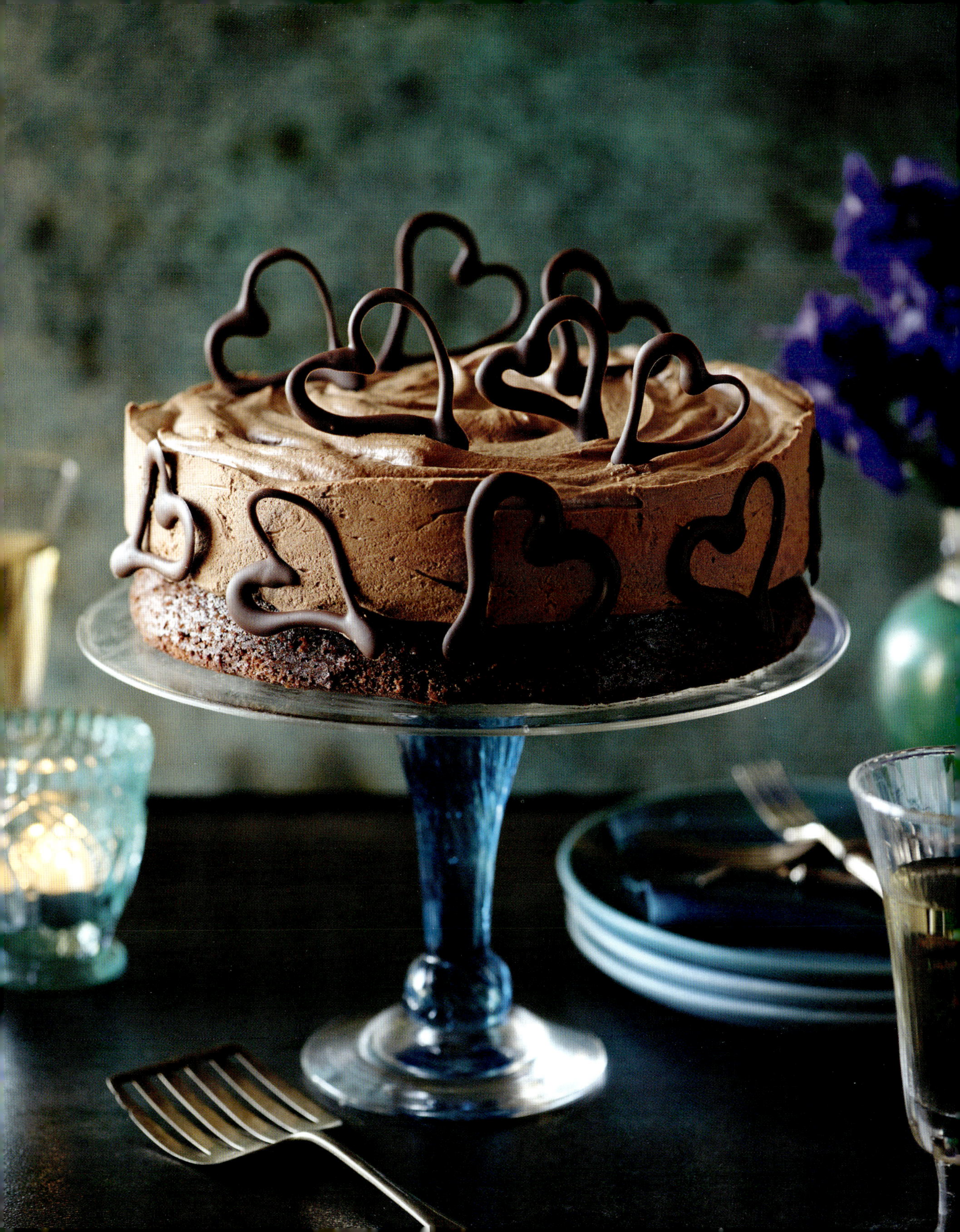

Hazelnut coffee gateau

Layers of hazelnut sponge sandwiched with a creamy coffee filling

SERVES 9
PREP TIME 20 mins
COOK TIME 45 mins

50g unsalted butter, melted, plus extra for greasing
3 egg whites, plus 3 whole eggs
150g caster sugar
150g ground roasted hazelnuts by Sainsbury's
75g plain flour, sifted
25g roasted chopped hazelnuts by Sainsbury's, to decorate

3 tbsp strong coffee, cold
Icing sugar and cocoa powder, for dusting

FOR THE FILLING
300ml whipping cream
25g icing sugar
2 tbsp strong coffee, cold

1. Preheat the oven to 200°C, fan 180°C, gas 6. Grease an 18cm square cake tin and line the base with baking paper.

2. In a large bowl, whisk the egg whites* using a hand-held electric whisk until stiff, peaks form. Gradually add 50g of the caster sugar, whisking until stiff and glossy.

3. In a separate bowl, whisk together the remaining sugar and the whole eggs until the mixture is pale and thickened. Gently fold in the hazelnuts and flour, then stir in a heaped tablespoon of the egg whites. Fold in the remaining egg whites until fully incorporated, then pour in the melted butter and fold gently to combine.

4. Spoon the mixture into the prepared tin, gently levelling the top. Bake for 40 mins, or until risen and golden and a skewer inserted into the centre of the cake comes out clean. Cool in the tin for 5 mins, then turn out onto a cooling rack to cool completely. Trim the top of the cake to level it, if necessary, then cut it horizontally into 3 layers.

5. Make the filling. In a large bowl, whip together the cream, icing sugar and coffee until the mixture holds its shape.

6. Assemble the gateau. Put one cake layer onto a plate or stand. Sprinkle over 1 tbsp of the coffee, then spoon over half the filling and spread to the edges. Scatter over half of the hazelnuts, putting extra at the edges. Top with the next layer and repeat. Finish by dusting icing sugar and cocoa over the top of the cake in stripes, using strips of paper as a stencil.

*See p191 for a list of recipes to use leftover egg yolks.

Each serving (114g) provides:

ENERGY	FAT	SATURATES	SUGARS	SALT
1788kJ 430kcal	31.5g	12.3g	21.3g	0.1g
22%	45%	62%	24%	2%

% of the Reference Intakes
Typical values per 100g: Energy 1569kJ/377kcal
Each serving provides:
27.7g carbohydrate | 2.4g fibre | 7.9g protein

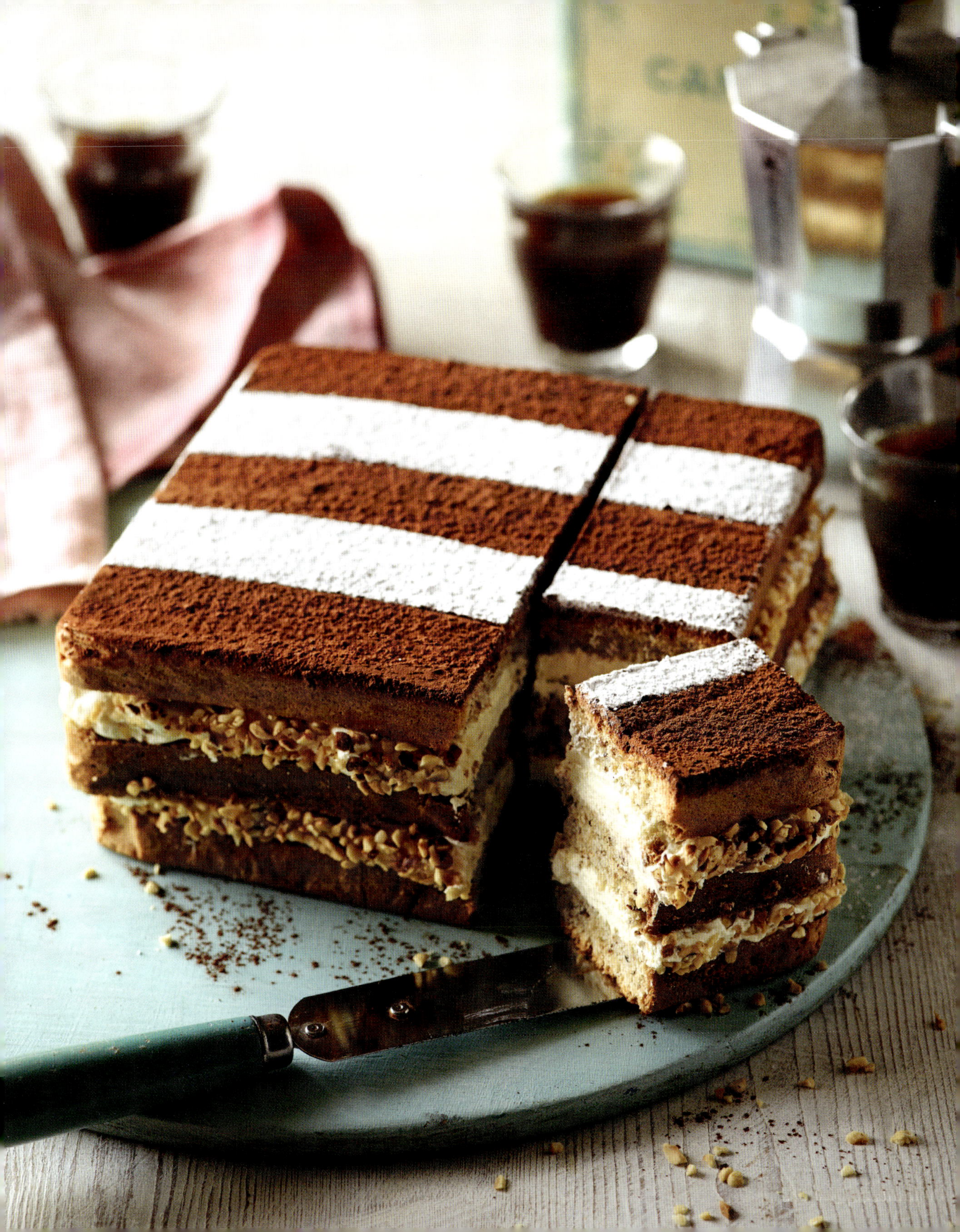

SERVES 14
PREP TIME 20 mins
COOK TIME 35-40 mins

Honeycomb cake

Rich chocolate meets golden honeycomb in this tempting creation

225g unsalted butter, softened, plus extra for greasing
4 tbsp cocoa by Sainsbury's
225g self-raising flour
½ tsp baking powder
225g light brown soft sugar
4 large eggs, lightly beaten

FOR THE HONEYCOMB
150g granulated sugar
6 tbsp golden syrup
1 ½ tsp bicarbonate of soda

FOR THE CHOCOLATE BUTTERCREAM
150g unsalted butter, softened
275g icing sugar, sifted
90g dark chocolate, melted

1. Preheat the oven to 180°C, fan 160°C, gas 4. Grease 3 x 20cm round cake tins and line the bases with baking paper.

2. Sift the cocoa, flour and baking powder into a large mixing bowl. Add the butter, brown sugar and eggs and beat with a hand-held electric whisk for 3-4 mins until smooth. Divide the mixture between the prepared tins and level the surfaces. Bake for 25-30 mins, or until risen and just firm to the touch. Cool in the tins for 5 mins, then turn out onto a cooling rack to cool completely.

3. Make the honeycomb. Grease a large baking tray. Put the sugar and syrup in a large pan and heat gently over a low heat, stirring, until the sugar has dissolved. Increase the heat and let the syrup bubble, without stirring, for 1-2 mins, until it turns a golden colour. Beat in the bicarbonate of soda (the mixture will bubble up), then pour onto the baking tray. Leave for 1 hour until cold and firm.

4. Make the buttercream. Put the butter in a mixing bowl and gradually beat in the icing sugar. Beat in the melted chocolate until combined, then beat in 2 tsp hot water until the mixture is smooth and glossy.

5. Assemble the cake. Cut two-thirds of the honeycomb into shards and roughly crush the rest. Put the buttercream into a piping bag fitted with a small round nozzle and pipe small blobs of buttercream all over each cake layer, then sprinkle some of the crushed honeycomb over each one. Stack the three cake layers together on a cake stand and top the cake with the honeycomb shards. Cut into thin slices to serve.

Each serving (104g) provides:

ENERGY	FAT	SATURATES	SUGARS	SALT
2129kJ 509kcal	26.4g	15.2g	51.3g	0.6g
25%	38%	76%	57%	11%

% of the Reference Intakes
Typical values per 100g: Energy 2047kJ/489kcal
Each serving provides:
62.4g carbohydrate | 1.6g fibre | 4.5g protein

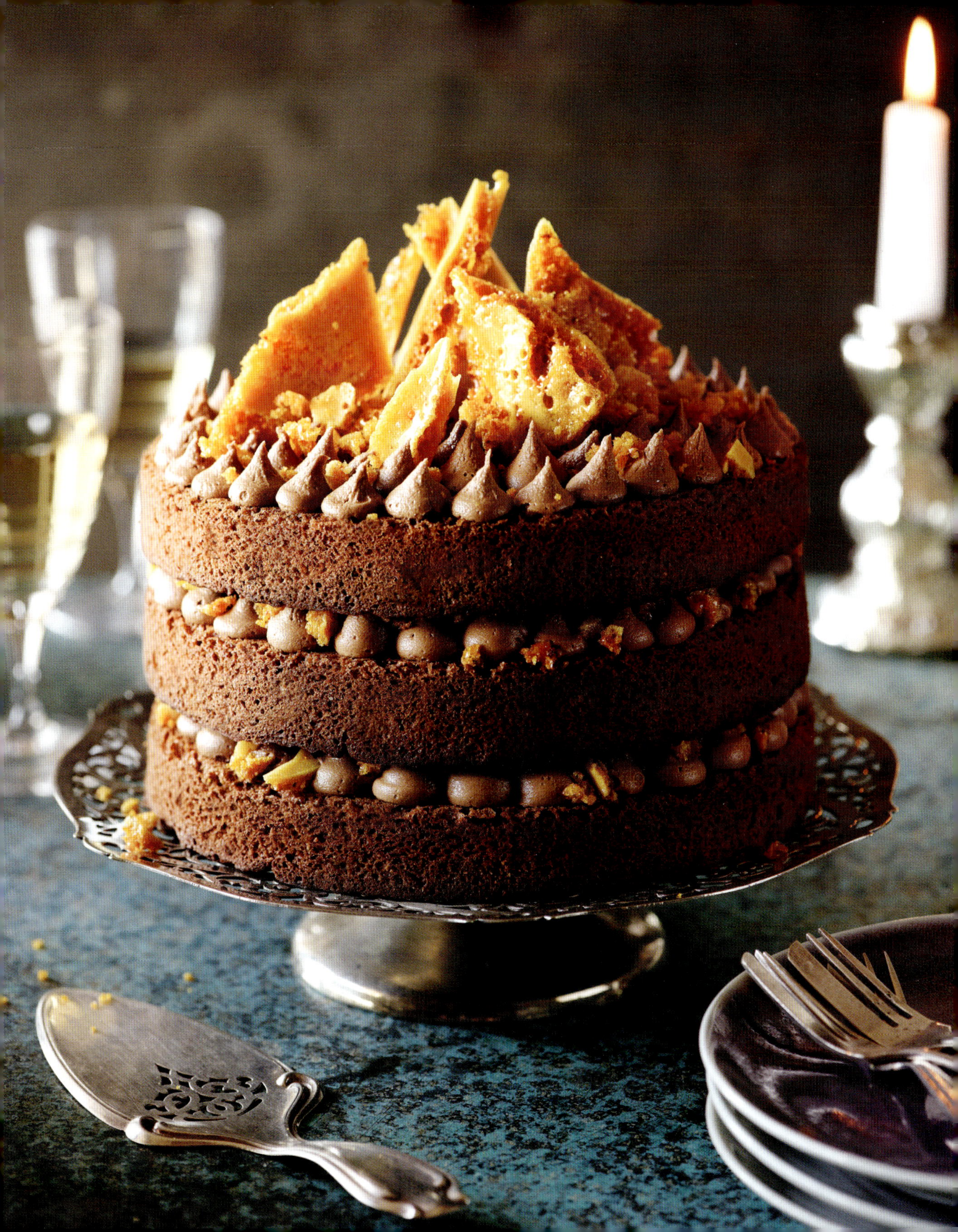

SERVES 14
PREP TIME 1 hour
COOK TIME 30 mins

Chocolate crêpe cake

If you love sweet pancakes, you'll really love this special-occasion cake made of stacks of crêpes layered with delicious chocolate ganache

300g plain flour
600ml semi-skimmed milk
3 large eggs
25g unsalted butter, melted
25g roasted chopped hazelnuts
by Sainsbury's

FOR THE CHOCOLATE GANACHE
300g Taste the Difference Belgian dark chocolate, finely chopped
500ml double fresh cream

1. Put the flour, milk and eggs in a blender or food processor and whizz for 30 seconds to make a smooth batter. Pour into a large jug.

2. Heat a 22-25cm non-stick frying pan over a medium heat. Brush with a little of the melted butter, then pour in 2 tbsp of the batter and quickly swirl the pan to coat the base with a thin layer of batter. Cook for 1 min until golden on the underside, flip the crêpe over and cook for a further 30 seconds. Remove from the pan and place on a sheet of baking paper.

3. Repeat with the rest of the batter, brushing the pan with a little melted butter each time, to make 14-15 crêpes in total. Stack the crêpes between sheets of baking paper and set aside to cool.

4. Make the chocolate ganache. Put the chocolate in a heatproof bowl. Heat the cream in a pan until almost boiling, then pour over the chocolate. Leave for 1 min, then stir until melted and smooth. Leave to cool, stirring occasionally until the ganache is thick enough to spread.

5. Assemble the cake. Put one crêpe on a plate or cake stand and spread with a thin layer of the ganache. Top with another crêpe and repeat the process, finishing with a plain crêpe. Spread the rest of the chocolate ganache over the top of the cake and let it drip over the sides. Decorate with the chopped hazelnuts and serve immediately, or chill until required. Serve on the day of making.

Each serving (122g) provides:

ENERGY	FAT	SATURATES	SUGARS	SALT
1721kJ / 415kcal	31.6g	18.6g	7.9g	0.1g
21%	45%	93%	9%	2%

% of the Reference Intakes

Typical values per 100g: Energy 1411kJ/340kcal
Each serving provides:
23.4g carbohydrate | 3.4g fibre | 7.4g protein

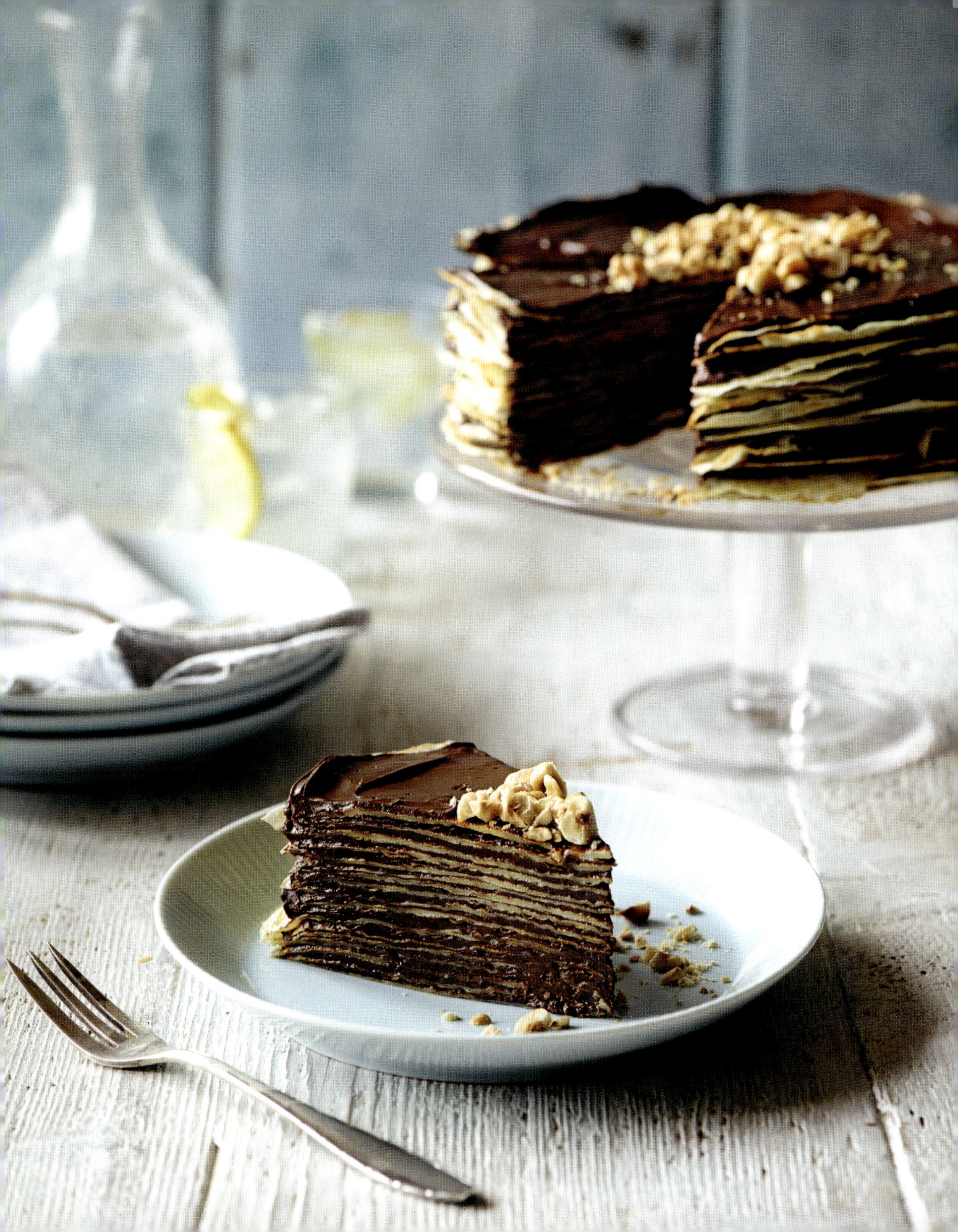

Mango meringue layer cake

Take pavlova to the next level with this towering tropical torte

SERVES 10
PREP TIME 40 mins
COOK TIME 1 hour

3 large egg whites
170g caster sugar
1 tsp cornflour
½ tsp cider vinegar
3 mangos, peeled, stones removed and flesh diced
450ml fresh double cream
150g Greek style natural yogurt by Sainsbury's

1. Preheat the oven to 140°C, fan 120°C, gas 2. Put the egg whites* in the bowl of a freestanding mixer with the balloon whisk attached, or use a hand-held electric whisk. Whisk for 3-4 mins until soft peaks form (see p7). While still whisking, slowly add the caster sugar, 2 tbsp at a time, until you have a stiff, glossy meringue mixture. Whisk in the cornflour and vinegar until combined.

2. Line two large baking trays with baking paper, fixing the paper in place with a tiny blob of meringue in each corner. Trace three 20cm circles onto the paper and, using a metal spoon, shape three large meringue rounds. Bake for 1 hour. Turn off the oven and leave the meringues to cool completely in the oven.

3. Meanwhile, put two-thirds of the mango into a food processor and process to a smooth purée. Chill until required. Whip the double cream with the yogurt until soft peaks form, and chill until required.

4. Assemble the cake. Put a layer of meringue on a cake stand and spoon over a third of the cream. Swirl some of the mango purée through the cream, then put another layer of meringue on top. Repeat with another third of the cream and more mango purée. Top the cake with the last meringue layer and spoon over the remaining cream. Decorate with fresh chopped mango, and drizzle over a little of the purée. Serve immediately with any leftover mango purée on the side.

*See p191 for a list of recipes to use leftover egg yolks.

Each serving (124g) provides:

ENERGY	FAT	SATURATES	SUGARS	SALT
1295kJ 311kcal	22.6g	14.2g	23.3g	0.1g
16%	32%	71%	26%	2%

% of the Reference Intakes
Typical values per 100g: Energy 1044kJ/251kcal
Each serving provides:
23.8g carbohydrate | 0.2g fibre | 2.9g protein

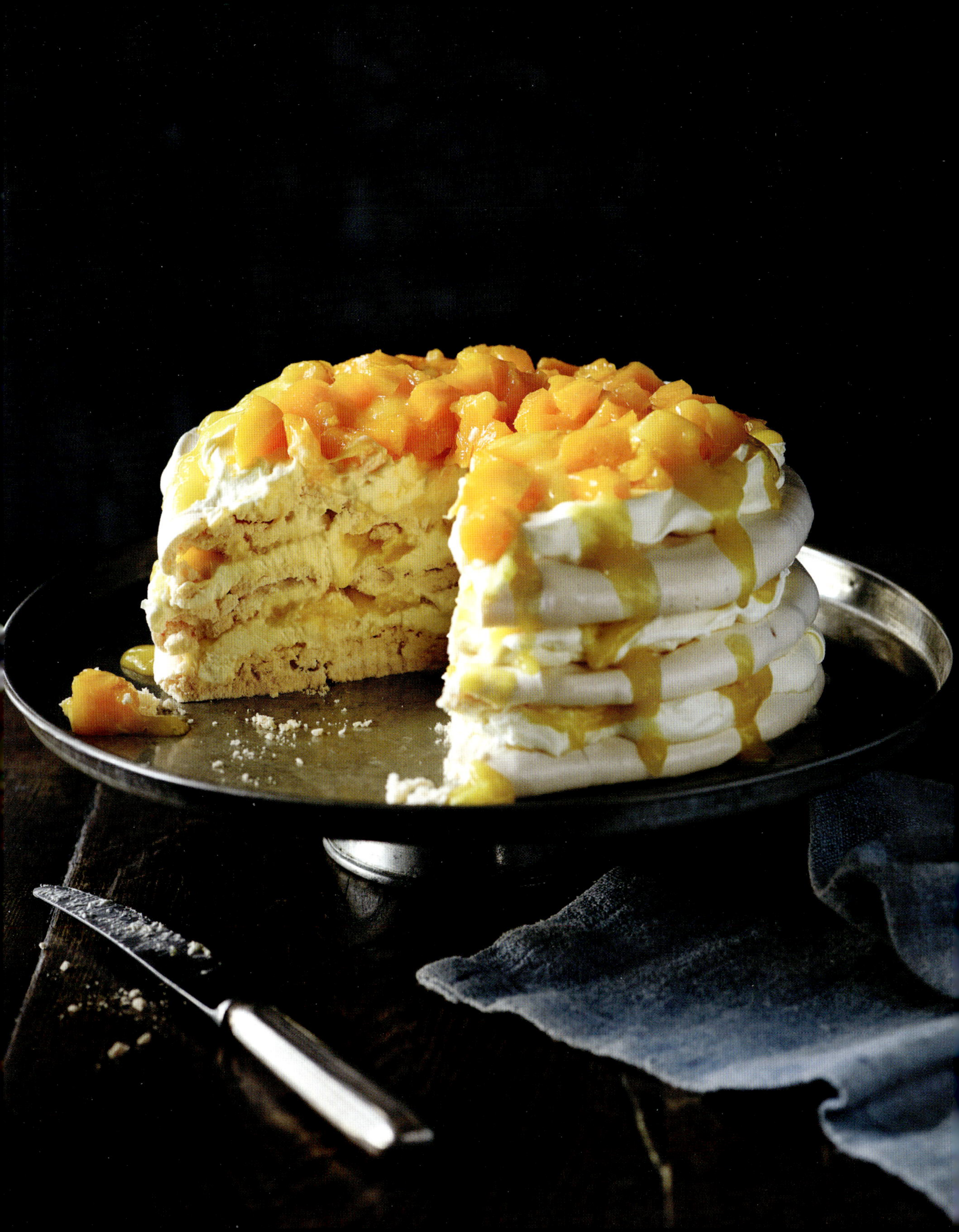

SERVES 14
PREP TIME 30 mins, plus freezing
COOK TIME 35-40 mins

Dulce de leche ice-cream cake

Serve up this decadent ice-cream cake at summer parties

150g unsalted butter, softened, plus extra for greasing
150g dark brown soft sugar
3 eggs, beaten
150g self-raising flour, sifted
300ml fresh double cream
300ml tub Sainsbury's be good to yourself fresh custard
40g jumbo honey roast cashew nuts by Sainsbury's, chopped
397g tin Carnation caramel, beaten until smooth
40g smooth dark chocolate by Sainsbury's, melted (see p7), to decorate

1. Preheat the oven to 180°C, fan 160°C, gas 4. Grease and line the base of a 20cm sandwich tin. Put the butter and sugar in a medium bowl and beat with an electric hand-held whisk for 1-2 mins until pale and creamy. Gradually beat in the eggs, then fold in the flour. Spoon the mixture into the tin and level the surface.

2. Bake for 30-35 mins, or until risen, golden and firm to the touch. Remove from the oven and leave in the tin for 5 mins, then turn out onto a cooling rack.

3. In a medium bowl, whip the cream until it holds firm peaks, then fold in the custard and cashews. Gently swirl two-thirds of the caramel into the mixture.

4. Line a 20cm springform tin with cling film, allowing the excess to hang over the top edge. Cut the sponge in half horizontally and put one half in the base of the tin. Spoon over the caramel and cream mixture, then top with the second sponge half. Freeze for at least 5 hours, until frozen.

5. Remove the cake from the freezer, release the side of the tin and remove, leaving the cake on the base. Spread the remaining caramel over the top of the cake. Put the melted chocolate into a small piping bag. Snip off the corner and pipe swirls of chocolate on top of the cake. Return to the freezer until required. Remove from the freezer 20-25 mins before serving and transfer to a serving plate.

Each serving (114g) provides:

ENERGY	FAT	SATURATES	SUGARS	SALT
1626kJ 390kcal	24.4g	13.9g	27.7g	0.2g
19%	35%	70%	31%	4%

% of the Reference Intakes
Typical values per 100g: Energy 1426kJ/342kcal
Each serving provides:
36.4g carbohydrate | 1g fibre | 5.6g protein

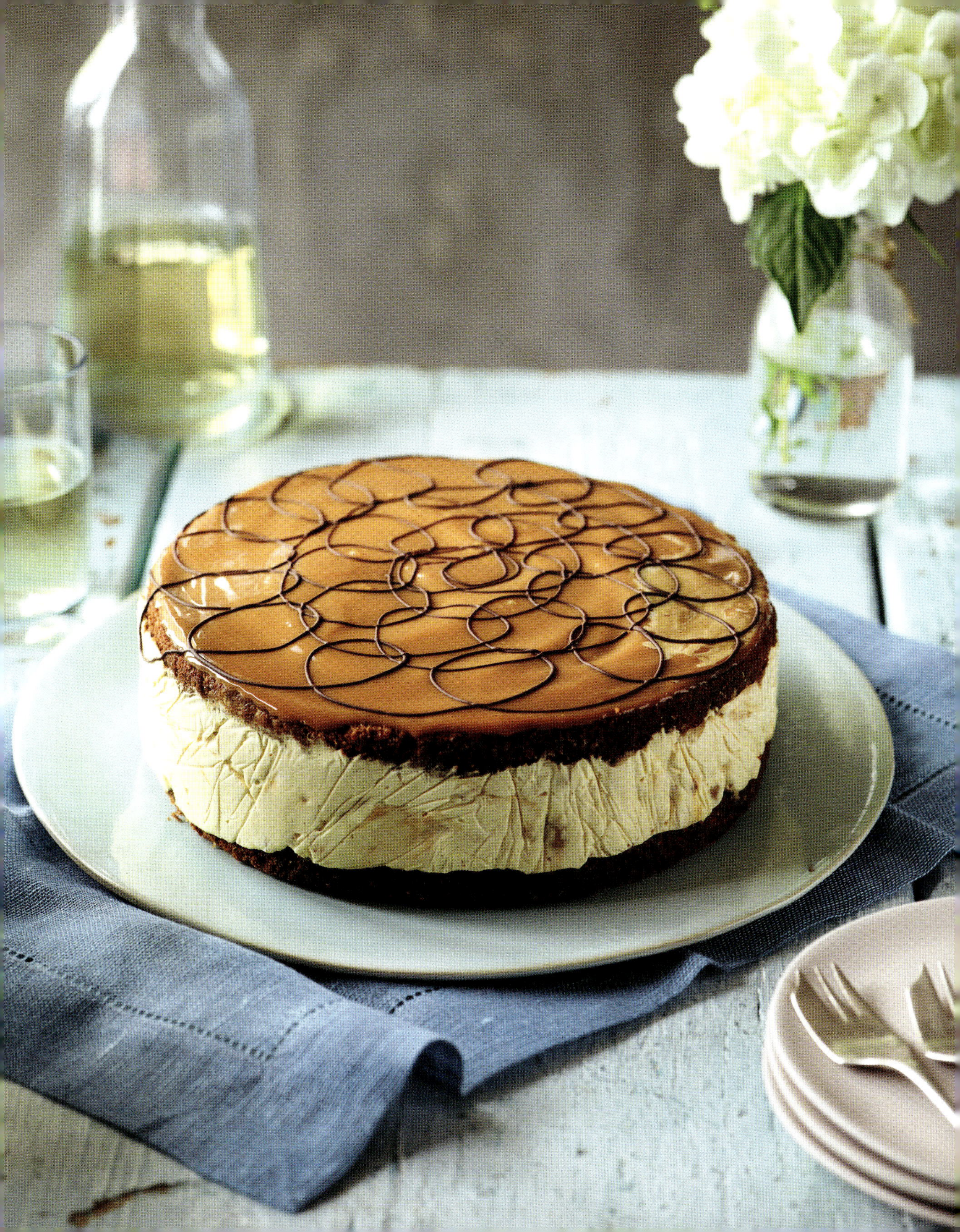

celebrations

SERVES 16
PREP TIME 25 mins
COOK TIME 40 mins

Tiramisu cake

Everyone's favourite Italian dessert turned into an irresistible cake

200g unsalted butter, melted, plus extra for greasing
60g cocoa powder
180ml freshly brewed hot coffee
200g self-raising flour
1 tsp baking powder
375g caster sugar
3 eggs
1 tsp Taste the Difference Madagascan vanilla extract
2 tbsp coffee-flavoured liqueur (optional)
250g Italian mascarpone by Sainsbury's
150ml whipping cream
200g pack Taste the Difference Italian Savoiardi sponge fingers, to decorate
Chocolate curls, to decorate (see Cook's tip)

1. Preheat the oven to 180°C, fan 160°C, gas 4. Grease and line a 23cm square cake tin. In a small bowl, mix the cocoa with 150ml of the coffee and stir until smooth.

2. Sift the flour and baking powder into a large bowl. Add 300g of the caster sugar, the melted butter, eggs, vanilla and the cocoa mixture, and beat using an electric hand-held whisk until smooth.

3. Pour the mixture into the prepared tin and bake for 30 mins or until a skewer inserted into the centre of the cake comes out clean. While the cake is still hot, brush over the coffee-flavoured liqueur, if using, then leave to cool in the tin. When the cake is cool, cut it in half to make 2 x 23cm x 11.5cm oblong pieces.

4. Whisk the mascarpone and remaining coffee in a large bowl until combined. In a separate bowl, whisk the cream and the remaining 75g caster sugar together until soft peaks form. Whisk both of these mixtures together until combined and form soft peaks again. Put one half of the cake on a serving plate, spread half the cream mixture over the top, then top with the other cake half. Spread the remaining cream over the top and sides of the entire cake.

5. Trim the sponge fingers at one end, then arrange them around the sides of the cake, sticking them to the cream. Top with the dark chocolate curls to serve.

Cook's tip
To make chocolate curls, spread melted chocolate (see p7) thinly over a baking tray. Leave until firm, then scrape a sharp knife along the chocolate at a 45-degree angle.

Each serving (103g) provides:

ENERGY	FAT	SATURATES	SUGARS	SALT
1729kJ 414kcal	23.7g	14.7g	29.9g	0.3g
21%	34%	74%	33%	5%

% of the Reference Intakes
Typical values per 100g: Energy 1679kJ/402kcal
Each serving provides:
43.3g carbohydrate | 2g fibre | 5.2g protein

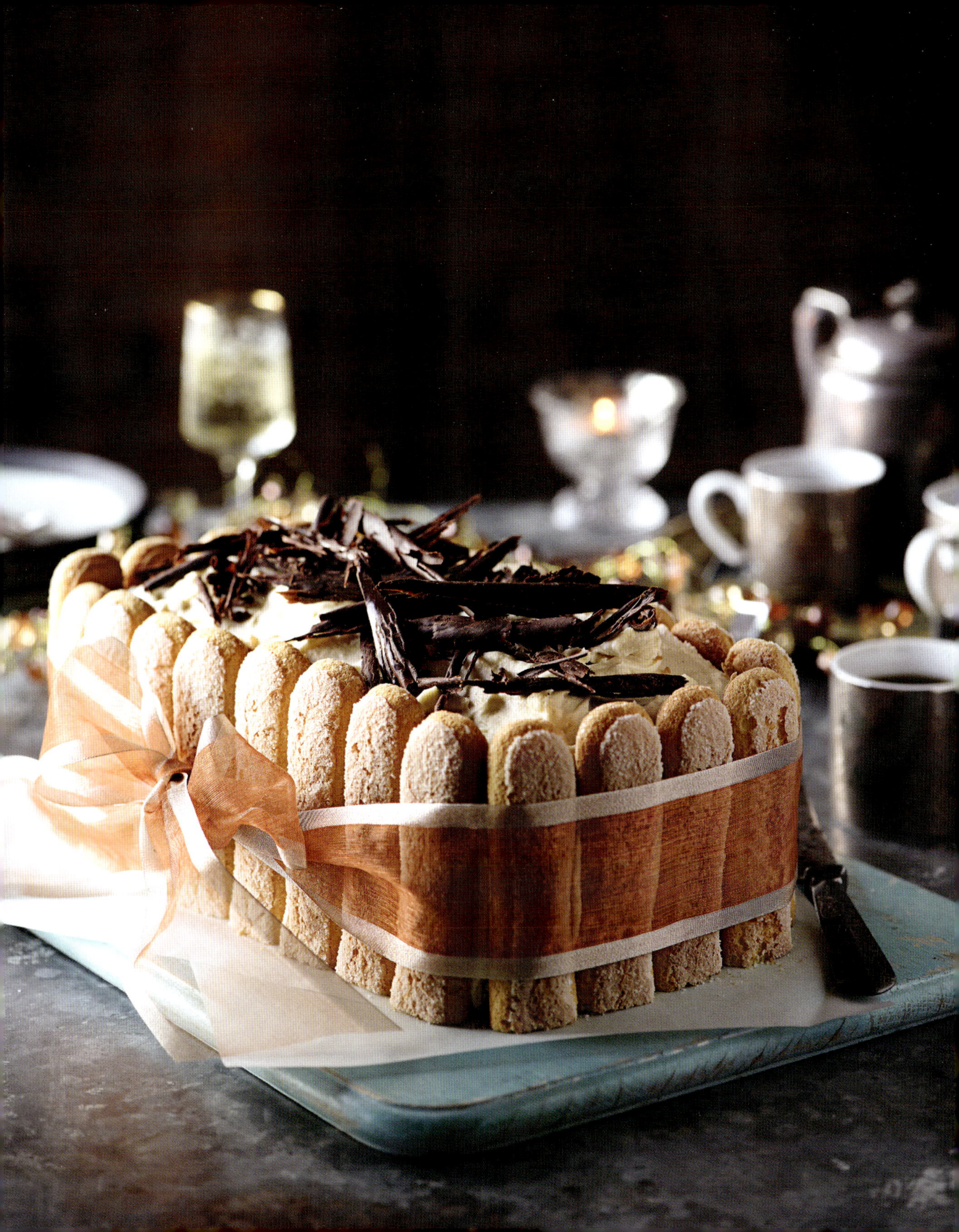

SERVES 14
PREP TIME
50 mins, plus cooling and chilling
COOK TIME
20-25 mins

Pink ombre cake

A colourful layer cake that's perfect for a teenager's birthday

300g butterlicious by Sainsbury's, softened plus extra for greasing
300g self-raising flour
1/2 tsp baking powder
300g caster sugar
5 eggs
2 tbsp semi-skimmed milk
1 tsp Taste the Difference Madagascan vanilla extract
Red food colouring by Sainsbury's

FOR THE BUTTERCREAM
200g unsalted butter, softened
1 tsp Taste the Difference Madagascan vanilla extract
400g icing sugar, sifted
Red food colouring by Sainsbury's

1. Preheat the oven to 180°C, fan 160°C, gas 4. Grease 3 x 18cm round sandwich tins and line the bases with baking paper.

2. Sift the flour and baking powder into a bowl and add the butter, sugar, eggs and milk. Beat with an electric hand-held whisk for 1-2 mins until pale and creamy. Divide the mixture equally between 3 bowls.

3. Gradually beat drops of the food colouring into each bowl to give three different shades of pink, ranging from pale to dark. Spoon into the tins and level the surfaces. Bake for 20-25 mins, or until risen and firm to the touch. Cool for 5 mins, then turn out onto a cooling rack to cool completely.

4. To make the buttercream, put the butter and vanilla extract in bowl and beat in the icing sugar until very smooth. Use a quarter of the buttercream to sandwich the three sponges together (put the darkest sponge at the base), then spread a thin layer over the top and sides of the cake. Chill in the fridge for 20 mins.

5. Put half the remaining buttercream into separate bowl and beat in a few drops of colouring to give a pale pink colour. Divide the rest of the buttercream between 2 bowls and add 1/2 tsp of the colouring to one bowl and 1 tsp to the second so you have one mid-pink and one deep pink buttercream.

6. Using a small palette knife, spread the deep pink buttercream around the base of the cake, the mid-pink buttercream around the middle and the lightest pink buttercream around the top, sides and over the top. Blend the shades of buttercream together slightly with the palette knife.

Each serving (118g) provides:

ENERGY	FAT	SATURATES	SUGARS	SALT
2010kJ 480kcal	23.5g	9.9g	47.6g	0.6g
24%	34%	50%	53%	10%

% of the Reference Intakes
Typical values per 100g: Energy 1704kJ/407kcal
Each serving provides:
62.1g carbohydrate | 1g fibre | 4.6g protein

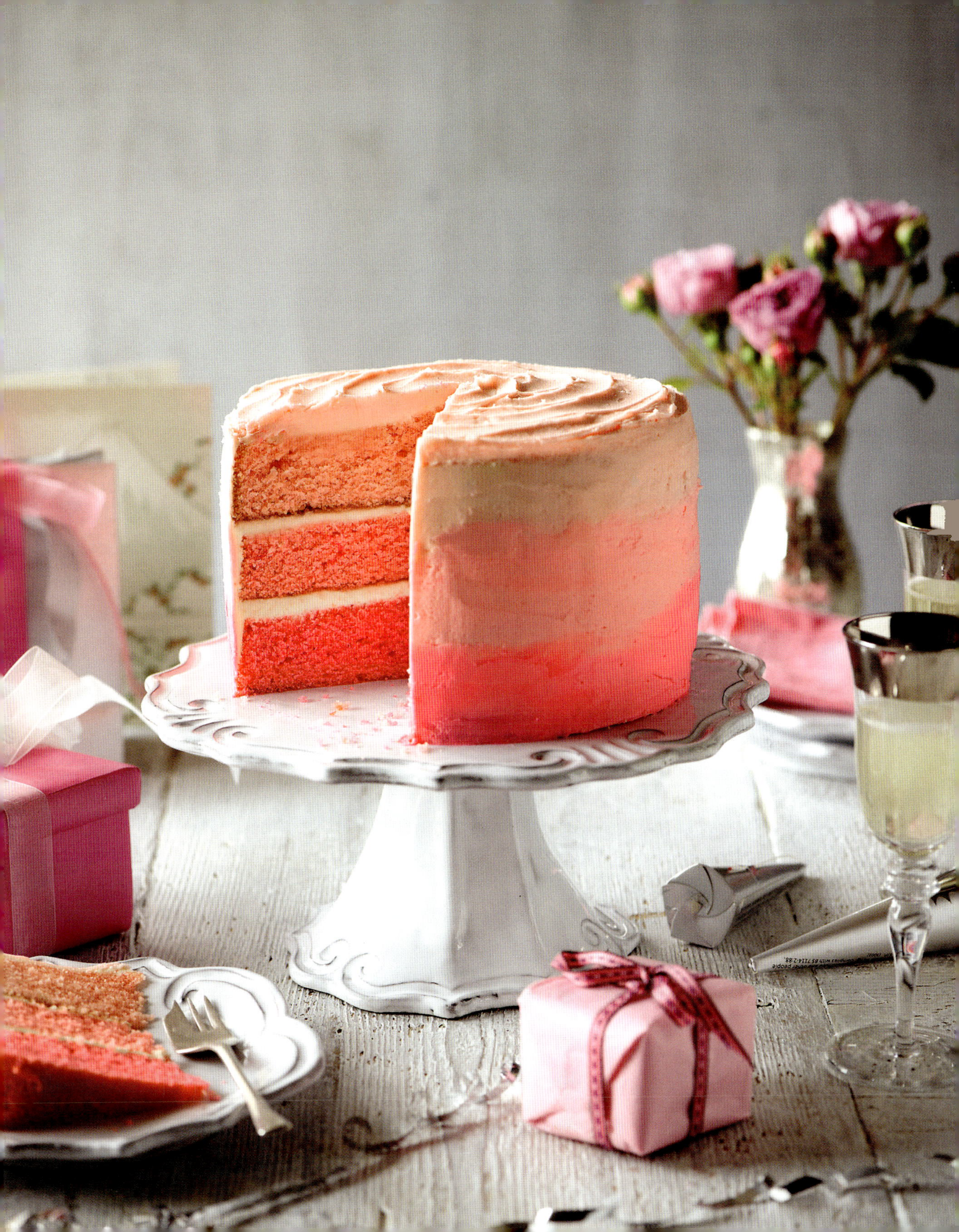

SERVES 8
PREP TIME 40 mins plus proving
COOK TIME 1 hour 5 mins

White chocolate & cranberry panettone

Make this sweet Italian-style bread at Christmas for added wow factor

500g strong white bread flour by Sainsbury's, plus 25g extra for kneading
2 x 7g sachets fast action dried yeast by Sainsbury's
100g caster sugar
Zest of 1 orange
1 large egg and 4 large egg yolks, plus beaten egg white, to glaze
150ml semi-skimmed milk, warm
125g unsalted butter, softened, plus extra for greasing
75g dried cranberries
40g white chocolate chips
30g cut mixed peel
Icing sugar, for dusting

1. Sift the flour into a large bowl and stir in the yeast, sugar and orange zest. Make a well in the centre and stir in the whole egg, egg yolks* and milk. Mix to a dough then turn out onto a floured surface and knead for 5-6 mins until smooth.

2. Gradually knead in the softened butter. The dough will become very soft and sticky, so add the extra flour as needed. Continue kneading for 2-3 mins until the dough is smooth and soft.

3. Return the dough to the bowl, cover with cling film and leave in a warm place for 2 hours 30 mins to 3 hours, or until doubled in size. Grease and line the base of a deep 18cm round cake tin. Line the sides with a double thickness of baking paper that extends 10cm above the rim of the tin.

4. Knock back the dough to release the air, then knead in the cranberries, chocolate chips and mixed peel. Shape into a ball and drop into the prepared tin. Cover with cling film and leave for 1 hour to 1 hour 30 mins, or until the dough has risen 2-3cm above the tin. Preheat the oven to 200°C, fan 180°C, gas 6.

5. Brush the top all over with the egg white. Bake for 20 mins, then reduce the oven temperature to 180°C, fan 160°C, gas 4 and bake for a further 45 mins, or until well-risen and golden (cover loosely with foil after 20 mins). Leave in the tin for 10 mins, then turn out onto a wire rack to cool completely. Dust with icing sugar to serve.

*See p191 for a list of recipes to use leftover egg whites.

Each serving (139g) provides:

ENERGY	FAT	SATURATES	SUGARS	SALT
2116kJ 504kcal	19.7g	10.2g	25.6g	0.1g
25%	28%	51%	28%	2%

% of the Reference Intakes
Typical values per 100g: Energy 1523kJ/363kcal
Each serving provides:
66.5g carbohydrate | 3.2g fibre | 13.7g protein

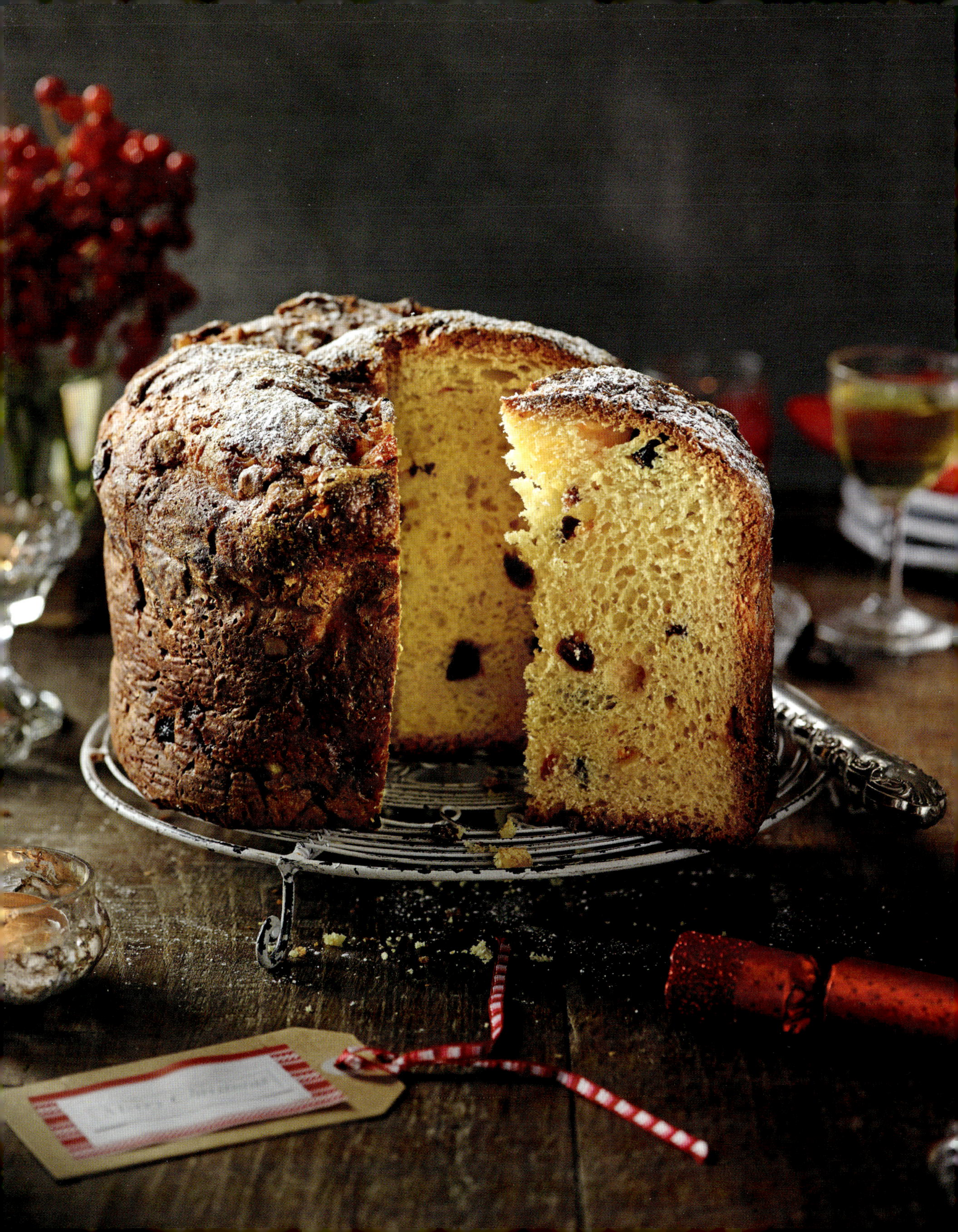

SERVES 24
PREP TIME 50 mins, plus cooling
COOK TIME 50 mins-1 hour

Naked cake

Let those lovely layers show through – this stunning cake is perfect for a special celebration, such as a wedding or big birthday

425g unsalted butter, softened, plus extra for greasing
425g self-raising flour
¾ tsp baking powder
425g caster sugar
7 eggs

FOR THE FROSTING & DECORATION
200g unsalted butter, softened
200g icing sugar, plus extra for dusting
200g full-fat soft cheese, at room temperature
2 passionfruit
12-14 physalis by Sainsbury's, papery cases peeled back
Edible gold leaf by Sainsbury's (optional)
4 small ripe figs, cut into quarters

1. Preheat the oven to 180°C, fan 160°C, gas 4. Grease 2 x 20cm round sandwich tins and 2 x 15cm round sandwich tins and line the bases with baking paper.

2. Sift 250g of the flour and ½ tsp of the baking powder into a mixing bowl and add 250g each of the butter and sugar, and 4 of the eggs. Beat with an electric hand-held whisk for 1-2 mins until pale and creamy. Divide the mixture between the 2 x 20cm tins and level the surfaces. Bake for 30-35 mins until risen and firm to the touch. Cool for 5 mins, then turn out onto a cooling rack and leave to cool. Repeat with the remaining cake ingredients to make the 2 smaller cakes, and bake them for 20-25 mins.

3. Make the frosting. Beat the butter in a bowl with a hand-held electric whisk until very soft. Whisk in the icing sugar until pale and fluffy, then beat in the soft cheese until smooth.

4. Assemble the cake. Halve the passionfruit and scoop out the pulp. Spread about half of the frosting over one of the large cakes, and a quarter of the frosting over one of the small cakes, then spoon the passionfruit pulp over the frosting on both cakes. Top each cake with its matching half.

5. Carefully stack the two pairs of cakes on a serving plate or cake stand. Swirl the rest of the frosting over the top tier. Cover the physalis berries with gold leaf, if using, then decorate the cake with the physalis and figs, and dust with icing sugar. Serve on the day of assembling.

Each serving (94g) provides:
ENERGY	FAT	SATURATES	SUGARS	SALT
1665kJ 399kcal	25.3g	14.6g	26.5g	0.3g
20%	36%	73%	29%	4%

% of the Reference Intakes
Typical values per 100g: Energy 1772kJ/425kcal
Each serving provides:
38.3g carbohydrate | 0.8g fibre | 4.3g protein

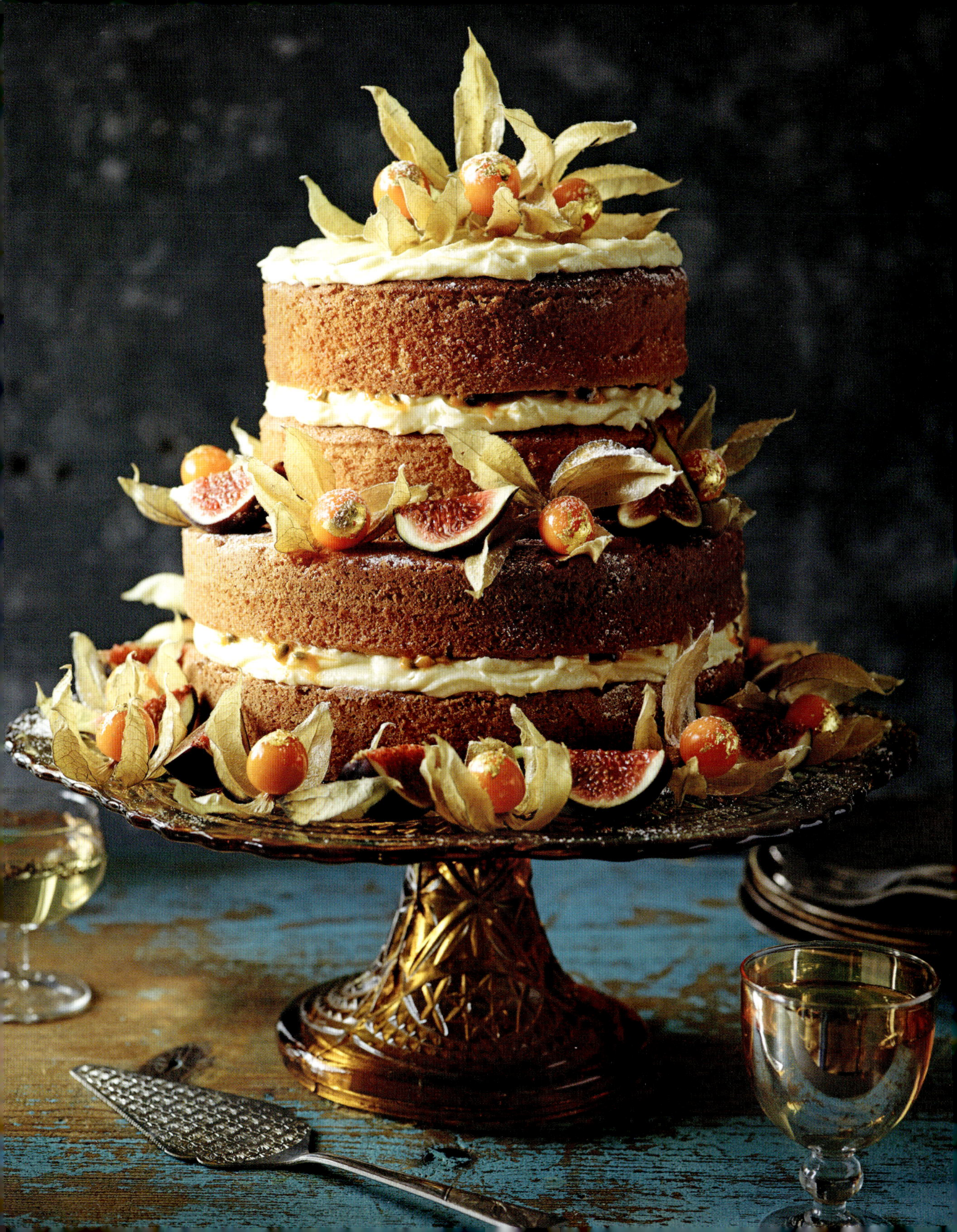

A-Z index

Apples
- Apple & Calvados tart — 106
- Apple & coconut cake — 112
- Apricot & stem ginger scones — 18

Bacon, broccoli & cheese bread pudding — 36

Banana
- Banana blondies — 44
- Salted caramel, banana and pecan muffins — 24

Berry angel food cake — 168

Biscuits
- Black pepper shortbread — 116
- Cheesy oatcakes — 130
- Cookie pizza — 86
- Ice cream sandwiches — 78
- Iced jewels — 94
- Lemon & almond butter biscuits — 46
- Pistachio & sour cherry biscotti — 164
- Popcorn cookies — 74
- Puzzle biscuits — 90

Black pepper shortbread — 116
Blackcurrant Bakewell tart — 22
Blueberry crumble squares — 56

Bread
- Bacon, broccoli & cheese bake — 36
- Courgette & oregano bread — 38
- Red pepper cornbread — 34
- Soft pretzels — 68
- Stromboli — 132
- White chocolate & cranberry panettone — 186

Brownies
- Black bean brownies — 60
- Salted caramel & peanut brownies — 110
- Townies — 62

Butternut squash
- Butternut filo parcels — 66
- Butternut squash, orange & rosemary loaf cake — 108

Cakes
- Apple & coconut cake — 112
- Berry angel food cake — 168
- Butternut squash, orange & rosemary loaf cake — 108
- Carrot & ginger cake — 28
- Chocolate & beetroot fudge cake — 16
- Chocolate crêpe cake — 176
- Chocolate dotty roll — 88
- Chocolate mousse cake — 170
- Chocolate olive oil cake — 104
- Coconut & lime Victoria sponge — 20
- Dulce de leche ice cream cake — 180
- Earl Grey tea cake — 114
- Ginger stout cake — 122
- Hazelnut coffee gateau — 172
- Honeycomb cake — 174
- Lemon fridge cake — 32
- Mango meringue layer cake — 178
- Naked cake — 188
- Orange blossom polenta cake — 118
- Passionfruit & lime drizzle cake — 10
- Pink ombre cake — 184
- Pistachio & apricot financiers — 52
- Plum & ginger upside-down cake — 12
- Rice pop cake — 82
- Tiramisu cake — 182
- Tosca cake — 162
- Zebra cake — 76

Cheese
- Bacon, broccoli & cheese bake — 36
- Cheese & mustard gougères — 64
- Cheesy oatcakes — 130
- Mushroom, pancetta & Taleggio tart — 128
- Spinach & feta tartlets — 124
- Tomato & mozzarella hand pies — 98

Cheesecake
- Chocolate spiced cheesecake — 158
- New York cheesecake — 150

Chocolate
- Chocolate & beetroot fudge cake — 16
- Chocolate & cherry meringue roulade — 148
- Chocolate & hazelnut millefeuille — 154
- Chocolate bark — 92
- Chocolate crêpe cake — 176
- Chocolate-dipped Madeleines — 54
- Chocolate dotty roll — 88
- Chocolate mousse cake — 170
- Chocolate olive oil cake — 104
- Chocolate spiced cheesecake — 158
- Honeycomb cake — 174
- Marshmallow fudge bites — 84
- Rice pop cake — 82
- White chocolate & cranberry panettone — 186

Chorizo-spiced sausage rolls — 126
Churros with cinnamon sugar — 160
Cinnamon & cardamom rolls — 14

Coconut
- Apple & coconut cake — 112
- Coconut & almond bites — 120
- Coconut & lime Victoria sponge — 20
- Mango & coconut tarte tatin — 138

Cookie pizza — 86
Courgette & oregano bread — 38

Cupcakes
- Mini cupcakes — 58
- Rainbow cupcakes — 72

Doughnuts
- Rhubarb & custard baked doughnuts — 30

Dulce de leche ice cream cake — 180

Earl Grey tea cake — 114

Fig & nut roll — 26

Filo pastry
- Butternut filo parcels — 66
- Greek milk pie — 144

Flapjacks
- No-bake fruity flapjacks — 80

Ginger
- Apricot & stem ginger scones — 18
- Carrot & ginger cake — 28
- Ginger stout cake — 122

Greek milk pie — 144

Ham & pineapple muffins — 100
Hazelnut coffee gateau — 172
Honeycomb cake — 174

Ice cream
- Dulce de leche ice cream cake — 180
- Ice cream sandwiches — 78
- Mini baked Alaskas — 156

Iced jewels — 94

Lemon
- Lemon & almond butter biscuits — 46
- Lemon fridge cake — 32

Lime
- Coconut & lime Victoria sponge — 20
- Passionfruit & lime drizzle cake — 10

Mango
- Mango & coconut tarte tatin — 138
- Mango meringue layer cake — 178

Marshmallow fudge bites	84
Meringue	
Chocolate & cherry meringue roulade	148
Mango meringue layer cake	178
Mini baked Alaskas	156
Passionfruit meringue pie	146
Peach Melba pavlova	142
Mini baked Alaskas	156
Mini cupcakes	58
Molten butterscotch puddings	140
Mushroom, pancetta & Taleggio tart	128
Muffins	
Ham & pineapple muffins	100
Raspberry & ricotta muffins	42
Salted caramel, banana & pecan muffins	24
Naked cake	188
New York cheesecake	150
No-bake fruity flapjacks	80
Orange	
Butternut squash, orange & rosemary loaf cake	108
Orange blossom polenta cake	118
Passionfruit	
Passionfruit & lime drizzle cake	10
Passionfruit meringue pie	146
Peach Melba pavlova	142
Pear & almond turnovers	50
Pies	
Greek milk pie	144
Passionfruit meringue pie	146
Tomato & mozzarella hand pies	98
Pink ombre cake	184
Pinwheel scones	96
Pistachio	
Pistachio & apricot financiers	52
Pistachio & sour cherry biscotti	164
Pizzettas	134
Plum	
Plum & ginger upside-down cake	12
Plum, vanilla & star anise galette	152
Popcorn cookies	74
Portuguese custard tarts	48
Puzzle biscuits	90
Rainbow cupcakes	72
Raspberry & ricotta muffins	42

Red pepper cornbread	34
Rhubarb & custard baked doughnuts	30
Rice pop cake	82
Salted caramel	
Salted caramel & peanut brownies	110
Salted caramel, banana & pecan muffins	24
Scones	
Apricot & stem ginger scones	18
Pinwheel scones	96
Soft pretzels	68
Spinach & feta tartlets	124
Stromboli	132
Tarts	
Blackcurrant Bakewell tart	22
Mango & coconut tarte tatin	138
Mushroom, pancetta & Taleggio tart	128
Plum, vanilla & star anise galette	152
Portuguese custard tarts	48
Spinach & feta tartlets	124
Townies	62
Tiramisu cake	182
Tomato & mozzarella hand pies	98
Tosca cake	162
White chocolate & cranberry panettone	186
Zebra cake	76
Recipes that use egg yolks	
Apple & Calvados tart	106
Chocolate & hazelnut millefeuille	154
Popcorn cookies	74
Portuguese custard tarts	48
Puzzle biscuits	90
Soft pretzels	68
White chocolate & cranberry panettone	186
Recipes that use egg whites	
Berry Angel food cake	168
Chocolate & cherry meringue roulade	148
Hazelnut coffee gateau	172
Mini baked Alaskas	156
Mango meringue layer cake	178
Pistachio and apricot financiers	50
Peach Melba pavlova	142

conversion table

Weights		Volume		Measurements		Oven temperatures		
							fan	gas
15g	½oz	25ml	1floz	2mm	1/16 in	110°C	90°C	
25g	1oz	50ml	2floz	3mm	⅛in	120°C	100°C	½
40g	1½oz	75ml	3floz	4mm	⅙in	140°C	120°C	1
50g	2oz	100ml	4floz	5mm	¼in	150°C	130°C	2
60g	2½oz	150ml	5floz (¼ pint)	1cm	½in	160°C	140°C	3
75g	3oz	175ml	6floz	2cm	¾in	180°C	160°C	4
100g	3½oz	200ml	7floz	2.5cm	1in	190°C	170°C	5
125g	4oz	225ml	8floz	3cm	1¼in	200°C	180°C	6
150g	5oz	250ml	9floz	4cm	1½in	220°C	200°C	7
175g	6oz	300ml	10floz (½ pint)	4.5cm	1¾in	230°C	210°C	8
200g	7oz	350ml	13floz	5cm	2in	240°C	220°C	9
225g	8oz	400ml	14floz	6cm	2½in			
250g	9oz	450ml	16floz (¾ pint)	7.5cm	3in			
275g	10oz	600ml	20floz (1 pint)	9cm	3½in			
300g	11oz	750ml	25floz (1¼ pints)	10cm	4in			
350g	12oz	900ml	30floz (1½ pints)	13cm	5in			
375g	13oz	1 litre	34floz (1¾ pints)	13.5cm	5¼in			
400g	14oz	1.2 litres	40floz (2 pints)	15cm	6in			
425g	15oz	1.5 litres	52floz (2½ pints)	16cm	6½in			
450g	1lb	1.8 litres	60floz (3 pints)	18cm	7in			
500g	1lb 2oz			19cm	7½in			
650g	1lb 7oz			20cm	8in			
675g	1½lb			23cm	9in			
700g	1lb 9oz			24cm	9½in			
750g	1lb 11oz			25.5cm	10in			
900g	2lb			28cm	11in			
1kg	2lb 4oz			30cm	12in			
1.5kg	3lb 6oz			32.5cm	13in			
				35cm	14in			

Sainsbury's food safety advice

- Remember to wash your hands thoroughly after handling raw meat, fish, poultry and eggs.
- Wash fresh vegetables, fruit, herbs salad and beansprouts before use.
- Public health advice is to avoid consumption of raw or lightly cooked eggs, especially for those vulnerable to infection, including pregnant women, babies and the elderly.
- Refer to ingredient packaging for full preparation and cooking instructions.
- Use separate equipment and surfaces for raw and ready-to-eat food, or wash thoroughly in between use.
- Cover raw meat and store at the bottom of the fridge separate from ready-to-eat food.
- When reheating leftover food, make sure it is piping hot throughout before consuming.

'Best before' and 'use-by' dates

- Food with a 'use-by' date goes off quite quickly and can be dangerous to eat after this date.
- Food with a 'best before' date is longer-lasting. It should be safe to eat but may not be at its best quality after this date.

Refrigerating food

- Keep your fridge temperature below 5°C.
- When preparing food, keep it out of the fridge for the shortest time possible.
- Cool down leftovers as quickly as possible (within 90 minutes) before storing them in the fridge. Eat them within two days.
- Store eggs in their box in the fridge
- Never put open cans in the fridge, as the metal may transfer to the can's contents - place the contents in a storage container or covered bowl instead.
- Clean your fridge regularly to ensure it remains hygienic and in good working condition.

Storing meat

- Store raw meat and poultry in clean, sealed containers on the bottom shelf of the fridge, so they can't touch or drip onto other food.
- Follow any storage instructions on the label and don't eat meat after its use-by date.
- Keep cooked meat separate from raw meat.

Freezing and defrosting

It's safe to freeze meat, fish and poultry as long as you:
- Freeze it before the use-by date.
- Defrost meat, poultry and fish thoroughly before cooking - lots of liquid will come out as meat thaws, so stand it in a bowl to stop bacteria in the juice spreading to other things.
- Defrost meat and fish in a microwave if you intend to cook it straightaway, or put it in the fridge to thaw so it doesn't get too warm.
- Cook food until it's piping hot all the way through.

Re-freezing

- Never re-freeze raw meat (including poultry) or fish that has been defrosted. It is possible to re-freeze cooked meat once, as long as it has been cooled before going into the freezer. But if in doubt, don't re-freeze.
- Frozen raw foods can be defrosted once and stored in the fridge for up to two days before they need to be cooked or thrown away. To reduce wastage, divide the meal into portions before freezing and then just defrost what you need.
- Cooked food that has been frozen and removed from the freezer must be reheated and eaten immediately once fully defrosted. When defrosted, food should be reheated only once, because the more times you cool and reheat food, the higher the risk of food poisoning. Bacteria can grow and multiply when food is cooled too slowly, and might survive if food isn't reheated properly.
- When reheating food, make sure it is heated until it reaches a temperature of 70°C for two minutes, so that it is steaming hot throughout.
- Foods stored in the freezer, such as ice cream and frozen desserts, should not be returned to the freezer once they have started to thaw. Only take out of the freezer what you intend to use for that meal.

Recipe nutrition

The nutrition information on each recipe shown in this book has been calculated using Sainsbury's own-brand products and is based on 1 portion, assuming equal division of the recipe into the suggested number of servings. The nutrition content will vary if other products are used or if the servings are not identical. Also, variations in cooking methods may affect the nutrition content. The nutritional information on each recipe also includes what percentage of Reference Intakes (RIs) - formerly known as Guideline Daily Amounts (GDAs) - a serving provides. RIs are a guide to the maximum amounts of calories, fat, saturates, sugars and salt an adult should consume in a day (based on an average female adult), and are as follows:

Energy or nutrient	Reference Intake per day
Energy	8400kJ/2000kcal
Total fat	70g
Saturates	20g
Total sugars	90g
Salt	6g

Nutrition and allergen information provided is correct at the time of going to press. For more information on food safety and nutrition visit sainsburys.co.uk/livewellforless and nhs.co.uk

credits

Food
Food editor Sarah Akhurst
Food assistants Linzi Brechin, Nadine Brown
Nutritionist Alexandra Harris
Recipes Sarah Akhurst, Linzi Brechin, Nadine Brown, Angela Drake, Matthew Ford, Emma Franklin, Georgina Fuggle, Lucy Jessop, Glynis McGuinness, Mima Sinclair

Editorial
Editor Ward Hellewell
Sub-editor Christine Faughlin

Design & photography
Head of design Scott McKenzie
Senior art director Pam Price
Prop stylist Morag Farquhar
Food stylists Jayne Cross, Angela Drake, Rosie Reynolds, Vicki Smallwood
Food stylist assistants Katy Gilhooly, Jessica Moxley
Photography Lauren Mclean

Acount management
Account managers Jo Brennan, Keeley Young
Client director Andy Roughton

For Sainsbury's
Book team Harry Bryan, Lynne de Lacy, Mavis Sarfo, Pete Selby, Louise Ward
Nutrition Annie Denny
Product safety manager Elizabeth Williamson

Production
Production director Sophie Dillon
Colour origination F1 Colour Ltd

seven.co.uk

© Produced by Seven Publishing on behalf of Sainsbury's Supermarkets Ltd, 33 Holborn, London EC1N 2HT.

Published January 2016. All rights reserved. No part of this publication may be reproduced, stored in a retrieval system or transmitted in any form by any means, electronic, mechanical, photocopying, recording or otherwise, without the prior written permission of Seven Publishing. Printed in Italy by Rotolito Lombarda. ISBN-13: 978-0-9934575-0-0

MIX Paper from responsible sources
FSC® C005461